THE ONE PILL FIX

THE ONE PILL FIX

a simple cure for an ailing planet

ANDY KIRKWOOD

To order additional copies of this book, contact:
Xlibris
UK TFN: 0800 0148620 (Toll Free inside the UK)
UK Local: 02036 956328 (+44 20 3695 6328 from outside the UK)
www.Xlibrispublishing.co.uk
Orders@Xlibrispublishing.co.uk
792719

CONTENTS

"The One Pill Fix", revealing the single, simple, evolutionary step that mankind must make to save our world, and ourselves.

'The first step in solving any problem is recognising there is one.'

It is 1963 and I am six. The whole school is assembled in the hall and we stand as head teacher, Mrs. Peach, tells us to be absolutely silent, 'so I can hear a pin drop' she frostily instructs. It takes a while, but eventually we are absolutely still and it is a weird sensation to be one of a hundred kids silently standing in lines. So strange in fact, that I crane my head right around to get the full picture. 'You!' the shout is loud and a shock to find out it is directed at me. I feel a sickness spreading in my stomach. 'We told you to be quiet and you turned around to talk!' 'No! I was just looking!' I reply in an effort to defend myself. 'That's his friend Nigel Papworth behind him!' shouts another teacher as if this proves everything. 'Right! I am sick of this incessant talking and we need to make an example of you!' shouts Mrs. Peach as she hauls me to the front by my right ear. My hand is held out by the wrist, palm down as Mrs. Peach reaches for a ruler. I know what is coming next and I start to sob 'I didn't say anything!' I plead. 'Yes, but you were going to!' I am scolded and with that the edge of the ruler comes down hard across the backs of my fingers. Three excruciatingly painful swipes and then I am made to stand at the front facing everyone as tears roll down my cheeks. I am physically hurt, but worse I have been wronged. I am furious about my treatment but am impotent to do anything about it, or even formulate the thoughts properly, so I just weep. I get home and tell my mother who consoles me. 'It isn't fair!' is all I can manage and she calmly replies 'life isn't fair darling.' 'But it should be!' I frustratedly retort. To this day my opinion hasn't changed one bit. Life should be fair. But it's not, and that has to change before anything else can.

52 years later:

It is 2015 and six o'clock. The sun is still bright on this spring evening as I find myself assembling for a hustings debate at a Weymouth church hall. This is my third attempt at winning the parliamentary seat for South Dorset. The usual suspects are taking their seats behind a long table: Lib Dem, Labour, UKIP, Green, and me. Oh, and the man to beat, Conservative, Richard Drax, (Richard Grosvenor Plunkett-Ernle-Erle-Drax to be precise), a tall, slim, ex-military, charmer, and the incumbent M.P. He has a cool manner that makes him almost believable, even if his family did make their millions in the slave trade, and still own their plantations in Barbados. That's not his fault, and neither is being the largest private landowner in Dorset, living at the 14,000 acre Charborough House, with its two miles of walls running alongside the A31, that lies in a different constituency to this one that he is contesting a parliamentary seat for.

The vicar has provided us with our opening question: 'why would Jesus vote for you?' (Really?!) The room fills with around a hundred people who, it appears, have nothing better to do on a sunny evening. The candidates answer in turn, most reading in monotone voices likely to bore. Richard talks of how essential our nuclear deterrent is for our security. I'm unconvinced that Jesus would vote for someone wanting to blow a cool hundred billion on a weapon that, if used once, would make the northern hemisphere uninhabitable. Surprisingly the Christian audience don't seem overly bothered about that detail. He finishes. I pick up my largely unneeded papers, move purposely to the lectern and begin.

'I think that Jesus would take a look at my esteemed combatants here and say 'forgive them father for they not what they do'.

I say this because – much as the other candidates here are, I'm sure, very charming and decent people, they are in fact the smiling face of politics that stops you, the public, perceiving the controlling monster that lurks behind the scenes.

You see, I think Jesus would have a discerning mind and the wherewithal to understand the motives of Chatham House – an institution dressed up as a 'Think Tank' which is really a select club of chief executive officers of banks and multinationals who make decisions based largely upon greed, and feed their agenda to the civil servant 'permanent secretaries', who in turn feed this to the government, who in turn feed it to us, the people.

I think Jesus would have the insight to smell a rat when these unelected permanent secretaries – who are mostly white, male, fifties and Oxbridge educated, remain unchanged even when a whole government is replaced, as in an election, including even that of the Prime Minister.

I think he would have seen how whipping M.P.s prevents them from having free speech or the opportunity to decide, and so I think he would quickly work out that elections are in fact an illusion of choice aimed at pacifying the masses.

I think he would have looked at the world around him with its ever-widening rich poor divide, the wars and the rape of mother nature and then I think he would have wept and prayed with all his heart to God saying 'Father please create something that enables the people of this wonderful planet to take control of their own destiny and put an end to the tyranny that is being wrongly sold to them as democracy for if something doesn't happen soon all of your creation shall be in vain'.

And God shall have smiled, as He always has the answer, and then He shall have created, through the ingenuity of man, the internet, which, while it has many faults, shall one day soon be revealed of its ultimate purpose: a way for all the peoples of the earth to join in fair and equal democracies through a simple online voting system, directly steering issues, not choosing strangers as representatives.

And God shall have said to Jesus 'you must now find disciples to help you spread this word.' And so it was that Jesus came to me in a dream in the far away town of Swanage and said 'Andy – lay down your clubs from the golf course and follow me for I am the way the truth and the light.'

'Verily you shall be my representative for South Dorset and you shall take your place in the evil citadel of Westminster, and once there you shall be the Trojan Horse that opens the doors and lets 40 million voting adults flood in – for I see that you alone of the candidates here do not want power for yourself, but only to share it equally amongst your fellow men.'

'To win your seat shall require a small miracle, however do not despair for I and my Son are on your side and we are pretty good at those, and one day you shall prevail. In the meantime, I notice that while you are not yet able to turn water into wine you do seem to have an aptitude for turning wine into water and that, I think, is a promising start.'

PROLOGUE

This book is, in part, a personal journey. Discovering the world in peril leads to soul searching of how any of us can really help. It examines different methods of how to make the difference that we hear so much about, but collectively feel so powerless to effect.

It reveals that, beyond reasonable doubt, we are being purposely misled by those who hold the reins of power, who would do anything and everything to maintain our corrupt and farcical political system that only serves themselves. It exposes perhaps the biggest insult, of how the elite fool us into believing they are acting in our best interests, when they are not, while only playing lip service to silence the most dissenting of voices.

This is not a depressing story, however, but one of discovery and opportunity leading to an understanding that the answer to mankind's woes today, and for every generation to come, is in fact, an extremely simple 'One Pill Fix.'

CHAPTER 1

The journey begins

'As you journey through life take a minute every now and then to give a thought for the other fellow. He could be plotting something.' - Hagar the Horrible

It is now 1987. Unexpectedly, and alarmingly, I find myself travelling the world. It turns out to be a roller-coaster of an adventure that opens my mind and changes the path of my life, but I have become unsettled. Having escaped from the hamster-wheel of day to day living my mind has time to wander and consider. I am using my senses better at assessing my surroundings and I have become more aware. And I'm troubled.

The first I hear of it was when I am in Florida with friends as we emerge from a restaurant in the early evening to find it teeming with rain. The car park is flooded and we hover in the doorway before making the mad dash for the protection of the car. 'This is really unusual' my friend Ned exclaims, 'the rains should have stopped over a month ago.'

I don't dwell on it, but Ned's comment has been subliminally filed, coming to the fore three months later when the wet season in north-eastern Australia is also remarkably late, hanging around producing grey days when everyone is expecting reliable blue skies and bright sunshine. By the time I get back to the UK a year later I have noted twenty such occurrences, the latest, the earliest, the wettest, the driest, the windiest, the coldest or the hottest it has ever been known to be, in all sorts of places around the globe. Something is going on. Of course, swings and deviations in the weather are normal, a nice summer, a wet winter, but what is not normal is for all records to be broken in a single year. Everywhere.

On my return I try to tell my friends and family of this discovery, that something is odd with the weather, but no-one is the slightest bit interested. I am humoured and ridiculed and the information goes ignored and then, a full year later, I hear on the news for the first time the expression 'global warming.' 'That's it!' I start 'that's what I have been talking about all this year!' but still, staggeringly, no-one pays any attention. Over the coming months I avidly read little snippets of articles in the press. There isn't much to go on and most of the predictions are extremely moderate. A bit of flooding in Bangladesh in a hundred years' time, which is way too far away, both physically and chronologically to worry about. But I'm unconvinced. Certainly, what I had witnessed first-hand did not appear to be something to welcome, or that should be ignored.

CHAPTER 2

Re-examination

'What I spent I lost; what I possessed is left to others; what I gave away, and the good I did for others and my Earth remains with me.' Epitaph.

To give you an insight of my greatest concerns, I shall use an example closest to my heart, the demise of beaches. Beaches are a miracle. I know science says that sand is just rock ground up over millions of years and that it just happens to be lying around everywhere at the water's edge, but it is the delightful combination of utilitarian effectiveness, softness and beauty that makes beaches such a thrill to go to. We all love beaches, so surely this is something that we would all want to fight for, to protect for generations to come?

You'd be hard pressed to make them any better with any technology or idea, and so by that standard it does appear to be almost of divine creation that this marvel is here for all of us to enjoy. I once asked a group how it was that my home town of Swanage in Dorset had a golden sandy beach, given that the cliffs to the east were white chalk and those to the west Jurassic grey Purbeck stone and there wasn't a golden rock anywhere to be seen. 'Ah well,' I was told, 'you see you've got your Jurassic coast and you've got your Triassic bit as well, not to mention the Cretaceous period.' 'Oh great, that's all clear now' I had lied.

A couple of years after my round the world-er I decide to take another longish trip. Not the eighteen months I had previously been away for, but just four. It was an escape from our UK winter. Naturally it was great to get away, but now my ears and eyes were open I found the experience troubling. The weather patterns continued to be erratic, but I also became aware of rapid physical changes that had occurred to places that I had previously enjoyed. The building boom was going into overdrive. I tried to be cool about it, reasoning that whenever you see a place for the first time it's normal to assume it has somehow always been like that. I mean, none of us feel bad about London no longer being a swampy forest do we? Why? Because, in our own life experience we have only ever known it as a stone paved city saturated with roads and buildings.

When I took my first trip to Kuta in Bali I loved it. It was busy and vibrant and I met great people, but I was initially unaware that just ten years before I had arrived it was the most stunning arch of pristine golden sand where, if you wanted to stay the night, your only option was to crash in the simple fisherman's huts at the back of the beach. If I had seen it like that would I have still been enjoying the buzzing little metropolis that I had discovered? Probably not. No, I would have been ranting at the speed of change and the amount of litter in the sea.

The garbage in the water problem, which is now a worldwide epidemic, was uncontrolled and increasingly out of control as the Balinese seemed to think it is fine to put their rubbish into shallow graves on the beach and wit for the tide to take it away. When the tide came in it did indeed become unearthed and moved but it was far from having disappeared. The last time I went, as I walked out with a surfboard I put my foot on rubbish drifting on the seabed six times before feeling sand under my toes. It was an utterly vile experience.

Plastic in the sea has finally become a big issue. Birds are dying in their millions from eating it and all manner of marine life is tangled and choked and drowned. It is a most miserable affair. When I heard the expression 'non-biodegradable' for the first time I was eight, making it 1965. At that time any thinking caring government should have understood where this problem was leading, and have made creating plastic packaging without a workable solution at the end of its useful life illegal. I was a schoolboy and I could see it.

Fifty years on the world is in trouble due to a complete lack of forward thinking because the government is in the pocket of the corporations, and companies just love plastic. It's cheap and shiny and good for business, until now. Only when many people recently started complaining and the corporations looked like they might start losing market share did they act.

When encountering paradise lost the easiest solution for the traveler is to strike out to ever more remote and less developed areas of the planet. Typically, the places that are hardest to get to prove to be the least spoilt. Returning to the lost island paradise of Koh Samui, that had received overnight acclaim and an international airport, was one of the saddest experiences of my life. The beautiful beach at Lamai that, when I had first visited in 1987 had no more development than half a dozen small groups of simple huts, had changed beyond recognition. The mile long pristine beach was stacked with discarded litter, and the coconut groves behind had been hacked away and replaced by a huge squalid complex of cheaply constructed bars and restaurants. Where there had been jungle vegetation, and choruses of frogs, there were roads with tuk-tuks racing by. The people themselves had become battle hardened by the unceasing onslaught of tourists hunting cheap thrills. No-one any longer gave a look of wonder at other cultures visiting their land, only sideways glances of an opportunity to make even more money from an overly wealthy fahrang fool.

The Thai's are very good at extracting money by providing a service, and businesses are set up in moments that sterilised and dumbed down the whole experience. Gone was the cut and thrust and feeling of satisfaction at having solved the travelling puzzle. The answers were now provided on the same page as the questions, and weren't even written upside down. The quality of the visitors dropped until the experience became just another Ibiza of brightly lit bars. Thailand used to be so much more.

My first sortie to the island of Koh Phang Ghan was with three other guys and the place was almost deserted. There were a dozen basic huts near the wide golden sweep of Hat Rin Beach where we had smoked a joint and chatted as the sun went down. We were the only ones there, until a group of four girls, who sadly turned out to be two lesbian couples (meaning we spent an evening playing charades as there was nothing else on the menu), arrived. The next time I went back was just three years later and I couldn't believe my eyes. Perhaps fifty thousand tourists were there for the full moon party. The coconut groves had become roads edged by bars and restaurants of all types. Big banana and parascending rides monopolized the bay as speed boats and jet-ski's carved up the water. It was a shock, and it was awful to see what the promise of wealth could do.

Worse, it was with something of a shock when I realized that *I* was part of the problem. When I had visited and had spent my money in that little guest house or corner restaurant what was I really thinking the owner was going to do with the earnings? Some was going to go to feeding the family. Good. Some, maybe, sent to the ailing parents, that's good too. But if the business was a huge hit, and Thailand remains a massively popular destination, then obviously the thought of opening another, even bigger operation would occur to the owner, and so it was essentially my money that was funding the destruction of the natural beauty of the country.

Similarly Gili Trawengen, off the coast of Lombok in Indonesia was once an idyllically un-spoilt island. It was how Thailand had once been. No electricity and so no TV's, simple bamboo huts and amazingly a simple breakfast was included in the modest overnight hut fee of about two dollars. The question took me by surprise. 'You wan' banana pankek, banana jaffol or froo' sala?' 'well,' I considered, 'I think a fruit salad would be lovely thank you'. When my breakfast arrived I was amused to find my fruit salad was in fact a single unwrapped banana.

Dolphins swam by every day and gorgeously pristine coral gardens of exquisite colour and delicacy were accessible right off the beach. We chose to take a boat to see one of the spectacular 'coral gardens', and while I was happily swimming around admiring the beauty, another boat arrived and I watched with horror as their anchor dropped onto the stem to a delicately filamented outcrop of pink coral the size of a coffee table, breaking it away for it to sink slowly down to the sandy sea floor. A hundred years of growth gone in the blink of an eye for no reason other than pure thoughtlessness.

I was sickened by the sudden realisation of what I was allowing myself to participate in. I went to the boat owners and said that as a matter of urgency they should get together and drop a single mooring buoy that they could then tie up to. I have now had that conversation a dozen times in different places around the globe, but no notice has ever been taken until it is too late and a loss of business is staring them in the face because the coral is ruined and no-one wants to pay to see the bleached bones of something that has died. Only when the money dries up does it seem that anyone regrets their actions and tries to do something to remedy them. The foolishness of the boat owners is manifest, but can we honestly say our attitude to our ailing planet as a whole is any different?

To re-visit a colourful reef that you have in your memory only to find a sea floor littered with shards of white broken coral and witness, where once there were tropical fish in their millions to dazzle and amaze, a few solitary individuals eking out a living around the last live lump of coral, is a heartbreaking moment. When I saw a family of Japanese holding hands bent double with their masks in the water while walking across the coral, unthinkingly smashing it with their feet I knew that, without action, the last vestige of hope for these living jewels of the seas, would soon be gone.

There is a great amount of talk about the demise of the reefs of the world. I have read about it extensively and have gazed quizzically at them pondering a solution. At Chandidassar in Bali, I was privileged to receive what I considered to be something of an epiphany. The tale of Chandidassar is a sad. So keen were the Balinese to make a quick buck from the booming tourist industry someone made the bizarre and vile decision to make the roads and hotels from the coral reef. It was dug up, crushed and made into concrete for westerners' bedrooms and bars. Next a storm came in and, no longer protected by the reef, the beach got washed away. So now with no reef and no beach, but with a lot of empty rooms, Chandidassar was in trouble. Why would anyone bother to go to such a place?

In an attempt to undo the mischief they had caused a new artificial reef was put in place. It was made from concrete sewer pipes, a meter across and one and a half long. They were arranged on end in a castle wall like fashion and filled with concrete to make them immovable. Some remnants of reef started growing on the pipes but it was sparse and a shadow of its former glory.

As I snorkeled out there from the waters' edge, a journey of a hundred meters, the sea bed sloped down to a level sandy bottom about twenty feet deep before rising up to the concrete reef. On the sandy bottom half way to the reef was a small but vibrantly healthy strip of coral. This puzzled me, so I duck dived down to investigate, and found myself peering into two of the concrete tubes lying on their sides. They were hollow and luxuriantly covered in coral of many types, and shoals of reef fish darted amongst them. As an act of bravado I swam through the tubes receiving a deep scratch on my calf as my reward, but as I came to the surface I realised I had worked out the answer that could save the coral reefs of the world.

Coral reefs notoriously take thousands of years to grow from scratch, but these pipes had only been dropped overboard in the last decade, so it had to follow that the time it takes for a coral garden to flourish must be considerably less if the conditions were right and spores from existing nearby coral were floating in the water to start the process. They just needed something suitable for them to attach to and grow on, situated with the right ambient conditions. Now it seemed to me that, as the coral was struggling to re-establish at the shallower depths but was thriving twenty feet down it must have a preference for the cooler water and dimmer sunlight down there. This fitted perfectly with negating the adverse impacts of increased ultraviolet radiation due to ozone thinning and rising sea temperatures due to global warming.

Using the growth of coniferous trees on an Alpine mountainside as an easy example, you shall always see a sharp line of altitude above which they can no longer germinate and grow and where there is only snow and rock. Perhaps coral is the same? Why wouldn't it be? The difference of a few meters of water may therefore be the difference between life and death in coral terms. It certainly looked that way. That being the case, the answer of how to save the reefs was easy. In the vicinity of an existing but struggling reef, just litter any piece of seabed that is a little deeper and cooler with concrete pipes or lumps of volcanic stone for coral spores to hang on to. Then all you have to do is sit back and wait a few years for the new garden to grow. A beautifully simple logical low-cost fix. But there was a problem I didn't expect.

I wrote to numerous coral conservation lobbies with this simple plan but was told that the coral problem was in fact a rise in the levels of carbonic acid in sea water due to increased levels of carbon dioxide in the atmosphere, and that that was the real killer.

At first I accepted their reasoning without question. After all they must know more than me, right? But then I started to think about that statement. While it is true that carbon dioxide levels have increased in our atmosphere causing all manner of problems, the 'natural' component is only 0.03%, or if you prefer three ten-thousandths, or twenty one people in the new seventy thousand seater Wembley stadium wearing CO2 scarves. That level has now risen to 0.05% which is surprisingly dangerous for the planet but surely the levels of carbonic acid in the sea can't have raised enough to kill coral? Really? I mean that is a pretty diluted solution of it when you consider the volume of water it is mixed with. It would be like suggesting the at the atmosphere has become poisonous to us because of the rise in CO2.

So, given that this appears to be a pretty remote possibility of that being the true cause of the demise of coral why has this theory been accepted the way it has? It lead me to notice a frequent and significant problem in the press of reporting findings in University theses, and it works like this. Postgraduate students, who I'm not suggesting are stupid by any means do, however, lack the wisdom that half a century on this planet gives you. They are continually pressured and struggling about what to write about in their dissertations for their final exams. I have read reports of many transparently nonsensical arguments or 'findings' based on biased experiments where a particular outcome is sought, anticipated and so contrived.

So let's assume a student studying marine conservation (or something of that ilk) decides to write a thesis about the demise of coral, and makes the sweeping assumption that increased levels of carbonic acid is the culprit, after all CO2 levels have indeed risen. Three months of scribbling and half a dozen flawed experiments later and there you have it. A few easily cooked results, a hundred pages of supporting rubbish and a dozen lines in a red top daily paper and the whole world thinks that because the thesis has 'from Oxford University' on it the writer must know what they are talking about and no-one seems to question any of it. Apart from me, that is. Urban myth wins the day and the coral loses out.

Ot how about the plight of the seahorse? In attempt to awaken the big players who could easily help these beautiful and rare creatures out I wrote an article which ran as follows:- Like many who have marvelled at their first sight of a seahorse, I had wrongly assumed that such an extraordinary and beautiful creature must hail from an equally exotic location; somewhere in the turquoise waters of the Caribbean, perhaps, or off some remote Pacific Island?

You can imagine, therefore, that it came as something of a shock for me to discover that this exquisitely evolved creature is commonly found in the cold, shallow, tidal waters of Britain. Indeed it is believed that until recently South Beach at Studland in Dorset, had the second greatest concentration of seahorses in the world coming second only to the Rio Formosa in Portugal. That, sadly, was five years ago, before the numbers plummeted.

Seahorses are not only strangely beautiful but are full of surprises as they are in fact an unusually evolved fish. They can be found in a myriad of guises but here in British waters, if you are lucky enough, you are most likely to encounter just two types, the (obviously named when looked at) Spiny and Short snouted. They are intelligent with good memories and are unusual in that they have a stomach-less digestive systems, forcing them to eat for most of the day. Perhaps most astonishingly of all, the male seahorse is the only father on the planet that will become pregnant and give birth to their young.

It's true that few of us are really likely to encounter a seahorse in the wild as they can be elusive, having the ability to change colour to merge with its background like a chameleon. They are timid creatures, and, at their largest, are under a foot in length with many measuring less than an inch.

It is good to know, however, that the seahorse is there and the image of pairs of them rather sweetly patrolling their small patch of sea bottom to meet up regularly to affirm their bond to each other is surely one that must melt the hardest of hearts.

Sadly this fascinating part of our planets evolution may soon stop being a reality and pass into legend, becoming nothing more than stories for our children, as the future of the seahorse now hangs by a thread.

The greatest threat to seahorses is the bogus use in Chinese medicines, which places it right up there with rhino horn and crushed tigers bones. This is an issue that should be dealt with at government level but that would require finding someone with integrity and power who is willing to put ethics before profits when dealing with the Chinese, which, looking at Boris' recent 'trade' visit to China doesn't look likely any time soon.

The other cause of their demise is closer to home and is one that you could be forgiven for thinking should be quite easy to address. It is the loss of the seahorses' natural habitat, the sea grass meadows.

Sea grass is not a sea weed but is truly an underwater grass with root systems that bind into the sand creating the basis of an ecosystem that provides refuge for a cacophony of creatures, of which the seahorse is just one. Further it holds the sea bed together, slowing or even halting erosion of sand that would otherwise be swept away by storms and tidal currents. So for all of us, and in a diverse number of ways, sea grass is an extremely valuable ally.

Sea grass meadows are most prevalent off sandy beaches which, understandably, attract recreational boaters who choose to moor up either to take refuge from inclement weather conditions or to enjoy the popular beach locations, and this is where the conflict of interests arises.

The Seahorse Trust have undertaken extensive research projects to evaluate and better understand the ecosystem of the sea grass and the resulting populations of seahorses and have discovered that both are seriously in decline. This is due to the practice of dropping anchors or the placing of traditional mooring buoys in the sea grass meadows. Simply, mooring and anchor chains scrape clear the sandy bottom by uprooting the sea grass as boats swing around in the tidal currents. A single mooring can easily scour a circle of 30 meter diameter as a secure anchoring requires chain to be let out equal to at least three times the depth of the water, as any good skipper will tell you.

We should be thankful, therefore, to know that there is a simple solution to the plight of the seahorse and the preservation of the meadows. This is by utilising sophisticated sprung buoys, secured by a single screw into the sea bed, that keep chains from the bottom thus providing sea grass friendly moorings. So you could be forgiven for assuming that this is problem solved, but sadly this is not the case.

The problem is now one of economics. These moorings come at a cost of around £500 each with around 50 of them being needed in Studland alone, and this is where the efforts of the Seahorse and Dorset Wildlife Trusts have stalled. Their idea to provide advertising on the moorings in return for sponsorship has proven to be a long drawn out affair eating up time that the seahorse can ill afford to lose.

A speedier remedy to this problem the answer would be to look for funding from the two multi-billion pound owners and profiteers of Studland beach and the seabed. The beach is owned by the National Trust (as part of the single largest gift they have ever received) and you can be sure that they make a tidy profit from their operations there. The car parking alone can bring in around £6,000 in a single summers day and when the profits from the 500+ beach-hut rentals, the two café's, the boat park and the various operating concessions are taken into consideration the total annual profits from that beach can easily be estimated into the millions. Indeed the NT 's accounts for 2013 shows an operating profit of a staggering £93million (with a financial float carried over of over one trillion pounds) and that is even with an applaudable annual budget for conservation and consultancy programmes of £25million having already been deducted.

Even more pertinently, perhaps, we should look to the Crown Estate. The Crown Estate Act of 1961 dictates that the Crown Estate (which is worth in excess of £8 billion and generated a profit of £252.6 million this year of which the Queen will take 15%) has ownership of all the sea bed around the British Isles to a distance of 12 miles 'to manage it on behalf of the nation'.

In 2011 the Crown Estate carried out a consultancy concerning seahorses at Studland which agreed that the staggering loss of sea grass coverage was an urgent problem, however the paper then goes on to generate financial arguments as to why they shouldn't have to do anything about it. Among other things it estimates ridiculous costs, including paperwork and consultancy fees, of nearly a million pounds, which they say would be needed for the installation of an (excessive) 200 mooring buoys.

Incomprehensively the consultants have vastly over-estimated the number of moorings needed as they have chosen to ignore the quite obvious fact that if a mooring is secure enough in rough weather (when one might expect only a handful of boats sheltering) it will surely be secure enough for two or more yachts (a common practice called 'rafting') when the weather is fine and the bay is at its busiest.

The saddest part of all for me was that the report was largely based on calculating how much to charge currently 'free parking' boats to turn the mooring buoys into a profit making business. We can be truly thankful that

Great Ormond Street children's hospital doesn't operate under the same principles.

What the Crown Estate seems to be unable to acknowledge is that they have awarded themselves almost 100,000 square miles of the Nations land for free, albeit under water, and are generating huge profits from almost every activity that takes place on it. For example, every single mooring buoy that you see in British waters has to pay an annual rental to them of £80 and there are over 1000 in Poole Harbour alone with several million dotted around the UK. Additionally they are starting to profit heavily from the introduction of wind farms that have to pay hefty land rentals even when placed well out to sea.

Their financial summary for 2012 states that the profits and land values for the 'marine estate' have increased about 20% in this last fiscal year alone to show an annual profit of £55million and a marine estate value of £725million. Now, given these massive sources of virtually free income I find it very hard to imagine what better cause there could be in their mandate of 'managing the sea bed on behalf of the nation' than to step in and solve the plight of the seahorses of Studland Bay for what could, if managed properly, be a comparatively measly £100,000. To put this in proportion the amount needed is about 0.03% of the annual profits of these two huge companies – the equivalent of someone earning £25,000 a year making a one off donation of just £8.30p.

Studland Bay sits adjacent to the World Heritage Site of the Jurassic Coast, so called because of the age and natural beauty of the rocks of the coastline and the wealth of fossils that can be easily found from that era, making the preservation of the tiny pre-historic looking seahorse in this area perhaps even more pertinent.

A further incentive to the Crown Estate must surely be that seahorses and their habitat are protected under the Wildlife and Countryside Act of 1981 which states that 'intentionally or recklessly damaging' habitat (in this case the sea grass) that supports a protected species (seahorses) is an offence punishable by up to a £5000 fine and six months in prison. It is a fact that sea horses legally have the same protection status as otters, water voles and great crested newts however out of sight and out of mind seems to be the approach of those organisations that really should know better.

I am quietly confident that any good prosecuting barrister would be able to successfully argue that deliberate inactivity by the owner of the land in instigating measures that are well documented to save the sea grass meadow habitat, thus knowingly allowing the demise of the seahorses that are dependent upon it, is criminal damage with the Crown Estate and the National Trust being complicit in this crime.

Significantly, in the case of an organisation failing its obligations, the sentence can be passed on to the most senior person with the law further stating that full punishment can be metered out for each organism involved. This means the loss of 50 seahorses could lead to a fine of £250,000 and 25 years in prison. Suddenly forking out a cool £100,000 to get on and do the right thing should look quite appealing to Sir Stuart Hampson who heads up the Crown Estate and Dame Helen Ghosh, Director-General of the National Trust.

Sometimes we all get the opportunity and the urge to do something for others, to put our hand in our pocket to help those who are not in a position to help themselves. And if we poorer folk can do this then these well healed organisations that love to proclaim the good works they do for the country, and are even obliged by law, can surely do the same, especially in the case of the owners of the seabed, the Crown Estate. After all, we are regularly reminded that Her Majesty really does love her horses. So what about it, Ma'am?

To write to support the movement to stimulate the Crown estate or the National Trust into action please write to either, or both, of the following.

Enquiries@thecrownestate.co.uk attn. Sir Stuart Hampson
Enquiries@nationaltrust.org.uk attn. Dame Helen Ghosh

But, as I said earlier, far more worrying than any of this was the discovery of the rapid decline of the planets' beaches. When I first stumbled upon this disaster, I tried to tell myself that I must simply have been mistaken. Perhaps the tide was out last time I'd visited? But then I started photographing beaches, logging the results and so proving without question that a massive global problem was occurring.

There are many examples I could give both in the UK and around the globe but the Gambia in Western Africa is a reasonably typical story. The first time I visited that country the beach was over two hundred meters wide. It was such a long walk to the crashing surf that drinks bars even popped up half way to help the tourists with their steamy trek to the ocean. The next time I went I could hardly believe my eyes. All of the sand had been eroded away and the water was washing up and around the foundations of the beach bars that sat on a low earth bund at the back of the beach. Trees had had their roots washed clean and had toppled over to lie forlornly on the sand as tourists picked their way around them at low tide.

The only place where there was any kind of beach on this stretch of coastline was at the Senagambia Hotel where they had decided to build a dock of huge mealy bags full of sand. It was about two meters high and enclosed a protected area of beach about fifty meters long and twenty wide. At high tide the sea would slosh against the sand bags and at every low tide a JCB would trundle up and rebuild the dock of all the half washed away mealy bags. Parasols and sun loungers routinely fell into the swirling water but the tourists either didn't notice or didn't care, and just sat there sipping their cocktails. I seemed to be the only one bothered by the demise.

The next time I was there the Dutch had arrived and, using international fund money and their considerable knowledge of keeping the sea at bay they were rebuilding the beach. They had a ship that sucked up sand from the entrance to Banjul Harbour, which apparently needed doing in any case to keep shipping lanes open, and then the ship would sit a mile out to sea belching black fumes as its massive pumps strained to squirt thousands of tons of sand down a two meter pipe onto the beach, where a really ginormous bulldozers was waiting to level it out. It was an incredible job and in all they rebuilt twenty kilometers of coastline two meters up thereby re-creating the two hundred meter wide beach. I know because I paced it out and it was gorgeous, as God had intended.

I made an appointment and visited the chief engineer of the project and asked him how long he thought the beach would last. 'Eighty years' he told me without the slightest hesitation. 'It may need a little repair here and there but we expect a minimum of eighty years from this work.' Two years later the beach had receded to just fifty meters and a two meter cliff had formed at the tide line where the new sand was being washed away in great chunks to the old beach level at every high tide. This gave tourists something of a challenge to get to the sea so ladders were intermittently placed along the 'cliff' to assist going for a swim.

The very next year the beach was gone. The sea was back up to the restaurants and the Sennagambia was again building their dock. And the cost of this re-instatement that lasted less than five years? A hundred million dollars, paid for from an international relief fund (that the British government contributes to by the way.) I just recently returned from a further trip and was not in the least surprised to see that they had gone for a new strategy that is cropping up all over the planet. This is to build a two meter wall of large rocks in front of the bars leaving the doomed beach to its fate. Another half meter in sea level rises will take the water over this protective shield and, unless another hundred million is spent rapidly, about half of the Gambia will disappear underwater. That event is just a few years away. The run for the hills has begun!

So, the obvious question has to be, why are the sea levels rising? Well, this is predominantly due to water temperatures rising causing the melting of ice that currently sits on land (glaciers or packed ice in Alaska, Northern Russia, Canada, Scandinavia, Greenland and the Antarctic being the main areas) and the even bigger factor of natural expansion. Water expands with temperature like mercury does, but not linearly thus making it unpopular for thermometers. As the volume expands the additional amount of water has to go somewhere and the lowest areas of land to flood are, sadly, the beaches.

If you are skeptical try carrying out these simple observations for yourself. If you happen to live in the UK you might first ask yourself why it is that not one, but two Thames barriers have been constructed within just twenty years of each other. Jeremy Corbyn's brother, Peers, personally told me they only built the Thames barriers to fool people into thinking there is a problem. I can't say that Mr Cobyn is one for obvious reasons, but I do think that only a nit-wit would suggest such thing. If you are unconvinced, simply buy yourself a new Ordnance Survey map and compare it with a five-year-old one and note that a blue 'mean high water' line has suddenly appeared. This new addition separates anything on the seaward side as 'foreshore' (sea bottom for at least part of the tide) when, until a few years ago it used to be all beach at any point of the tide. The O.S. are cheating by their own rules as land covered by water at any point of the tide should be brown, so are they trying to make the demise of the beaches less shocking and less obvious? Next time you walk on a beach note the highest line of seaweed, and you will quickly see that line is near, or perhaps way past, the top of the beach.

You might also like to look for trees near beaches that have had their roots exposed due to sea erosion. No tree in the UK grows with its roots above ground level, and palms do not either, so if you can see roots the level of the ground must have eroded away. Erosion causes small 'cliffs', anything from six inches to three feet in height, to form in sand parallel to the sea. This phenomenon and steep stepping in shingle beaches both point to a problem of rapid erosion. Sand bars forming where the water shallows a few meters from the beach before going deeper again are caused by sand picked up by the waves then settling out of the water as the current slows. Sea defenses are prevalent and are continually built, ranging from concrete structures, piles of rock, sand bags, walls, and dykes. You can see them everywhere.

I went for a swim south of Melbourne and was staggered by the un-saltiness of the sea water. Honestly, it was like tasting tears. I could only conclude that this was because Antarctic ice melt fresh water, being less dense than its saline cousin, floats on the surface, thereby avoiding comprehensive mixing, and was drifting up on the sea currents in such quantities as to make the sea almost drinkable. You would need a lot of ice cubes to achieve that wouldn't you?

Now the next thing I want you to imagine is slowly running the tap in your bath and trying to stop the bottom being covered with water. You can build a barrier half way up perhaps, but what happens when that is over-run? As the battle to save the bottom (which represents the beaches) is lost the water continues to rise eventually coming to the brim of the bath. In desperation you can keep building up the baths edge but at some point it is going to become unstable and water will inevitably flood into your room. So surely the only sensible solution, and the easiest thing to do, would be to just turn off the taps?

And when will all this stop you may ask? First you should note that I don't ask when it will start, as it has already started but isn't yet in full swing. Well, when the melt cycle has completed, conservative estimates think sea levels will have risen by about forty feet, but many say closer to two hundred and eighty feet. So look at your OS map, find the forty foot, and two hundred and eighty foot, contour lines and do some shading. What I can promise you is that there won't be much land left. Every coastal city without exception shall have perished along with most of the good agricultural land. This is why you need to engage yourself in saving this planet, unless you want to be holding yourself gripped with regret and shame like the fishermen of the Gili Islands with their avoidably dead coral.

Now the good news is that I wouldn't be bothering you about all this if there wasn't a simple solution, so don't go and drink that bottle of vodka and paracetamols quite yet. Better to turn that tap off, don't you think? Our government knows all about this of course, but are doing very little to solve the problems. That is a shocking truth that may take a little while to sink in, but your job for now is to try and work out why they aren't acting, and to understand how you can. This may sound like a big ask but don't fret, you are not alone, and this book will help you find your way.

CHAPTER 3

A homecoming – of sorts

'It's easier to resist at the beginning than at the end.' -
Leonardo da Vinci

When I arrived home my mind was made up. Something had to
be done. I had to act, to do my bit. But do what? It is far too easy for
'real life' to take over and immerse yourself in petty problems while
putting other issues to the back of your mind, however I found that
the longer I procrastinated the worse the feeling of dread within me
became. I felt a desperate urgency that time was running out and I was
still doing nothing other than participating in fruitless conversations
with friends and family.

So then I struck upon the idea of just starting a website, putting
all the information I had gathered on it presented in an easy pictorial
form, and maybe someone would see it and act upon the initiative. It
seemed a long shot but it was all I could think of at the time. I wanted
to call the website 'sanity' and planned to put conflicting images of all
that we love and all that we hate and, assuming that most of us love
and hate the same things, to request people to click on which they
prefer, and so to try and get them to see the harm we as a species were
causing.

I planned to load up an image of a traffic jam next to that of a
speeding bus in its empty lane, of war opposite next to peace and
harmony, nature next to factories and cities, free creatures next to
farmed animals, freedom next to slavery (us working) and so on.

I was considering the problem of how to get people to see it, when I thought of a much better idea. I would start a political party.

When I first thought of the concept I believed it would be daunting to go through the paperwork and get myself registered but actually it was quite simple. I chose a name that made people laugh and so remember it, and so the 'Personality *And* Rational Thinking? Yes!' Party, or P.A.R.T.Y. Party was born. The concept was simple: introducing common sense, transparency and fun into politics, encouraging people want to engage just for the sheer enjoyment of it.

The party logo I designed was of a happy jumping dolphin with a Union Jack party hat on, encapsulating a message of a better environment, fun and a little patriotism. My candidates picture was flippant: me with sunglasses on and a bottle of pink champagne in front of tickertape draped over three flags, a Union Jack, a cross of St George and a skull and crossbones. It was an exciting moment.

CHAPTER 4

The P.A.R.T.Y. Party

'We will not agree on every issue. But let us respect those differences and respect one another. Let us recognize that we do not serve an ideology or a political party; we serve the people.' - John Lynch

From the website written in 1992.

The P.A.R.T.Y. Party is the brain child of a few individuals who became frustrated with Britain. Don't get us wrong, we love Britain, it is a unique country with so much to offer. It is beautiful, steeped in history, is financially strong, its people have humour, talent, passion, individuality, intelligence, creativity and resilience. Most people believe in the good basic principles of life, like truth, justice, honesty and fair play, and do their best to uphold them. Most people believe in tolerance and working together. So why is it we see so little of that reflected in the way our society runs and the systems placed upon us by government and what is reported in the press?

We are all fortunate to live in a land of milk and honey, so why is it such a struggle for most people to make a good life for themselves? Why are there so many fussy rules? Why is anything that is fun considered borderline in its legality, or illegal? Why are our wildlife and countryside in demise? Why is it every time you open a paper you can hardly believe the negativity you are reading? Why is it that the courts seem to make decisions that outrage the sensibilities of the common people? What happened to truly free speech and common sense?

It would appear that today's Britain is having a love affair with red tape, ever tightening laws, middle management and the abuse of the good will of the people. Does anyone believe that the needs and wants of the British public really come first by our government, whichever party may be in control? If so, where is the evidence of that? The taxes are outrageous, the waste of public money even more so, the rules stifling, the waiting lists long, the classes overcrowded, the system unfair, working life is too demanding and there is little or no emphasis on fun or quality of life. We have become so used to being bullied and threatened by an over controlling Government that most of us accept it as normal.

Have you ever wondered why the party in power swings from Conservative to Labour and back again like a pendulum? Could it be that it is because neither party are really solving any issues? Could it be that as memory fades, and it becomes clear that the 'party of today' are not making a blind bit of difference, that people just go for the 'other' option? And next time guess what? The same thing happens and we all give the other one another go. Have you considered that perhaps it is because they really aren't in control at all? That they are the puppet of the moneyed people that persuade us there is nothing better for us? If that were the case what sort of future can we possibly have?

So here at the P.A.R.T.Y. Party we decided to do something about this. It would be easy just to carry on being aghast at the poor decisions, the ever tightening ratchet constraining freedom and choice but we decided to try and provide a real alternative to this dead end the situation, by starting a new political party aimed at injecting some fresh thinking into a stale, unfair and outdated system.

Unlike our established opponents we do not claim to have all the answers. We do not claim that we are 100% right in everything we say. And we do not want to change everything - many of the systems in place are good and simply need a tweak. What we do claim is that we have recognised many areas which could so easily and painlessly be improved. We have seen places where the appliance of just a smidgen of common sense and fresh thinking, unshackled from the control of banks and corporations, would make enormous strides to make life better for the people almost overnight. We are brave enough to talk about them and, given the opportunity, bright enough to implement them.

We believe that there are many people out there who are as disillusioned as we were, and feel as strongly as we do that things can really get better. All we ask is that you take the time to read what we have to say, give it some thought and see if your heart can support this new movement. Britain could be so wonderful - so why not help to make it that way?

So, who would vote for the P.A.R.T.Y. Party?

Well, if you ever....

. . .think that life could be more fun than this.

. . .feel you are working too many hours, too many weeks and still struggling to make ends meet or to spend enough time with your family?.

. . .feel like you are on the travellator of life running as fast as you can and getting nowhere.

. . .wonder why we in the U.K. wait months for operations while the French have the capacity to take our overflow.

. . .think that the wealth in Britain should be spread more evenly.

. . .sympathise with the public sector - police, teachers, nurses etc. - over the amount of time they are forced to waste (that you and I pay for) on meaningless paperwork.

. . .think that you don't see good a good value return in services on the taxes you pay

. . .feel a pang when you see yet another field covered with roads or houses.

. . . are concerned about Britain's diminishing wildlife.

. . .think things are confused and muddled for the sake of it.

. . .think you are expected to take life just too damn seriously.

. . .watch politicians gassing on and wish that they would just shut up and disappear.

. . .wonder why, no matter what the government does or says, the opposition parties always runs them down (unless it is about someone who has died and then they all agree that that person was fab!)

. . .wish that Britain made its own mind up and didn't spend so much time playing the lap dog to the U.S.A., the Chinese or Europe.

. . .think council tax is too heavy and that the money is not properly reaching the sectors that service the needs of you, the public.

. . .think that the legal aid system is a license to print money for the lawyers.

. . .feel bad about how little support there is for the hungry and homeless.

. . .feel that thieves should be fair game if they threaten you or your family.

. . .wonder how your parliamentary member can best act on your behalf when they are told how to vote and act by a party whip.

. . .wonder why our taxes on alcohol and tobacco are so much higher than that of our nearest European neighbours.

. . .get sick and tired of hearing the same old empty promises from the two main parties.

. . .think your freedom is being whittled away.

. . .despair at who you might vote for.

. . .are concerned that nothing ever changes and all you get is repackaged mediocrity.

. . .dream that you should be free to live life the way you choose.

. . .hope that love, respect, compassion, thoughtfulness and caring should be at the heart of the decisions that Governments make.

. . .fear that the introduction of ever tightening control laws are an unnecessary burden to a free society and erode your birthright freedoms

. . .feel concerned about where the past trends of our country's history will be leading us to in the future.

. . .worry for the health of the planet we rely upon.

. . .pray that mankind can live in harmony.

. . .get the feeling that you are working flat out to make the super-rich richer.

. . .feel that there is little common sense in the law and the way things are done anymore.

. . .think things could be done simpler, better and more effectively.

. . .believe that all politics should be open and accountable.

. . .feel frustration for your voice not being heard and experience powerlessness when trying to dealing with the establishment.

Well if you have had those thoughts on any of the above then you are ready for a refreshing break! If it is over half - 18 or more - then you really should give the P.A.R.T.Y. Party a go! What have you got to lose? After all - what difference will one more Conservative or one more Labour M.P. going to make in Parliament anyway? I'll tell you - none! At least with the P.A.R.T.Y. Party you get individuals with fresh ideas and the freedom and passion to stand up and talk about them.

Who would be unlikely to vote for the PA.R.T.Y. Party?

In all honesty, the Party Party isn't for you if you. . .

. . .believe that generating as much money as possible is the most important thing in life.

. . .believe that man's activities are not having an adverse effect on the state of our planet.

. . .believe that it is O.K. for individuals to seek extraordinary wealth at the cost of everyone else.

. . .believe that animals have no feelings or rights and are there purely there as a convenience and a commodity for people utilize and profit from.

. . .believe it is better to spend public money on middle management paperwork rather than at the front end getting the job done.

. . .believe that it is fine keep archaic systems in place simply to fuel work for overpaid 'experts.'

. . .believe the loss of countryside and its wildlife does not concern you.

. . .want to keep the British public working flat out to support an outdated class system.

. . .are happy to abuse the people of the third world to save a few pounds.

. . .believe that it is O.K. for a few individuals to play around with the genetic make-up of our planet, risking everything we know and rely on, just so they can make a lot more money.

. . .are happy for huge numbers of people in Britain to suffer chronic health problems because of the burden of their work load.

. . .really think 48 weeks on and 4 weeks off is a reasonable proportional work leisure ratio.

. . .think it is right for the adult British public to be told what time to go to bed.

CHAPTER 5

The Election

'People never lie so much as after a hunt, during a war or before an election.' - Otto von Bismarck

The run up to the election was a panic. There were hoops to jump through for the Electoral Commission, but everything was pretty simple except the deadlines. While going through the process it dawned on me that because small parties like mine don't have a cats' chance of winning we are encouraged as it looks good if you are trying to sell the concept of a an open, free and fair democracy.

'Look at how many small parties are running in the election! Everyone can have a go! That is the kind of fair and equal land we live in! Anyone could be the next prime minister!' Bollocks. I worked my arse off, went to all the hustings debates that I could get in to speaking about common sense solutions and had the longest lines of audience participants queuing to talk to me after each event. The result? 107 votes. Jim Knight (Labour) won with about 18,000. Rubbish!

I was surprised to learn that hustings debates were held in church halls, or even in the church itself, with the vicar as the timekeeper and referee. That had me wondering what the church have to do with elections? Why were they getting involved? Is this just another bit of subliminal programming so people sub-consciously link church and government as one happy organization working together to make our lives better?

What I can say for sure is that while they claim to be impartial, the vicars are not. On my very first experience it took me by complete surprise that the vicar ruled that the current member of parliament should be given three minutes for each answer, the next party two and the others, including me, one. What the fuck is that about? We all know what the guy who is currently part of the government is going to say. We have been hearing about their policies on the news for the last five years. And they are the favourite in the race. They should be giving the underdogs, who have something fresh to say, the extra time.

Imagine if they had the same rules in the Olympics. 'Well, as Hussein Bolt won the hundred meters last time, he only has to run sixty meters this time, and the guy who got silver has to do eighty and the rest of you have to do the full one hundred, except the contestants we never heard of mcan start in the car park outside the stadium. We'll give you a call when the gun goes off. Oh, and good luck with your race by the way!'

In the same vein the party election broadcasts are also unfairly rigged. The government gets three of them, the second placed guys get two and everyone else who has enough candidates (with representation in one sixth of the constituencies), one. And who do you think it is who unilaterally gets to choose the time that the Party Election Broadcasts (P.E.B.s) go out? The BBC. That's democratic isn't it? A TV station unilaterally chooses the times, which is why the main parties get their broadcasts around peak viewing times of seven in the evening and others, such as the Greens, get theirs at ten thirty at night. If you are starting to smell a rat you - are right to.

At the hustings debates several other things started to occur to me. One, the candidates could say whatever they wanted with utter impunity. No-one held them to any commitments or promises they might make. That meant, for example, that the conservative candidate can, without any fear of being taken to court, claim that his top priority was to bring about equality of earnings, and improvement of conditions for the poor was his highest priority. To sit there and listen to him saying this, even though it was utterly at odds with the proven policies of his party that were widening the rich/poor gulf into the Grand Canyon by driving people into zero hours contracts and internships, (where people are expected to work for *nothing*), was simply staggering.

It was also interesting to see the guys who were a candidate of a larger party struggling with their answers as, apart from the odd blatant lie, they could only echo what was in their parties manifesto. This meant their answers for the most part were stuttering and guarded as they struggled to remember what they were supposed to say, not what they wanted to say from the heart. That struck me as taking the whole point out of the meeting. I mean why not just send everybody a copy of the manifesto and let them get on and read what you are going to say. Any person in the room could predict what 'yes man' Jim Knight was going to say and so really there was no need for him to be there at all.

Incidentally Jim stood for three terms as labour MP before being ousted, and in all that time never once voted against his party leader, and he then lost an election but immediately became Lord Jim Knight of Weymouth. Oooh! I wonder how our political system, that we are told at school is the envy of the world, works?

All that said I did enjoy the hustings. It elevated me out of the frustrations of being in the audience on to the rostrum where I could have my two-penneth worth. I am pretty good at thinking on my feet and like talking in public. I can also like making people laugh and while I suppressed that, occasionally it surfaced. After all I was standing for the ridiculously named Party Party.

At the debate in Weymouth a lady stood up and asked a question dear to everyone who lives in Dorset's heart. 'My three daughters are unable to afford to buy properties in Weymouth where they want to live. Does the panel recommend that they go to London and work for ten years to get a deposit together or do they think they should get pregnant and so get provided a property by the council?' This wasn't a question. This wise old bird had already thought out the only two options that presented themselves to her daughters and was making a statement of this highly unsatisfactory state of affairs.

The candidates tried to out-do each other with the number of affordable houses that would be built if they got in. 'We would build ten thousand new homes', 'we would build twenty thousand.' When it was my turn I said 'before I answer the main part of this question can I just say to the lady that should any of her daughters decide to go down the pregnant single parent route I would be more than happy to help them out with that part of their problem at least!' I waited for the laughing to subside before adding 'the solution shouldn't be about building more houses, we all love living in Dorset because it is beautiful and rural, so the thrust should be about making it financially painful for people to have second homes that they use solely for investment and holidays. Houses should be homes and to own one you should have to live in it and work in the area. There are plenty of properties around but they are all empty. Some villages are eighty per cent empty. The school has no children, the busses are empty, the pub can't survive, the post office and shop are closed down and that to my mind is unacceptable. Who wants twenty thousand new houses? You want to live in Sheffield-on-sea? And guess what? If you did build them who would end up buying those houses? Some banker from London who is collecting them. And why? Because there is nothing to stop him. It would cost almost nothing to implement and would solve the housing dilemma not just for this lady's daughters but for everybody who wants to live and work in Weymouth.' Huge round of applause. The people agree! They are impressed with an honest logical answer! 107 miserable votes. Fuck me.

I was accused by a disgruntled conservative supporter who clearly didn't want to hear anything fresh 'you don't like rules do you? Do you observe double yellow lines?' I replied 'I am perfectly capable of deciding where it is safe or unsafe to park so for me there are more important things to concern myself about.' So then he asked 'how do you feel about paying tax?' and I answered 'I wouldn't have a problem paying tax if the government were like my wise uncle who loved me and who spent my pocket-money carefully and frugally, putting aside some for a rainy day, spending a little on things that were essential for my welfare while letting me have enough to enjoy myself. But they are not. They are like my wicked uncle who likes to keep most of my pocket money for himself and chooses to spend it on controlling me and waging war in my name.' Big round of applause, 107 votes (although if I were to have met those 106 people, I did vote for myself obviously, I would be humbled and feel indebted to them.)

The questions were drying up when someone who was in an anti-abortion group stood up and asked 'where does the panel sit when it comes to the lengthening of abortion deadlines?' 'Bloomn' 'eck', I thought, 'why on earth would anyone want my opinion on that?' You may like to know that my answer now would be 'every baby, a wanted baby and the mother should have all the facts and absolute authority.' But luckily the legalise marijuana candidate was before me and he said 'what a woman does with her vagina should be her concern and us men shouldn't be trying to stick our noses in.' Well you don't miss an opportunity like that do you? So I just blurted out 'bloody 'ell mate, speak for yourself!' It brought the house down.

After the Weymouth debate ended the 'big boys' were driven off by their election agents while the rest of us candidates kind of stood around in the car park chatting and finding out more about each other. I discovered that all of us deserved a vote more than the established parties. We all of us had a take on something that we believed in and were prepared to sacrifice our own time and money to try and put our case across. Good for us. At the lower end of the car park was a pub and I asked if anyone fancied a pint and was impressed that we all did, even if in fact it was only the four of us, the 'Legalise marijuana party', the 'Independence for Wessex party', the 'Green Party' and me.

At the entrance to the pub we were astounded to see a plastic bush that had leaves that were unmistakably in the shape of a cannabis plant. The shape of the bush was all wrong (I happened to know being such a smart-arse) but that famous five fingered leaf was all over it. The legalise marijuana man was in raptures and saw it as a sign, and I could only agree that it did seem an unlikely coincidence. We took photographs of him with it and laughed at them over a couple of pints. We got on so well that the marijuana man invited us back to his flat where he promptly rolled a couple of the biggest fattest spliffs I had seen for a long time. In my stoned state I couldn't help finding it ironic to have been up on the stage an hour or so ago telling people to entrust me with their votes and here I was, this fine upstanding member of the community, laughing my head off, lying on some strangers floor. I suspect much worse happens behind the doors of power (and there is a great deal of evidence of really sordid goings on that the police will not act upon) if we were only to hear the truth.

When I got the results I was miffed that the electoral commission had got the name of my party wrong and had simply called it P.R.T. It was disappointing because the whole reason for calling the party such a ridiculous name that was funny and interesting had been lost in the lists that would now appear in the press and the archives. It's only a small thing but the joke was spoiled, and that was disappointing. Purposefully? Well perhaps.

CHAPTER 6

An attempt to unify

'If we expand our experience into wilder and wilder regions of experience - every once in a while, we have these integrations when everything's pulled together into a unification, in which it turns out to be simpler than it looked before.' - Richard P. Feynman

The was a problem. I was doing this completely on my own and decided I needed to gather a large number of candidates together to stand under a single banner, and came up with the title of 'Alliance of Free Speaking Independents'. I wrote to every minor party in the Electoral Commissions register stating that we needed to band together in order to get the necessary numbers to qualify for a Party Election Broadcast and that it should be possible for us to do that as long as we could agree a format that every candidate adhered to. It was a pretty tricky proposition to balance, for example, to get the 'anti-abortion party' and the 'free choices for women party' candidates sitting at the same table.

I did get about fifty responses from the six hundred independent candidates and minor parties saying they would be interested but it was difficult to get excited about furthering it on that level of interest so I diverted my attention to campaign organisations instead. There are many of these in Britain, the highest profile ones being 38 Degrees, Avaarz and Zeitgeist. I mailed the executives of each of these suggesting that while it was great organising protests to persuade elected representatives to do the right thing, surely it would be better to be on the inside and make the decisions for yourself.

I likened it to trying to cook the perfect omelette by shouting instructions through the letterbox rather than being in the kitchen and being able to turn the gas down yourself. Because a lot of my thoughts were going into protecting the environment I also contacted Greenpeace and Friends of the Earth to see if they had any interest. I argued that most people cared about the creatures we share this planet with. When a whale comes up the Thames estuary by mistake the whole city stops to watch. That would suggest that people have more empathy for the natural world than they are credited for. However their position was that they were non-political and that they wished to remain that way, which is fair enough, but I still think they're missing a trick.

It was all looking like an uphill battle so I decided to remove every policy from the manifesto except the introduction of a true democracy. While it was interesting for me to be looking at how problems might be solved it was simpler by far to just say that I stood for the introduction of a free and fair democracy for the people, run by the people and that whatever the people might decide would be what the people would get.

The most common argument that people launch against this suggestion is that there are a lot of un-thinking, un-caring people about and letting them have an equal part of the vote would bring about complete chaos. I understand the concern, but this could never be the case because mathematics takes over. If you ask ten people their opinion you can form some idea of the result, if it's a hundred you iron out some quirks, a thousand is better still but if you ask forty million then you are sure to arrive at the right answer. Because of probability curves and the way the maths works there can be no other outcome than the collectively right result. Add to this that most people want the same sorts of things, peace, freedom, fun, security, clean air and water, affordable homes and transport, a sustainable future, child care, equality, an efficient health service, good pensions, a comfortable retirement and a sunny future, then surely most people are going to vote with policies that point way.

Even if a sizeable proportion didn't have a clue, the maths still takes over, as the wayward thinkers would randomise, thereby negating each other and so not distorting the underlying curve. Ask a family that includes four small children what the square root of eighty one is and the children might give nonsensical answers. The fact that there is a consensus from the others, even if it is only two of them who know the answer is nine, is enough to produce the right result. In the game show 'Who wants to be a millionaire?' the 'ask the audience' help line is by far the most reliable assistance to the contestant. In Norway the producers expanded it so that anyone in the country could answer the question and guess what? Collectively they never got one single answer wrong in three years. That tells you a lot.

CHAPTER 7

Movement for Active Democracy (M.A.D.)

'If liberty and equality, as is thought by some are chiefly to be found in democracy, they will be best attained when all persons alike share in the government to the utmost.' - Aristotle

So I had run in an election. It had turned out to be less fruitful than I had hoped but I had learnt a lot, and was awakened with the absolute knowledge that anyone standing as an independent or for a minor party, was not playing on an even field. The main parties had it all sown up. It wasn't a matter of which candidate had the best policies, as I had naively believed, but indoctrination of children in their formative years, of press domination and the bogus fear programmed into each of us of 'the other party' getting in. In the run up to the election many people had said to me 'I would love to vote for you but I simply can't risk (insert name of the party that wasn't the major one they usually support here) winning.

I'd had my two minutes of fame. A couple of pieces on the radio, a few lines in the press, a couple of public showings and that could have been the end of it, however I believed more strongly than ever that the future of mankind and the planet relied on shattering the corrupt system controlling government that was driving us to oblivion and so, with that in mind it was uncomfortable to let it lie and go play tennis.

I thought about the P.A.R.T.Y. Party gambit and decided that, while it had been fun having a poke at the system, and I had enjoyed the ride for my own ego's sake, I really had stumbled onto something important and possible. I realised that if this were to be furthered then the care-free image had to go. I umed and ahed about what to replace it with, as I wanted a catchy acronym. I decided I needed something that would be slogan-able and bumper sticker-able, with revolution to a true democracy being the heart of the campaign.

Most people mistakenly think we are already living in a democracy, and that isn't surprising. We are always being told that, but it simply isn't true. A 'representative democracy' is what we have, and that isn't the same thing at all. So, Campaign for Real Democracy? True Democracy? How about an 'Active Democracy, where the people take a key role in the decision making process? Surely that could be the way forward? And so after thumbing through the dictionary for a day for inspiration I came up with the 'Movement for Active Democracy.' The acronym is M.A.D. which struck me as being pretty attention grabbing. I was envisaging tee shirts with 'Don't go crazy. Go M.A.D.!' or 'If you aren't M.A.D. you must be nuts!' on them. Well, something like that anyway.

I knew there might be a downside with people assuming that this was another 'Monster Raving Looney Party', but reckoned that anyone who took any time to find out about it would soon realise their mistake. I decided to go with it as I really didn't want it to blend into the grey background and boring mediocrity that is British politics. The party was re-registered and work began on generating a new logo, image and website.

At the heart of the campaign was the logo of the upside down pyramid, based on an inversion of the one on the back of the dollar bill that I drew up myself. The front page of the website read – "following is a brief 'elevator pitch' of the fantasy land that has been constructed for you. A list of myths that most people believe in so strongly that they can become angered at the merest suggestion that their truths that they cling to are no more than a shallow fabrication.

Myth 1 – You live in a Democracy.

You vote therefore you live in a democracy, right? But what do you vote for? An M.P? Is that all? So you can choose between parties or people to represent you but that is the limit of your involvement other than extremely rare (twice in my lifetime) referendums. That is not democracy, but *representative* democracy and it is a very different thing, incorrectly labeled to hinder you realising your exclusion from power.

Myth 2 – The Government are at the top.

The pyramid that appears on the back of the dollar bill and the MI5 logo is a masonic symbol, has a divide toward the capstone. The wide bottom of the main pyramid represents you and I, the people, many of us but with no power. The top of the lower section is diagrammatically represents the Presidents and Prime Ministers. Significantly, this is not at the top. There is a break before we the capstone, with the all seeing eye and powerful light rays emanating from it. This represents the tiny minority, the wealthy elite, the 1% club that is made up from banking families (like the Rothschilds who alone are worth around $100 trillion), and CEO's of huge corporations. Often referred to as the 'Illuminati', these people control government by sitting on boards that feed and dictate the government agenda. This capstone remains unchanged and in control no matter who the electorate might choose as their puppet leader, and it is from this position of power that the politicians receive their orders.

Myth 3 – The Government makes the important decisions.

Your Prime Minister does not wake up in the night and suddenly decide that the people need a war, but receives instructions from the elite. This is achieved through a visible yet little understood chain of civil servants (Permanent Secretaries) who in turn receive their orders from 'Think Tanks' like Chatham House that consist of self-appointed wealthy committee members that manipulate government policy to meet their own ends.

Myth 4 – Elections matter as they effect change.

Elections, in their current form, are an elaborately played out charade. Being encouraged to vote for one of the 'traditional' parties is promoted by those parties as being the opportunity for the people to effect change. The truth, however, is that this is nothing more than a trick to fool the people into believing they are 'involved', 'listened to' or 'asked opinion of', when they are not. An illusion of choice to pacify and control the unaware masses by making them believe they are deciding the future of their country, when they are not.

Myth 5 – Your well-being matters to the Government.

The people are treated little better than a 'peasant class, or like animals in a field that are only there to serve their masters. A largely disenfranchised population is being effectively controlled as, because all traditional parties are dictated to by the same elite group, there can never be, nor is there meant to ever be, any significant change that would benefit the ordinary people of Britain.

Our role is simple - to do the work that the elite have no interest in doing themselves and in doing so become part of the tax-farm. Our life's efforts fund the ambitions of the elite. It is our taxes that makes everything possible and pays for all government activities whether those activities serve the people or not. While every decision is sold to the people as being in some way or other in our interest, mostly they are not. They don't want to actually fight in their wars, they don't want to clean their streets and they don't want to carry out their operations, drive their taxis, dig their fields, teach their children, or even police their people. In fact every job you see being done, other than sitting in a swiveling leather chair barking orders, is carried out by one of us who will never be a member of the elitist club.

Without us, however, the elite would be sunk. For that reason and that reason alone we are allowed some simple pleasures to make life tolerable. We can have a few weeks holiday each year, we might even have enough money to go somewhere nice. We can watch football and paint our houses and go to the pub, walk the dog, take the kids to school and have sex with our partners. Don't ever forget though that the price we pay for these simple 'liberties' is that we must go to work for forty eight weeks out of the fifty two, five days out of the seven and eight daylight hours out of the eleven.

Myth 6 – You are not bright enough to form opinions about the world around you and need a 'clever' representative.

When someone questions a decision that clearly is going to cause them degradation or loss of life style the governments normal response is to simply say that that person doesn't understand the greater good they shall be benefiting from. If pressed and exposed the Government will simply blame a 'scape goat', or put up some smokescreen saying they made 'mistakes' and it was their 'own stupidity.' This is normally swallowed without question as in normal life no-one wants people to think they are stupid. This is the governments most effective escape route, as people thinking they are stupid will laugh and look no further, and this is their best cover. They will never reveal the identity of, or point out the normally greed motivated directions of the elite class who are secretly behind the policies partly because most M.P.s are themselves unaware that they are virtually powerless and just part of the system of deception.

Myth 7 – A 'representative democracy' is a 'democracy'.

Britain's democracy is founded on the document of Magna Carta, of which there are several versions but is usually referred back to the revisions of 1216 or 1297. At that time, and since, 'democracy' in Britain has normally only made allowance for the people of the country to periodically vote on a choice of representatives, who themselves are not selected by the voting population, but by a 'party', which is a privately run, self-serving, profit making corporation that files profit and loss accounts with Companies House, in the same way that B.P. or Lloyds Bank does.

These candidates, who become MP's if elected, are then relied upon by the people to go to Parliament to supposedly put forward views on behalf of those who voted them in (and those who did not). Other than extremely rare referendums the people have never been allowed to vote on individual issues for themselves.

The original reason for having a representative M.P. was the physical limitations involved in travelling to Westminster to join in a voting process. In the past it simply wasn't feasible for everyone to make that journey when it took several days, and so a simplified system was implemented.

While this was a poor and restricting manner in which to conduct the matter there was, at that time, little choice and no better solution available. Hence the creation of the concept of a 'representative democracy', which has been widely adopted throughout the world. This approximation is almost always referred to simply as 'democracy' when it is not one. 'Representative democracy' is a very different animal and the blurring of the two as being one and the same is perhaps the biggest lie of all.

Myth 8 – Your MP will represent and argue your views for you.

At a local level this may well be the case. M.P.s are loaded down with trivial work to perform for their constituents. When their time is taken up in this manner they are not acting as a member of parliament, but as a glorified councilor but with no actual power to influence local decisions other than by making their opinion known. If you want the swing in the playground fixed or a late bus putting on your M.P. can be very useful. This, however is not the role your M.P. should be playing.

When it comes to national issues, the problem with a 'representative democracy' is that it is clearly impossible for any one person to accurately represent the views of any one other person, let alone the varying views of some tens of thousands of constituents who will have conflicting views with each other

Myth 9 – Each candidate stands by their own principles.

Because each candidate is selected by their 'party' and not by their constituents, they are expected, and often ordered (whipped), to cast their vote in accordance with the party's aims, and not allowed to exercise their personal good judgement. All M.P.s are rewarded by the party for being 'good' (towing the party line, agreeing with the party leaders and supporting party policy) and can expect high profile roles in the cabinet (an inner steering group) and possibly a seat in the House of Lords as a reward at the end of a loyal stint in the House of Commons. They receive enhanced media attention and financial rewards related to both of those positions that flatter and massage the M.P.'s ego.

Myth 10 – When a Government loses an election everyone associated with that government changes.

While the government, that is made up of the party in control (providing the faces we see on the television) changes, the permanent secretaries (including the Prime Ministers), do not. As such it appears to us that a change has taken place, but it hasn't at all. It's just smoke and mirrors. It's like saying you have moved house because a different car is parked in the driveway.

So the answer to all this? True 'crowd-sourced' democracy. Involve the people in deciding about their circumstances and their future, passing their desires to an impotent government, who's only mandate was to act upon that will, as back office implementers, (civil servants, but ones that actually *serve* rather than dictate to us as they do now.) This would remove power from the banks and corporations. Which is why the M.A.D. inverted pyramid logo depicts the people at the top, celebrating their new found freedom, the government under us doing our bidding (for a change), and the capstone at the bottom with the eye closed and powerless.

Now I accept that some peoples' opinions shall be laughably ridiculous. I happened to listen to Talk Radio discussing crime and punishment. A lady came on and with sincerity suggested 'I would just take all the criminals and send them to the deepest darkest parts of Africa' to which the shows' host responded 'well, I'm not sure what the people who live in the deepest darkest parts of Africa would have to say about that but thank you for your comment anyway.' Of course, her opinion was not really a bad one if Africa were, as she surely had in her mind, a Tarzan jungle stretching for thousands of uninhabited miles. After all, this what we did with Australia. But that is alright. Some people will always have whacky and diverse opinions. It is good honest and balanced information that is the key to minimising tangential thoughts like this. Ultimately, if everyone had the authority to participate in the decision process and the results averaged out, all daft, ill-informed or extreme suggestions would get smoothed away by the simple maths of the majority.

When someone questions a decision that clearly is going to cause them degradation or loss of life style the governments normal response is to simply say that that person doesn't understand the greater good they shall be benefiting from.

If pressed and exposed as being at fault though endless lobbying and protests the Government will firstly try to blame the opposition party, saying the mess was created when they were in power. If that fails, they will then blame a scape goat, and lastly they fall back on saying they are stupid. 'Mistakes were made', 'we are only human' 'we got it wrong.' Putting themselves forward as being stupid may sound like a victory for the common man but actually it is the smartest smoke screen of all.

Who in their right mind likes to say they were stupid? But if your absolute agenda is to never reveal the identity of, or the greed motivated directions of, an elite class who are secretly behind the policies that have been exposed as not being in the common interest, what better way can there be to stop all further investigation in its tracks than to fool the blind into celebrating a hollow meaningless victory. A laugh on 'Have I got news for you?' at the governments expense.

Because they are not at the top, the government's role is not to create policy, but to 'sell' the proposals they have been given by the elite classes who control them, to us, the people. Voting therefore is little more than choosing the face on the television that is relaying the bad news to you and I.

And why don't the ruling elite want us to live in a true democracy? Because this would cause a serious erosion of the power and influence of a tiny minority. How would they be able to sustain their massive profits and tax burdens if the people had a chance to have their say?

The more I thought of this abomination of our system that, once considered, is so transparent and yet virtually ignored in the press, the more motivated I became to start the change. To get the message across the 'Movement for Active Democracy' website was loaded with a slew of video clip links. This gave me great pleasure, and tried to make them informative and entertaining, hoping people would watch the next clip purely for the fun of it.

You need two people to form a political party but I had three. Myself, and my friends Jill and Simon, who are now married. The first attempt at the videos was laughable. A company was brought in to film, with Jill asking the questions one after the other, and I answering them in the same fashion. The two sets of takes were then edited together. I took one look at the result and burst out laughing. It was so utterly amateurish, with Jill doing little anxious sideways glances at the end of each question like she was doing something really naughty, and me trying to be professional in my answers oblivious of my hair sticking out from my head at some bonkers angle.

Next, I bought a camcorder and set it up in my conservatory with a ripped and stained George Cross backdrop (patriotic but not too establishment, and suggestive of a struggle) and was delighted with the results. The recording quality was perfectly adequate and putting all of the clips on YouTube turned out to be a simple process. The clips mounted up quickly as every time I thought of a funny way to open people's minds I would sit down and add another to my website.

Sadly, they were too long for the modern world. My friend Owen told me that as soon as he saw a two minute bar at the bottom he just turned off. I had hoped that I'd made them entertaining enough for people to want to watch them. Some did, but not nearly enough.

Also, it was only me doing the clips. What further evidence was needed to know that this was essentially a one man show? A large part of the website was dedicated to inviting people to join the party. I believed that finding more candidates would be simple, but it wasn't at all.

Publicity is everything and so the next goal was a Party Election Broadcast. Smaller parties only get the one broadcast and the BBC would probably choose a time like ten thirty in the evening but even so, three minutes of terrestrial TV could change everything. To qualify I needed a candidate standing in every sixth constituency, which then was only one hundred and eight in the whole of Britain. Surely there had to be that number of people in the country who were disgruntled enough to put up a five hundred pound deposit and pay for a little printing and perhaps a website, in return for having a role in a PEB and furthering the cause to solve man-kinds ills? Wrong again. I was on my own.

CHAPTER 8

The Gazette

'Trying to determine what is going on in the world by reading newspapers is like trying to tell the time by watching the second hand of a clock.' - Ben Hecht

One day I unexpectedly bumped into John on the high street in Swanage. John was a charming portly guy whom I only knew in passing. He edited the local paper, the Gazette. I was surprised when he told me that he had admired the stand I was taking and offered me a hundred pounds towards the party funds. I had said that was very generous of him but I couldn't take his money with a clean conscience as no-one else had donated and I was feeling a little in the doldrums with it all.

His spirits unquenched, he replied 'ok then, I'll tell you what I'll do, I'll give you a page in the Gazette' which is the free monthly publication that was eighty per cent advertising, but with just enough content to make people want to open it. Although one of my best friends in Swanage said his went 'straight into the bin' which wasn't overly encouraging, it boasted a circulation of about sixty thousand so there had to be some merit in it.

I thanked him but didn't give it too much thought until a week before print-deadline when I sat down and started to write, pretty much for the first time in my life, and found that I enjoyed it. The thoughts tumbled out and I asked for the page to be called 'Outside the Box' as there was a lot of lateral thinking in the articles. I liked choosing a topical issue, airing it and exposing the problems, but also putting forward simple and affordable fixes.

The articles gained popularity and the feedback was good. One of the local teachers started reading them to their class for general studies, getting the kids to debate them. Several people started dropping in at my pitch and putt course and that was hugely encouraging. I tried to emulate a jaunty Bill Bryson-esque format hoping people might be entertained even if they didn't agree with the content. Following are some of the pages I wrote.

I have subsequently added news articles that were written some years afterwards to each to give you some idea of the more recent position that we find ourselves in. The common theme is one of a lack of action or intelligent problem solving by government, which should not surprise anyone.

CHAPTER 9

Housing or Second Homes

'Housing is absolutely essential to human flourishing. Without stable shelter, it all falls apart.' - Matthew Desmond.

My very first article for the Gazette was published in June 2005. It read:-

So another Parliamentary Election has come and gone, Jim Knight has been returned once again to represent South Dorset, and can I say what a pleasure it was to be sat momentarily in the spotlight with him and the other runners in my capacity as leader of the P.A.R.T.Y. Party - Personality AND Rational Thinking? YES! Party.

Well I read with interest that Jim has some plans to tackle the thorny issue of providing low cost housing in Dorset that I find, shall we say, just a little wishy washy. At the Q. & A. sessions running up to the election the Lib Dems were advocating the building of 10,000 new houses in the county, (a bit like John 'smack 'em in the face with a left hook' Prescott's bright idea - that's right lad - 10 million more houses all over the place that's what we need to improve quality of life in Britain) but who wants to live in Birmingham-on-Sea? Ed Matts of the Conservatives was his usual crisp self (now that is a very important question that is very dear to my heart - er - what was it again?) and Jim blinded us all with percentages, apparent differentials and meetings with Kofi Anan that, while no-one understood any of it, surely proved that he was so much more intelligent than us mere mortals that he had to know what he was twittering on about and was bound to be right!

And so the great idea (that incidentally is new since the Q. &A.'s) is? To change the planning law to provide for low cost housing on the outskirts of villages. Hmmmmm...well this sounds kinda like the 10,000 new houses 'idea' so let us think this through for a moment.

First, how low cost can they be? After all even with the Government giving away land the Builders Association say it would be a challenge to provide houses for £60,000, so add £40K for the plot and you are into six figures. And what would happen to these not so lovely cheap houses surrounding all our pretty Dorset villages? They would be snapped up by speculators before they even got built and sold on completion for £150,000 to - er - locals? No! Someone with plenty of cash up in London who can afford to speculate with their pocket money. The countryside will have gone, the villages ruined and nothing will have changed. And there lies the problem.

The Channel Islands saw it coming decades ago. Everyone would love to have a holiday home in Guernsey so did they 'solve' the problem by building 10,000 new cheap houses all over the island? Thank God no. They introduced a bit of legislation that said there are one set of rules on buying a property if you are born there and another set (making it unprofitable for speculation) if you come in from outside. Simple, quick, easy, cheap and it works! Go and have a look for yourself, the place retains its beauty and the communities, with full houses, are thriving.

So here we are - ghost villages of empty property, holiday homes, second, homes third homes, twelfth homes, seventy fifth homes, closed post offices, empty busses, struggling pubs, village schools closing down and no-where for local people to live. This clearly has to stop. Homes are a necessity, not a luxury, and these empty houses have got to become available as prime residences only for people who work and live full time in Dorset.

So how to do this? Well there are many ways, 100% purchase tax on property for people purchasing from outside the County without a full time job is one. Or perhaps increasing Council Tax on second homes by 1000%. Yep - that should do it. Think how less attractive it would be to sit on your empty house in Langton Matravers with an rates annual bill of £20k waiting for you when you popped down for your second weekend of the year. Sure there would be a lot of upset people, but houses are built to be homes. As a result property would be sold, the market would be flooded, prices would fall (yes I hear a groan at that one but hey - you cant want affordable housing for your kids and have your two bed flat being worth half a mil - it just doesn't work like that) and there would be enough - even more than enough affordable housing for us all. And no building on our green and pleasant land.

So come on Jim - how about it? You have the power, so why not do a bit of thinking outside the box and use it creatively!?

Maybe what Britain needs is a country wide campaign - the Campaign Against Second Homes - C.A.S.H. - and John 'which Jag shall I use today?' Prescott who, if he gets his way, is going to mess up this country permanently, can stick his thoughtless blinkered plans up his exhaust pipe.

So what has actually happened in the ten years since? Olivia Rudgard, social affairs correspondent in the Telegraph, on 19th August 2017 wrote:-

"One in ten British adults now owns a second property, research has found.

She states that the figures published by the Resolution Foundation show that the number of people with multiple properties *'rose from 1.6m to 5.2m between 2000 and 2014 - a 30 per cent increase in the proportion of adults who owned more than one home.'*

Olivia reveals that just 3.4 per cent were letting property out, meaning that 6.6 per cent of the population, or 3.4m people, have extra properties that they leave empty as an investment or use as holiday homes. That his was confirmed by Laura Gardiner of the Office for National Statistics who found find that while overall home-ownership plummeted, second home-ownership had risen dramatically.

Laura stated that properties not being used for rental included "holiday homes, flats that adult kids live in for free, empty properties being speculating on, MP's with London flats and constituency houses."

Paula Higgins, of pressure group the Homeowners Alliance, called the figures *"shocking"*, adding *"you shouldn't be making more money off your house than you do from going to work."*

In summary Paula stated *"It's really the haves and have nots - there's a generation of people being locked out of owning their own home and all the benefits that go along with it, and there's another generation who's got the leverage to benefit from rising house prices.*

We need to get homes that are for living in and not for investment."

Well needless to say I am with Paula on this one. Second homes are a travesty. Oh yes, I understand the benefits of having one, but the impact on the loss of real homes that people desperately need and the carving up of yet more countryside to replace the stock is unacceptable, unless of course you happen to be a greedy property developer - then of course it is great!

CHAPTER 10

Housing again

'Much of the social history of the Western world over the past three decades has involved replacing what worked with what sounded good. In area after area - crime, education, housing, race relations - the situation has gotten worse after the bright new theories were put into operation. The amazing thing is that this history of failure and disaster has neither discouraged the social engineers nor discredited them.' - Thomas Sowell

Authors note: Apologies for some duplications between the two housing articles. Originally written several months apart they tackle different areas, but clearly the problems caused overlap. For authenticity's sake I chose to include the whole article rather than to edit.

Later I wrote:-

So let's face it - no matter how wealthy we think we are in Britain due to the fabulous price tag on our houses the reality is that, unless you don't plan to have a property anymore, no-one is better off. Well that isn't quite true is it? Because if you only have one house and then you buy another while selling the first you are not better off, but if you collect houses now you can start creaming it.

The big question is whether this is an acceptable way for individuals to act. Britain is a small place and we are running short on space. There are plenty of houses in Britain for pretty well each family to have one, but the problem is that quite a lot of us want more than one. Some people even want more than a hundred, and this is leading to the shortage and is unacceptable and unsustainable.

Empty holiday homes have the knock on effect on small communities in beautiful locations, which cease to function because there is no-one there. There are no kids to go to school, no-one to use the corner shop or the post office, no-one to use the busses and no-one to drink in the pubs. Young people who are on comparatively very low wages are unable to compete with the city house collectors and so have no choice but to move away. Many of our loveliest towns and villages are becoming ghost towns and I think that is a tragedy that has to stop.

I utterly oppose the governments answer to build a load more houses. We do not have that much green space left on this crowded island and even if they did build 10 million more homes what would happen? Yep you guessed it! The greedy house collectors would snap them up and speculate on their values leaving the countryside gone and the problem unresolved.

Well how about this? Imagine if the tax rules were changed to make it financially unviable for anyone to own more than one dwelling. Think of all the housing stock that would become available. Prices would tumble (I hear you grab your wallet close to your chest - but hey you can't make a killing on your own place and demand low cost housing for your kids!) and property would once again be available and affordable to those who actually lived in the area.

And no-one need lose out because when you sold your old house at a lower price perhaps, you would get your new one also at a lower price.

A home is not a luxury, it is a necessity. Water is a necessity. Food is a necessity. Is there any law to prevent someone super wealthy buying all the food in a city for a week? No. Would they make a lot of money selling it on to the starving? Probably. Would this however be considered unacceptable behaviour? Yes.

It is as simple as this, nine bears, ten caves, harmony. One of the bears takes over four of the caves, well, we have a problem Houston!

CHAPTER 11

Homelessness

'People can be so apathetic. They continue to ignore the real people trapped in poverty and homelessness. It's all most maddening.' - Daphne Zuniga

This article read:-

I have never been homeless and I have never had to worry about where the next meal is coming from, but I can imagine how tough that situation must be.

Because of this I struggle to understand the logic of legislation that ensures supermarkets and restaurants destroy perfectly wholesome food just yards from where a destitute person might be going hungry. Food hygiene laws are generally a good thing but they have got out of control, and now go far beyond a reasonable and safe standard.

If a little compassion were exercised and these laws relaxed a little it would be simplicity itself to introduce inner city schemes of hygienic food collection and re-distribution. I would support a scheme whereby restaurants and supermarkets would be encouraged to save unsold food for collection later that night, and, as an incentive, those establishment supporting the scheme would receive awards to place on the menus and in their windows recognising the fact that they are compassionate enough to support the less fortunate. This would enable the public to make their choice of restaurant or supermarket at least in part based on conscience. In this manner a vast food supply could be made available at minimal cost.

It is all very well sitting in a nice centrally heated office with a full stomach blocking such a proposal on hygiene grounds - it is quite another being unfortunate enough to be experiencing it first-hand.

So, what has happened in the ten years since I wrote that? Patrick Butler, the social policy editor for the Guardian, on 8th November 2017 wrote:-

"More than 300,000 people in Britain – equivalent to one in every 200 – are officially recorded as homeless or living in inadequate homes, according to figures released by the charity Shelter.

He goes on to say that by using official government data and freedom of information returns from local authorities, it was estimated that 307,000 people were sleeping rough, or accommodated in temporary housing, bed and breakfast rooms, or hostels – an increase of 13,000 over the year before.

Despite this huge number he was told by Shelter that the figures were an underestimate as they did not include people trapped in so-called *"hidden homelessness"*, who have nowhere to live but are not recorded as needing housing assistance, and end up *"sofa surfing."*

He goes on to say that in London at that time, one in every 59 people were homeless, and the city remained Britain's homelessness centre. Of the top 50 local authority homelessness *"hotspots"*, 18 were in Greater London, with Newham, where one in 27 residents are homeless, being worst hit.

Patrick explained that the problem was becoming worse in commuter areas bordering the capital, such as Broxbourne, Luton, and Chelmsford with big regional cities seeing a substantial year-on-year increases in the rate of homelessness. *'In Manchester, one in 154 people are homeless (compared with one in 266 in 2016); in Birmingham one in 88 are homeless (was 119); in Bristol one in 170 are affected (was 199).'*

He said that Polly Neate, chief executive for Shelter, said: *"It's shocking to think that today, more than 300,000 people in Britain are waking up homeless. Some will have spent the night shivering on a cold pavement, others crammed into a dingy hostel room with their children. And what is worse, many are simply unaccounted for.*

On a daily basis, we speak to hundreds of people and families who are desperately trying to escape the devastating trap of homelessness. A trap that is tightening thanks to decades of failure to build enough affordable homes and the impact of welfare cuts."

Patrick added that although public perceptions of homelessness are dominated by rough sleeping, Shelter points out that the single leading cause of recorded homelessness is the ending of a private tenancy, accounting for three in every 10 cases, and often triggered by a combination of soaring rents and housing benefit cuts.

He rounds off with Shelter's figures that showed as of April 2017, 281,000 people were living in temporary accommodation in Britain. A further 21,300 were in single homeless hostels or social services housing, while 4,500 were rough sleeping.

What a great country we have. 300,000 people with no homes, and, looking at the report on housing previously, 3.4 million empty properties that are for financial speculation use only. How can that be allowed unless the corporate elite view homeless people simply as a nuisance? After all, they don't bring anything useful to the table, do they? They make a mess of the streets, don't do much work, they don't pay tax, they make you feel guilty about that new Roller and Rolex you've been promising yourself, and they hold their filthy hands out as you walk by. No, they shouldn't get any help at all. Poor people, I just despise them. Why don't they just piss off and get rich?!

CHAPTER 12

Crime and Punishment

'If people are good only because they fear punishment, and hope for reward, then we are a sorry lot indeed.' - Albert Einstein

The article read:-

I do not agree with locking people up as the only form of punishment. Certainly it is a deterrent, which is good, but it is archaic and expensive, and so I would choose for this to be just one of the options available.

For those who were placed in confinement, other than those who presented a real risk to the public, I would make their services available to us all. After all they represent a huge work force sitting around doing not much at our expense. Paying their debt to society or creating one? - that is the question we have to consider here. Think of the good that this number of essentially free manual workers could do for society. Beach cleaning, litter picking, park maintenance, lamp post painting, pavement laying, canal digging, recycling sorting, the list is endless. With carefully chosen work projects this would not jeopardise jobs.

Further I think that young offenders often need assistance to obtain a new perspective on their lives and help to broaden their horizons. I suggest having them sent to third world projects where they could live very simply and work to the benefit of the local community, away from the trappings of our modern and materialistic society. I believe that in time friendship bonds would develop and both parties would benefit. Spending time with people who are living with very little would create a greater understanding of how comparatively privileged even the least fortunate in Britain are. Opposed to idolising millionaire footballers as role models, and seeing how far down they are, thereby creating discontentment, this would show young people how very fortunate and better off they are.

I believe that in some circumstances corporal and public punishment would be acceptable. Naming and shaming, as in the stocks, would be a good cheap deterrent! More importantly however this needs to be followed by a 'bringing back into society' ceremony if the offender is seen to be mending their ways. A tearing up of the record, a genuine fresh start and support to make real an opportunity to do better.

In Britain we are very good at making criminals of our young people and who can honestly say they never made mistakes when they were young? Records that stay with you for life are a terrible thing and destroy the chance to move on and to forget about mistakes made. Even if you are older it is the easiest thing to make a mistake and suddenly be daubed as a 'criminal'. This makes victims of people and creates bad feeling toward society, creating a much greater likelihood to re-offend.

I am not a Christian per say - although it is not a million miles from my spiritual viewpoint and I live in a predominantly Christian society, so where is the forgiveness? The turning of the other cheek? Government should be the ones to set a good example on this.

My proposal therefore would be to consider every prisoner for public works service, to provide life experience punishment for young offenders, and to put as much effort into re-introducing an offender back into society as was put into convicting them in the first place.

Kevin Marsh of the Guardian on the 28th July 2008 wrote:

"Moral, social and political arguments for and against prison are all very well. But what about value for money?

He tells us that in 1993, the UK prison population was 44,000, while in 2008 it was over 83,000. This trend was set to continue with the government announcing an extra £3.8bn to create 20,000 more prison places.

As a breakdown of the costs Kevin explained that in the UK it is estimated that each new prison place costs £119,000 and that the annual average cost for each prisoner exceeds £40,000. He suggests that such huge public expenditure should not occur without question. Value for money models were widely applied in other state services like healthcare, but have rarely been used to test the value of the criminal justice sector.

He questioned that while it might be true that incarceration reduces re-offending, the cost of the prison system still had to justify that reduction, and asked *'is the cost of cutting offending through prisons too high? Could alternatives provide better value for money?'*

From information gathered by the Matrix Knowledge Group using data from the US and the UK from 1996 measuring the net benefit of alternatives to prison, they found that alternatives to prison seem to deliver a better return on public money.

As an example, they suggested that residential drug treatment programs offered a £200,000 net benefit over prison over the lifetime of an offender. This was because drug treatment programs are cheaper to run than incarceration systems as they deliver lower re-offending rates. Similarly, using surveillance instead of cells saved £125,000 per convict.

He says that these findings could be used to argue that if corners were cut and we McDonald's-ise our cells, prisons still wouldn't deliver value for money. Once the numbers were crunched, investing more in prisons per head actually delivered increased savings in the long run. *'Because of associated reductions in re-offending rates, prisons which include educational and vocational programmes save society £50,000 for each inmate, whilst prisons with drug treatment saves £125,000.'*

Other work supported the findings, with some key studies indicating that prison, as we know it, is completely unjustifiable on economic grounds. Cynthia McDougall and colleagues from Matrix point out that *'for every $1 spent on prison, only $0.24 to $0.36 is saved on avoiding offending. This contrasts to spending on probation, which delivers $1.70 in benefits for every dollar spent.'*

Kevin summarized by saying *'the debate for and against prisons has historically focused on the moral, political and social arguments for sentencing. But public money is scarce; we need to make sure that the benefits of our prisons outweigh their costs. Whatever penal policy we decide to pursue, ignoring the economic dimension to this argument is something we can no longer afford to do.'*

CHAPTER 13

The Police

'There's only two people in your life you should lie to... your girlfriend and the police.' - Jack Nicholson

My article read:-

In Britain the police do a pretty good job under ever increasingly difficult circumstances. I think though, with a little help in a few areas, they could do a much better job and be more popular with the public.

For example, I don't think that the police time should be spent on traffic law enforcement. They could still play a role should a situation requiring them to be involved arise, but they are an expensive option to take on the full role. They are over-trained, overqualified, over equipped to be used in this manner. It also does nothing for public relations and the one thing the police need is the public one hundred per cent on their side.

I would make life simpler for the police officer on duty by removing or cutting back on onerous paperwork and giving officers the freedom to use their discretion to take reasonable and appropriate personal action without fear of prosecution and providing a fast track justice system for petty offences. Measurement of effectiveness would not be taken from meaningless numbers of arrests and convictions, but from the feedback from the community as a whole - after all if the public are satisfied then the objective has been achieved.

Taking ideas from officers at the front end force and implementing them would be high on my agenda, after all who knows more about the problems of policing than the police out on the streets, right?

It also saddens me to see the police used as the bouncers to the corporate machine. Causing trouble at peaceful marches by kettling (or worse), victimising protesters who have been ignored at every turn and now are left to the last option of hindering fracking lorries and basically being used to arrest anyone who tries to get their point of view over against the capitalist agenda the only ways they can.

I would put an end to I would propose cutting red tape, trimming down the management and consultant teams and stopping hugely expensive computer systems in favour of placing more local bobbies on the beat doing what the police force should be all about – deterring criminals before they offend, and catching them if they do.

So any changes since then? Tom Whitehead, Home Affairs Editor of the Telegraph wrote on 05 Jul 2009:-

'Police spending half their time away from front line as paperwork increases Police officers are spending an increasing amount of their time on paperwork, despite the Government's claim to have cut the burden of red tape, new figures have disclosed.'

He goes on to say that official Home Office data appeared to suggest its moves to cut bureaucracy are working, with police spending a larger proportion of their time on what is called *"front line policing"*. However, this definition included time spent on *"incident-related paperwork, such as preparing files for court cases or filling in stop and search forms. which has actually increased by a fifth in just five years, new figures show."*

This meant that almost half of an officers' time was taken up by dealing with paperwork, red tape and other duties away from patrolling the streets.

Tom expanded to say that opposition MPs accused ministers of using *"sleight of hand"* to disguise the fact that police officers are increasingly chained to their desks, with Chris Grayling, the shadow Home Secretary, saying: *"These figures will come as no surprise to any front line police officer, but it just beggars belief that the Government is yet again manipulating figures to make a false claim that things are getting better adding "We'll only tackle policing problems properly when we really do get rid of all the red tape they have to deal with, and not when Ministers pretend that's happening."*

Tom summarises with *'This means officers now spend almost half of their time carrying out some form of paperwork and other duties away from the front line.'*

CHAPTER 14

Less Work

'All paid jobs absorb and degrade the mind.' - Aristotle

My article read:-

So, have you ever wondered why you have to spend so much of your life working? Here you are with the good fortune of living in one of the wealthiest countries on the planet and look how much of your life you have to run around for someone else just to get by. Most workers are at it 40 hours a week, 48 weeks a year. Think about that for a moment - 48 weeks on- 4 weeks off, five days on and two off - doesn't that strike you as being a little one sided and excessive? Add time to get to and from work plus over time that many people are expected to put into their work for nothing, and it is hardly any wonder that many people have little quality home life, miss their kids growing up and are suffering from stress related illnesses.

In Britain we work longer hours and more weeks each year than any of our European neighbours. Ask a Frenchman to do a bit of free overtime and see what he has to say: Mais Non! Tell the Germans that they are only getting 4 weeks holiday a year and check out the reaction: Nein meinen leiberchick! Maybe the Spaniards wouldn't mind missing their famous siestas to help the economy along a bit? No mucho gracias, Hose!

Take a look what happens when we have a bank holiday. One measly extra day out of the week and the country goes mad. The beaches are packed and the roads are so jammed many people spend most of their free day sitting in their car.

I would suggest to readdress this by getting the work schedule in line with our European neighbours - longer breaks, shorter weeks and at least one more weeks holiday a year for everyone. Right away the we hear the governments arguments. What about productivity? Where would the money come from?

Well, for our start, if our neighbours can do it, then we can do it. The British worker carries the huge financial liability of the super-rich. There is a finite amount of money in any country and when huge amounts are being sucked away by the multi-property owning, overpaid directors and shareholders, the man on the street has to run around flat out just to make ends meet. This is why I would look at a maximum earnings limit (£1million a year perhaps?) before going over 100% taxation, thus making generating even greater earnings creating a loss exercise so shut the greed merchants up a bit. You see, while it is a deadly sin, there is no law against avarice and there lies the problem.

I also believe that if we all worked less hours the productivity in the remaining time would rise to fill the void, with greater levels of motivation, less fatigue and so less time being taken as sick leave.

I believe that life is for living, not working. As they say: if working were so great, how come the rich don't keep it all for themselves?

And since writing this? Richard Dyson and James Connington in the Telegraph 20th July 2017 wrote:-

"Teenagers and those in their twenties can expect to work to age 70 as the state pension age rises to cope with an ageing population and longer lifespans.

He pointed out that there was already a number of age increases planned, but that process was beginning to accelerate, and that the Government had just announced that a planned increase to 68, due to happen between 2044 and 2046, will now take place between 2037 and 2039.

They said this occurred in response to a report, by John Cridland, which outlined ways in which future pensioners might be able to delay taking their state pension in exchange for cash meaning around six million people in their 40s will need to wait or work longer than anticipated to receive their state pension.

Even with the boom of robots increasing productivity in the work place it seems we shall never be free of the yolk of an overburdened working schedule. I agree people are living longer but surely a robot workforce should be seen as a good thing, enabling people to enjoy more of their lives in peace without that 6a.m. alarm, not as an opportunity to squeeze even more toil and tax from an already overworked population.

CHAPTER 15

Cars

'Life is too short for traffic.' - Dan Bellack

I gave this emotive subject the following airing:-

Given what we know of what we are doing to our planet through the burning of fossil fuels it would seem to be wrong to continue putting more cars on the road.

Changes in the way we view transport need to be made. Dependency upon private cars eats up natural resources, pollutes the environment we rely upon, is causing chaotic weather patterns and puts pressure on building even more roads in a country fast running out of green space.

Cars are great! Of course they are! That is why most of us have got one! They are convenient and shiny and make you feel fab. But there is just a little tiny little downside to all of this and even the most ardent unbeliever is beginning to wake up to it. They are probably going to kill us all in the end. Now I know that may sound dramatic but it is true!

Cars are the biggest burners of fossil fuels by miles - if you don't believe that think about how much your heating or other travel bills are over the year and compare this with the amount you spend on petrol (true there are other factors like tax proportions but this still gives you a pretty simple indicator anyway.) So what do you think happens to all that petrol that magically disappears out of your tank? Has it gone away? You can't find it anymore can you so it must have gone! The trouble of course is that it hasn't gone away at all - it has just been converted into a whole load of pollution and CO_2 and been dumped into the atmosphere.

Air pollution causes illnesses but that is the good news here! The bad news is the cost in perhaps irreversible damage to the fragile ecosystem of our home planet. If this were resulting from pretty much any other activity other than using the cars that are so close to our hearts it would be outlawed. I mean - would we put up with this for a moment if it were - say - badgers that were driving around? No - we would get out there and kill the lot of them!

Now, let's take an example of any artery road heading into any city in rush hour and look at the cars and their drivers. Most of the vehicles you would see are expensive luxury company cars with one person in them. Now companies do not hand over vehicles like that to idiots - so we have to assume that the drivers of these vehicles are, by and large, intelligent, articulate and aware. So why are they happy to leave home in the full knowledge that they will crawl along at average speeds sometimes of less than ten miles per hour? Why do they put up with it? Surely this is a bad habit that needs breaking and to do this you need viable and attractive alternatives.

Consider this - one single two litre saloon car driving for one hour at 60mph kicks out enough exhaust to fill 10 double-decker busses - and that is just one! And consider also just how much time is wasted every day in this ridiculous exercise. If 30 million people take one hour longer to travel to and from work than it would take when the roads were empty (conservative estimate), then that would mean 30 million hours of qualified educated peoples time wasted each day - 150 million hours each week - 7,500 million hours each year. Or if you prefer about 937 million working days each year! That is enough time for all working adults in Britain to take six weeks off each year - without losing any productivity at all!

So here is the question. Accepting that walking to the minibus is less glamorous than jumping in your own car, and that walking to take one would in itself take time, so reducing the estimates here, would you be happy to change the way you travel in return for one month of extra paid holiday? Suddenly not using your own car doesn't look quite so unattractive does it?

Now here is the thorny part. For the transport system to work there has to be a change in attitude by everyone - and that includes the rich. I don't subscribe to the consensus of simply making it more expensive, as that only hurts the lower earning bracket of our society, but I would propose to limit everyone as to the quantity of private journeys they can make by limiting fuel availability. Yep - rationing.

With the exception of emergency services and those dependent upon vehicles for their trade (and no, carrying a brief case doesn't qualify) everyone would have to comply - that is the only way it can fairly work.

Remember when the petrol strike was on? Everyone still got to where they wanted to go - and there was no planning to that at all. People shared journeys, looked to public transport as a viable alternative, worked from home, let the kids walk to school, cycled, and jogged. And if by chance you did have a few gallons, wasn't it a joy to use the roads? Britain was quieter, cleaner and more efficient.

Imagine for a moment that every other car were suddenly off the road. How freely would the traffic flow and how quick would the journeys become? Imagine now public transport so regular that you need never carry a timetable. And imagine it being reliable, quick and virtually free.

To make this possible there has to be a re-shaping of bus and private taxi services into affordable hop on hop off minibuses that would ply set routes and run as regularly as the tube. This way the journeys of twelve people would be efficiently carried out by just one vehicle.

I would place greater reliance on the train network with an increased in rolling stock and journey prices being slashed. It would be far more enjoyable to relax while traveling from London to Manchester for under a tenner, knowing that a minibus would whisk you off within minutes of your arrival - no timetable needed. Surely that has to be better than sitting behind the wheel for hours?

I suggest abolishing road tax and cancel all road building schemes putting the money instead into public transport initiatives. Because use of private vehicles would be limited and as so many people would now be utilising public transport it would become highly profitable and successful proposition, even with low, low fares.

And remember the other side of the coin - everyone gets the equivalent of four weeks EXTRA holiday a year to as a thank you for supporting the scheme.

And since then? BBC News - 20 January 2016 said '*The number of cars on England's roads has risen by almost 600,000 in one year. Latest figures show there were 25.8 million licensed cars in the third quarter of 2015 compared with 25.2 million in the same period of 2014. Since 2011, the number has increased by about 1.6 million in England, 142,000 in Scotland and 69,000 in Wales'.*

They went on to say that *"the largest rise has been in south-east England, with 373,200 more cars over five years and added that the Society of Motor Manufacturers and Traders said there had been 2.63 million new cars made during 2015, a 6.3% rise on the year before. Production also hit a seven-year high."*

Unbelievable insanity. No effort to reduce cars on the roads. The public transport networks continue to be overpriced and ineffective. This doesn't serve the people. Who in their right mind wants log-jammed roads, air pollution and climate change? But you can bet that the car manufactures and oil producers will be rubbing their hands in glee. Most cars are now bought on HP, meaning more debt, so happy bankers too!

CHAPTER 16

Financial Meltdown

'If we are really serious about preventing another crisis like the 2008 meltdown, we should simply ban complex financial instruments unless they can be unambiguously shown to benefit society in the long run'. - Ha-Joon Chang

My article in the Gazette read:-

Who thinks that the global financial meltdown happened accidentally? Is it really possible that numerous different and unconnected financial institutions could all be making the same fundamental and significant mistakes - at the same time? Could over-zealous and irresponsible sales people have so infiltrated such formalised and controlled businesses as banking and mortgage lending that all these financial institutions collapsed all together?

Surely this would be like every car manufacturer in the world suddenly realising that they haven't been putting tyres on their vehicles. Unlikely to happen for one, but surely impossible for them all to have been making the same catastrophic mistake at the same time.

So what happens when someone can't, or doesn't, make their mortgage payments? The bank steps in and takes over the property. O.K. - the bank may have lost the money, but don't they now they own a cute little house in New Orleans or somewhere? There could be a loss in this but surely these places have some residual value? And if so many have been repossessed - where are they? Because if people could get a holiday home in the U.S.

for 5 G's then I reckon they wouldn't have any trouble shifting them, global meltdown or not.

When you can no longer furnish your repayments the bank simply takes back your home or car. Then surely it follows that the bank should have to live or die by those same rules. When they couldn't produce the money that their customers had invested and became insolvent what did the government do? They stepped right in and supported them, by giving them shed loads of our, the tax-payer's, money. That doesn't happen for you and I, so why should it happen for them?

I personally would have chosen to make an example of the first financial institution to register a problem and have forced them to sell all assets including all branches and offices with their contents around the world, all company cars, all directors assets and pensions, and redistribute the funds raised in proportion to the investors who had put their faith in them. If there were a shortfall then, and only then, the government could have looked at making up that difference.

This would have acted to both give warning to banks who were considering filing for bankruptcy and have made those responsible pay, not the innocent victims.

And did you see what happened when the government poured money into the financial markets? The graph took a huge leap up. There was celebration in the streets of Tokyo, London and New York. Yep, those nice friendly traders who have been sucking money out of the system for decades, money that otherwise would have been around for you and I, were partying their arses off. And then they sold out at the top, creaming all our money that our government had given them right off the top and putting us all right back where we were a few days before - but without the reserves.

And then we find that the government themselves are having to borrow money to do all this. And where do they get the money from? That's right - the bank! Am I beginning to smell a rat here!? Nice one guys - thanks for all your help! What would we have done without you?!

So if this is constructed as I believe, why would they bother? I mean things were ticking along quite nicely weren't they? Well here are three things to consider.

One, you cannot continue to grow indefinitely. Anyone can work that out. It is obvious. So sometime or other you have to have a downward period so you can start growing again. So better to have a huge and fast downward trend so you can get back on track for growth as soon as possible rather than to have a longer drawn out period of stagnation (if you are in the business of making money by riding other peoples' horses for free that is).

Second, if you happen to know when a global meltdown is going to occur then you know which horses haven't been drugged so betting becomes a sure fire way to make a huge amount of cash by being in the know, getting out early and letting the suckers (you and I) pay for it all.

Imagine conceiving a plan to hoodwink, (or more probably to work with as your co-conspirator), the government into pouring billions into YOUR institution so you can make vast profits even when everyone else is losing? Not a bad trick if you can get away with it. And they seem to have!

Third, the world is a changing place and the writing is on the wall, in fact just about on every wall, for anyone who wants to read it. Populations are growing, resources are getting scarcer, climate change is putting huge pressure on communities and countries, and globally things are not looking good. If you are not in the money or in control, have a view on life that is not only centred around you and your profits and have qualms about the suffering of others, it is time for you to act.

At the heart of the problem is the population growth, and the plan, that we are not informed of, is to reverse that trend through malnutrition. Let us take an example of Angola. That country has the second highest food prices in the world at the same time being one of the poorest African nations. How are people supposed to feed themselves on a dollar a day?

It doesn't add up, which is the way those in control want it. Impossible you say? They will never get away with it? Well who is going to stop them? You? Me? Of course the one force that they still have to pussy foot around, although not that carefully these days, is the people. That IS you and I. But now we would love to help out all those unfortunates in Africa, and ordinarily there would be a huge outcry about it but guess what? We have just had a global meltdown and now we are running scared about our own situations.

Yep, it's our old friend 'control through fear'. The same one that makes us give away our liberty to save us from bogus terrorism. The same one that keeps us working in jobs that have no meaning, other than to make money in the name of security. It's all control through fear, and most governments are masters at it.

So here is the crunch. Maybe these two events are not unconnected. The shrinking of the world population is a plan that is now in place and, to keep our eyes off the ball and stop us reaching out with empathy love to assist our fellow man, we are being dealt the fear card of global recession to shut us up.

What a terrible thought. Is this really the world we had planned for our children? A world of ceaseless greed and manipulation. A world where entire civilisations could be at risk just so others can make a quick buck? Yep, it would appear so. So is there an answer to all of this? Is there anything any of us can do? YES! Insist that a true democracy is born where the people have their say in everything thereby creating a world where, as the dictionary promises, the supreme power is held by the people. Where we make the choices and we know our truths.

The Guardian on 29th March 2018 had this to say about some of the banks involved in the crashes dubious activities: *"Barclays has agreed a $2bn (£1.4bn) settlement with the US justice department over the sale of mortgage-backed securities in the lead-up to the 2008 financial crisis.*

The settlement follows a three-year investigation into allegations that the bank caused billions of dollars of losses to investors by "engaging in a fraudulent scheme" to sell Residential Mortgage-Backed Securities (RMBS) between 2005 and 2007'.

They added that the British bank was said to have misled investors about the quality of the mortgage loans backing those deals, and that the justice department alleged violations of the Financial Institutions Reform, Recovery and Enforcement Act of 1989, based on postal, wire and bank fraud as well as other misconduct.

They told us that two former Barclays executives had also reached a settlement. Paul Menefee, who served as the lead banker of its subprime RMBS securitisation unit, and John Carroll, who worked as the head trader for subprime loan acquisitions, would pay a total of $2m.

Richard Donoghue, US attorney for the eastern district of New York, said: *"This settlement reflects the ongoing commitment of the Department of Justice, and this office, to hold banks and other entities and individuals accountable for their fraudulent conduct.*

They summarised by saying, however, that *'the fine was less than City analysts had expected and less than the penalties paid by other foreign banks facing similar claims. In December 2016 Credit Suisse paid $5.3bn as a settlement and to consumers. Deutsche Bank settled at $7.2bn a month later."*

CHAPTER 17

Civil Servants

'The film of tomorrow will not be directed by civil servants of the camera, but by artists for whom shooting a film constitutes a wonderful and thrilling adventure'. - Francois Truffaut

A favourite dig of mine in the Gazette read:-

I believe that there is far too much valuable time and financial resources being wasted in the Public Sector. This includes the police, medical staff, teachers, fire officers and pretty much every other public service funded through the government and local authorities.

I my opinion there is too much red tape, too many forms, too much testing, too much worry over political correctness and fear of being sued for doing no more than a good job. The people trying to do the jobs are finding it increasingly difficult and frustrating. Morale is low and expensively qualified and vital staff are leaving in droves.

In their place it would appear that we are getting an ever expanding army of middle management justifying their position by incessantly meddling with things that they appear not to fully understand, introducing meaningless reporting, targets and assessment systems which in turn creates an ever increasing paperwork burden for those on the front line.

You don't have to take my word on this. Ask any police officer what they think of the forms that have to be filled in. Ask any teacher what it is like dealing with a difficult children. Ask any nurse how their ward could be better organised. Ask any builder what they think of the current level of health and safety rules.

I would propose that this this trend be reversed. For teachers not to be in fear of children who know how to work the system. For police to act as they see fit when dealing with suspects and for medical staff to make appropriate decisions without fear.

I would allow the people doing the job to be the ones who get to say how they think it would be best done. I would cut down on the middle management hordes and spend the money where it is needed - in staffing, training and facilities for those who are doing the job and providing the service.

I would thin out the dead wood at the local council offices. Ask almost anyone working Council offices and they will be able to tell you who is providing a good and efficient service to the community and who is not. By streamlining the organisation a real and significant reduction could be made to council tax bills without the public loosing anything in services received.

And since then? Writing for the Telegraph, Jamil Mustafa on the 29th August 2016 told us:- *"More than 700 civil servants, officials and "quangocrats" earned more than £100,000 last year costing the taxpayer more than £100million, according to official figures.*

He said that an analysis by The Daily Telegraph found that the number of officials earning six-figure salaries has risen by nearly a fifth over the past two years.

And that the number of officials earning more than the Prime Minister's £142,500 salary has risen by a quarter to 332, with the highest earner paid £750,000.

Adding that more than 200 of them have enjoyed pay rises despite a cap by the Government and deep public spending cuts under the Conservatives, while others have boosted their pay packets with bonuses, six-figure pension contributions and official cars. Some were given six-figure payoffs after leaving their posts.

Jamil reported that Andrew Bridgen, a Conservative MP, said *"It's clear that the Paymaster General needs to get a grip on the culture of senior civil servants awarding themselves six figure salaries. It seems extraordinary that over 300 civil servants in Whitehall should earn more than the Prime Minister and these figures do not even include the thousands of local government officers earning six figure salaries."*

He pointed out that the highest earner was Simon Kirby, the chief executive of High Speed 2, who was paid a salary of £750,000. He has previously said he would provide *"value to the taxpayers by delivering the £56 billion project on time and on budget."*

Jim Crawford, a managing director at HS2, is paid a salary £395,000 while 32 other officials at the organisation earn more than £100,000.

When he turned his attention to the NHS, the body which runs the health service, he found that 23 officials earn more than the Prime Minister. The highest paid was Paul Baumann, the organisation's chief financial officer, who earned £210,000 in 2015 and had a pension pot worth nearly £500,000.

He said that these details of the high earners emerged as the NHS was drawing up a formal list of hospital departments to be shut in an attempt to ease the worst financial crisis in the history of the health service.

The Ministry of Defence has more than 100 officials earning over £100,000, he said, while at the Department of Work and Pensions, the total stood at 57, while HMRC, which has been heavily criticised for its "appalling" standards of customer service, has more than 35 officials earning over £100,000."

What can I say about that that you didn't already grasp? Or gasp at?! There was a time when being a civil servant was about serving the community and in return a nice steady safe job, low working hours, good conditions and a reasonable pension was reward enough. Times have changed. Greed has got into the public service sector. Councils have become self-serving money grabbing corporations in their own right. Most worryingly of the above for me is the HS2 conglomeration. A white elephant of a project that no-one wants, especially if you happen to live within two miles of the proposed route. A £56 billion budget? Salaries of £750k and £395k? A gang of 32 employees rewarding themselves over £100k? All to cut twenty minutes off the time to travel from London to Birmingham? And not one meter of track laid to date. Well there doesn't seem to be any hold on public money being ploughed into the corporations who are involved, so let's just move on shall we?

CHAPTER 18

America

'My fellow Americans, I am pleased to tell you I just signed legislation which outlaws Russia forever. The bombing begins in five minutes.' Ronald Reagan

My Gazette pop at our transatlantic cousins read:-

Now, I do not care for Britain following America. It appears to me the America is not the world peace keeper it wishes to portray itself as but in my opinion a country embroiled in invasive foreign policy that serves only its own purposes. This increasingly is becoming a threat to world wide stability.

O.K., Obama is in now but I personally do not believe that the American position or attitude will significantly change (save for a little rhetoric and some high profile changes that will make little difference.)

I am concerned by the tightening of liberties that we are experiencing as a hand down from the American way of life. Based upon what I believe to be a bogus threat of worldwide terror, we are being dealt blows to our personal freedom in the form of ID cards, surveillance, car tracking, monitoring of phone calls and e-mails, DNA databases and so-forth. These have all been inherited from the U.S.

I am alarmed by the American term of 'zero tolerance' which has invaded British life. While it charmingly has the word tolerance in the title, it actually means that no measure of understanding will be afforded to you for any mitigating circumstances whatsoever. Think about the implications of that for a moment. Nothing in life is undertaken with zero tolerance, there is always a little give and take or all things become impossible. It puzzles me that we just accept and adopt fascist terminology like this out of hand.

I do not like America's foreign policy and I do not like them, or us, occupying other people's countries, especially when they are clearly misleading us about their real ambitions. For example did you know that America has drone planes in Pakistan (and probably elsewhere) which they can solely authorise the launching of, and which have the capability to bomb settlements or groups of people without any communication to the Pakistan government and that they regularly blow up innocent civilians by this method? That is going to make us a whole bunch of friends isn't it?

I dislike the authoritarian manner in which legislation is introduced. The health and safety fiasco is an example. Red tape so thick people cannot get the job done and innocent people are being prosecuted for just trying to get on with things.

The lunacy of suing for damages for the most innocent of inconveniences or trivial of mistakes or accidents (that incidentally costs our NHS service about one seventh of its entire annual budget) regularly closes businesses down and puts well-meaning individuals into the courts. This is unacceptable, and inherited from the U.S.

Because it makes no sense for us to be this close to American principles, it suggests to me that we are not being told the whole truth about our 'special relationship' and the real reasons for these ties are being kept from us. This is deeply worrying.

My proposal would be for Britain to rebalance all of the laws pertaining to health and safety and rights to sue, and to retain the absolute right to form our own foreign policy decisions for ourselves.

And ten years since then? Ashley Cowburn, Political Correspondent at the Independent, on Friday 7th April 2017 wrote:-

"UK involvement in Syria: Would the Government or Labour back military intervention after US air strikes? Downing Street issued a statement saying the Government 'fully supported' the actions of the US President in Syria."

Ashley tells us that the United States military launched at least 59 tomahawk cruise missiles [valued at about $1 million each] at al-Shayrat military airfield near Homs, Syria, in response to the Syrian military's alleged use of chemical weapons in an airstrike in a rebel held area in Idlib province EPA. which killed dozens of civilians in the Idlib province of the war-ravaged country.

Ashley said that as Donald Trump urged other so-called "civilised nations" to join the US in its effort to "end the slaughter and bloodshed" in the region, the Independent examines the position of the UK Government, the opposition parties and whether it is likely Britain will now step up its military intervention in Syria.

And the reaction from the UK Government?

As news of the airbase assault filtered through, Downing Street, which was notified beforehand by the American administration, hastily issued a statement saying it "fully supported" the actions of the US President in the early hours of Friday morning. Government sources added they believed the action was *an appropriate response to the barbaric chemical weapons attack launched by the Syrian regime, and is intended to deter further attacks*".

I rest my case.

But touching on the Syria issue in particular for a moment, what disturbed me when I looked through the Reuters website was the slating of President Assad of Syria for the use of gas, which the article says it finds puzzling. Mohammad Bazzi of Reuters wrote, '*Why would Syrian President Bashar al-Assad, whose regime has consolidated control over Syria's largest cities in the past year and put the rebels on the defensive, risk a new international backlash by using chemical weapons? If he's winning, why would Assad take such a risk?*'

In my opinion, the simple answer is that he didn't. The article goes on to suggest it was a calculated risk that went wrong, but if a little research is carried out away from the main stream media, combined with interviews with Assad himslef, it appears highly likely that the trail leads to these atrocities being carried out by the U.S., as they have the vested interest in putting the blame on Assad, thereby destabilising the country, justifying the bombing and possibly invasion and the setting up of a puppet government aligned to U.S. policy in Syria, as they have done an many other countries.

I mean, we never saw anything like that before did we? Not in Iran? Not in Iraq? Not in Lybia? Pnanma? We are only doing it to restore democracy! Of course you are! You would think the U.S. would come up with a new lie by now. That one is getting a little old, don't you think? The U.K., as usual, is the puppy meekly following at the heels of mighty America, hoping to get a share of the spoils. We never heard much about the two dedicated floors of B.P in London that now heads up the U.K.'s oil and gas interests in Iraq did we? Well, like they always said, it never was about the oil. Was it?

The U.S. is clearly obsessed with protecting its oil supplies, and so just wants to control as many gulf countries as they can. The added bonus is ring fencing the threat from the dreaded Chinese.

As a background, Syria has no Rothschild controlled bank, does not owe money to the International Monetary Fund, does not import or produce genetically modified organisms, has valuable gas and oil reserves, does not support Israeli apartheid and is the last secular Arab nation in the world. Might all that not upset the banks enough for them to start yet another campaign? And so Mohamad Bazzi, in his position at Reuters at a stroke has written a piece that shall be swallowed and regurgitated by most of the mainstream press around the world, and another war is justified to the people who are yet to remove their blinkers.

In each of these events the test of truth is to simply ask yourself who it was who benefitted from such a dastardly scheme. Well it wasn't him or his country that's for sure, but the Americans got the excuse they needed. Hmmmmm.

CHAPTER 19

Genetic modification

'Transhumanism is the ethics and science of using things like biological and genetic engineering to transform our bodies and make us a more powerful species.' - Dan Brown

The article I wrote for the Gazette on this massively important subject read:-

I do not agree with genetic engineering. I don't subscribe to the, in my opinion, bogus arguments given by corporations like Monsanto about helping to feed the third world or improve our quality of life. It is transparent that this is a smoke screen and that the multinationals involved are concerned only with controlling the world food supply in the interests of returning vast profits.

Take Monsanto, if they really cared about feeding the third world why don't they start by about pledging a proportion of their vast profits to that cause?

Genetic engineering is meddling with nature. No-one knows exactly what might happen as a result of such dabbling but every time something is changed an adverse and unexpected down side has appearsed

Take Monsanto's Roundup weed killer tolerant wheat. Grow it and you will never have to worry about those pesky weeds again because you can spray the whole crop with Roundup and the wheat will continue to live - mmmmm - two loaves please! But the hidden trick is that Monsanto's wheat germ is sterile (but still packed with goodness I bet?) so when the farmer wants to get seed for next year's crop they can no longer keep 10% back for that, as they have done since farming began. They have to go back and buy it all again from, yes that's right, Monsanto! Get that into every farm and they are making mega-bucks! Their plan is to get the whole world food supply dependent on one firm! Great idea......for the shareholders, but what a grim price to pay for the rest of us.

And if I can plant a little seed of my own here, what happens if that sterile gene gets out and starts effecting other plants? Hum - sterile plants taking over? Could cause more than a bit of a problem for us in a few years don't you think? How can any company risk the future of life on earth in the interests of profits? No - I am very happy for my wheat to be natural and organic thank you Monsanto.

So while we are on the Monsanto thing did you know that they have developed genetically modified pigs that they have patented? This means that if any pigs turn up in any future generation with that modified gene in, the farmer will be unwittingly breaking patent laws opening him/her to prosecution unless they pay a licence fee to Monsanto. Thanks guys, anything else?

Well actually I could go on all week but in essence I believe this dabbling with Mother Nature is inherently wrong and should be stopped. We are already inflicted with GM tomatoes that look fab but taste of nothing, GM roses that look fab but smell of nothing and GM trout that are easy to see in the water but get cancer from sunburn. All huge successes then!

The World Health Organisation WHO have already put forward proposals for all animals for human consumption to have been treated with antibiotics which will stay in the animal flesh after slaughter and cooking. We all know the more you use antibiotics the less effective they become - so is this really in our best interest? I would say not.

My proposal therefore would be to ban genetically modified crops and genetic engineering forthwith, and to bring farming practices steadily back to all organic.

And since then? On February 10, 2014, Dr. Mercola of the Organic Consumers Association wrote:- *"For thousands of years, farmers have saved seeds from one farming season to another. But when Monsanto developed genetically modified (GM) seeds that would resist its own herbicide, the glyphosate-based Roundup, it patented the seeds.*

The Doctor then goes on to state that he United States Patent and Trademark Office, for practically all of its history, refused to grant patents on seeds, viewing them as life forms with too many variables to be patented. He adds that in 1980, the U.S. Supreme Court allowed for seed patents, in a close run 5-4 decision, which laid the groundwork for plenty of corporations to start gaining control of global food supply.

His opinion was that *the patenting of seeds is only one of the different ways that Monsanto affects food, farming, and your future health.*

He revealed the shocking insight that over the past 15 years, a collection of five giant biotech corporations - Monsanto, Syngenta, Bayer, Dow, and DuPont - have bought up more than 200 other companies, allowing them to dominate access to seeds.

Monsanto has become the world leader in genetic engineering of seeds, winning 674 biotechnology patents, which is more than any other company. It in now the case that if you are a farmer who buys its Roundup Ready seeds, you are required to sign an agreement promising not to save the seed produced after each harvest for re-planting. You are also prohibited from selling the seed to other farmers. In short, you must buy new seeds from Monsanto every year.

Dr Mercola said that *'Because saving seeds is considered patent infringement, anyone who does save GM seeds must pay a license fee to re-sow them. This results in higher prices and reduced product options, as well as the increased need for pesticides and herbicides required by GM crops.'*

He said that this means that given their current powers, Monsanto puts pressure on farmers, farmer's coops, seed dealers, and anyone it suspects may have infringed its seed patents. Its shadowy army of private investigators and agents secretly photograph and videotape farmers, co-ops, and store owners, they infiltrate community meetings and gather news from informants about farming activities, confronting farmers on their land and trying to pressure them into signing papers that give Monsanto access to their private records.

'These Monsanto agents and investigators are called the "seed police" by farmers, and they are said to employ "Gestapo" and "mafia" like tactics.'

He points out that farmers are caught up in a lose-lose situation. They end up with a far more expensive crop that has the potential to fail more frequently than conventional crops and can be very dangerous to the animals and humans who consume them.

According to Phillip Howard from Michigan University, as quoted by The Ecologist,' *the increasing power of seed companies is "incompatible" with renewable agricultural practices, and one solution to restricting their control would be through banning the practice of granting patents on seeds, plants, and genes.'*

He adds that one very alarming sign that change is needed today, is the wave of farmer suicides in India, which has greatly increased, for instance, since GE cotton was introduced in 2002.

A publication from the New York University School of Law shows that in 2009 alone, 17,638 Indian farmers committed suicide, which translates to one farmer every 30 minutes. A great number of those affected are cash crop farmers, cotton farmers in particular.

He says that a shift from polyculture farming (diverse crops) to monoculture farming (primarily cotton) had depleted the soil and increased pest infestation on crop. Limited water supplies, periodic drought, decreased monsoon rainfall, poor access to irrigation, a lack of government support, grossly inadequate government relief programs, and predatory salesmen all added to the problems.

'Monsanto has been ruthless in its aim to use India as a testing ground for GE crops, giving you a clear picture of what could happen for the small farmers of the world if GE seed conglomerates are allowed to continue this practice.'

To make matters worse this chilling update was taken from the Monsanto-Bayer website after their multi-billion dollar cash paid merger:- *"Joint Statement: Monsanto, Bayer CEOs meet with new administration 'Werner Baumann, Bayer CEO, and Hugh Grant, Monsanto Chairman and CEO, had a very productive meeting last week with President-Elect Trump and his team to share their view on the future of the agriculture industry and its need for innovation. The driving force behind the Bayer-Monsanto combination is increasing and accelerating innovation to help growers around the world address challenges like climate change and food security. This becomes increasingly important as we all work together to feed a growing population in a sustainable way"'*
Ohhh nooooooo!

And how about this one from that Greenpeace Feature story released on 2 August, 2005.

"It's official. Monsanto Corporation is out to own the world's food supply. The dangers of genetic engineering and reduced biodiversity notwithstanding, they've pig-headedly set about hog-tying farmers with their monopoly plans. We've discovered chilling new evidence of this in recent patents that seek to establish ownership rights over pigs and their offspring.

In the crop department, Monsanto is well on their way to dictating what consumers will eat, what farmers will grow, and how much Monsanto will get paid for seeds. In some cases those seeds are designed not to reproduce sowable offspring. In others, a flock of lawyers stand ready to swoop down on farmers who illegally, or even unknowingly, end up with Monsanto's private property growing in their fields.

One way or another, Monsanto wants to make sure no food is grown that they don't own -- and the record shows they don't care if it's safe for the environment or not. Monsanto has aggressively set out to bulldoze environmental concerns about its genetically engineered (GE) seeds at every regulatory level.

So why stop in the field? Not content to own the pesticide and the herbicide and the crop, they've made a move on the barnyard by filing two patents which would make the corporate giant the sole owner of that famous Monsanto invention: the pig."

They go on to say that the patent applications were published in February 2005 at the World Intellectual Property Organisation (WIPO) in Geneva. A Greenpeace researcher who monitors patent applications, Christoph Then, uncovered the fact that Monsanto is seeking patents not only on methods of breeding, but on actual breeding herds of pigs as well as the offspring that result.

Then added that if these patents are granted, Monsanto can legally prevent breeders and farmers from breeding pigs whose characteristics are described in the patent claims, or force them to pay royalties. It's a first step toward the same kind of corporate control of an animal line that Monsanto is aggressively pursuing with various grain and vegetable lines.

Greenpeace say that there are more than 160 countries and territories mentioned where the patent is sought including Europe, the

Russian Federation, Asia (India, China, Philippines) America (USA, Brazil, Mexico), Australia and New Zealand. WIPO itself can only receive applications, not grant patents. The applications are forwarded to regional patent offices.

They add that *"the patents are based on simple procedures, but are incredibly broad in their claims, saying that in one application (WO 2005/015989 to be precise) Monsanto is describing very general methods of crossbreeding and selection, using artificial insemination and other breeding methods which are already in use. The main "invention" is nothing more than a particular combination of these elements designed to speed up the breeding cycle for selected traits, in order to make the animals more commercially profitable. (Monsanto chirps gleefully about lower fat content and higher nutritional value. But we've looked and we couldn't find any "Philanthropic altruism" line item in their annual reports, despite the fact that it's an omnipresent factor in their advertising.)"*

According to Then, *"I couldn't believe this. I've been reviewing patents for 10 years and I had to read this three times. Monsanto isn't just seeking a patent for the method, they are seeking a patent on the actual pigs which are bred from this method. It's an astoundingly broad and dangerous claim."*

He tells us that other patents refer to pigs in which a certain gene sequence related to faster growth is detected. This is a variation on a natural occurring sequence – so Monsanto didn't invent it.

"But again, Monsanto wants to own not just the selection and breeding method, not just the information about the genetic indicators, but, if you pardon the expression, the whole hog."

We are told that they also requested patents for a pig offspring produced by a method, a pig herd having an increased frequency of a specific gene, a pig population produced by the method, and a swine herd produced by a method.

This means the pigs, their offspring, and the use of the genetic information for breeding will be entirely owned by Monsanto, Inc. and any replication or infringement of their patent by man or beast will mean royalties or jail for the offending swine.

When it comes to profits, pigs are big. Monsanto notes that *"The economic impact of the industry in rural America is immense. Annual* *farm sales typically exceed US$ 11 billion, while the retail value of pork sold to consumers reaches US$ 38 billion each year."*

The chilling fact is that at almost every level of food production, Monsanto is seeking a monopoly position.

Greenpeace go on to tell us that the company once earned its money almost exclusively through agrochemicals. But in the last ten years they've spent about US$10 billion buying up seed producers and companies in other sectors of the agricultural business. Their last big acquisition was Seminis, the biggest producer of vegetable seeds in the world.

The big picture is chilling to anyone who mistrusts Monsanto's record disinterest for environmental safety.

And if you're not worried, you should be: central control of food supply has been a standard ingredient for social and political control throughout history. By creating a monopoly position, Monsanto can force dangerous experiments like the release of GMOs into the environment on an unwilling public. They can ensure that GMOs will be sold and consumed wherever they say they will.'

They sum up by saying that by claiming global monopoly patent rights throughout the entire food chain, Monsanto seeks to make farmers and food producers, and ultimately consumers, entirely dependent and reliant on one single corporate entity for a basic human need. It's the same dependence that Russian peasants had on the Soviet Government following the Russian revolution. The same dependence that French peasants had on Feudal kings during the middle ages. But control of a significant proportion of the global food supply by a single corporation would be unprecedented in human history.

The rt.com website tells us of the health effects on pigs fed a GM diet as follows:-

"UK Environment officials praise GMO crops as 'safer than conventional' ones, but a recent study reveals more sobering evidence that the world urgently needs to ask fundamental safety questions about genetic engineering of the human food chain."

They say that the new pig study was the first attempt to seriously and independently test over the typical life of the pigs the effects, if any, of the most widely used mix of GMO feed. They add that, astonishingly, at least to those who might assume that US Government agencies entrusted with animal and human health keep a close watch on GMO product effects, US and EU regulators do not require animal feeding studies on mixtures of GMO feed.

We are told that EU labeling laws require a product to state if it contains more than 0.9 percent GMO products, but the EU Commission, under lobbying pressure from the giant US grain cartel—Bunge, ADM, Cargill— granted a giant loophole that allows EU food to be contaminated with huge amounts of GMO.

They point out that the digestive tract of a pig is very similar to that of humans. The most shocking discovery was that the GMO fed pigs had uteruses that were 25% heavier than non-GMO fed pigs and that GMO fed pigs had a higher rate of severe stomach inflammation with a rate of 32% of GMO-fed pigs compared to 12% of non-GMO-fed pigs. The severe stomach inflammation was worse in GMO-fed males compared to non-GMO fed males by a factor of 4, and GMO-fed females compared to non-GMO fed females by a factor of 2.2.

Yet again we see government support for the big greed driven corporations. Genetically modified pigs that can trick a farmer into landing in court, GM foods that cause heath issues, insecticides that slaughter our wildlife and little help for farmers who, we are told, are killing themselves at a rate of one every 30 minutes in India as a result of Monsanto's messing with the structure of the plants which are at the heart of their businesses and their lives, and with the full approval of Donald Trump. Great.

Perhaps the final insult is the fact that while a company like Monsanto is breaking all the natural laws to achieve world domination of genetically modified foods that they say will fight starvation, a huge amount of what is produced is simply thrown in the bin.

Hazel Sheffield of the Independent told us on the 10th of January 2017:-

"How the UK's household food waste problem is getting worse As many as 8.4 million families in the UK struggle to put food on the table – and yet, 7.3 million tonnes of food waste ends up in landfills each year."

Hazel goes on to make the point that household food waste in the UK increased by 4.4 per cent between 2012 and 2015, the Waste and Resources Action Programme said and that the UK Government had failed to meet its target on household food waste. Statistics from the Waste and Resources Action Programme (WRAP) show household food waste in the UK increased 4.4 per cent between 2012 and 2015, despite a target to cut household waste 5 per cent by 2015. That brings the amount of food sent to landfill in 2015 to 7.3 million tonnes, costing UK families £700 per year.

Hazel added that *"the rise in food waste is shameful at a time when 8.4 million UK families are struggling to put food on the table, the equivalent of the whole population of London. As many as half of these families regularly go a whole day without food. The UK is in the bottom half of European countries for food insecurity, even as we keep throwing more and more food away."*

Food waste activists The Real Junk Food Project said the food industry, not the consumer, must take responsibility.

They say *"I'm sick of the food industry passing their responsibility onto the consumers as though it's our fault,"* said Adam Smith, founder. *"More and more people are composting than ever before. More and more people have less food than ever before and this Christmas period, food sales were down due to a 14 per cent increase in food prices for Christmas lunch."*

No surprises there then. The more we throw away the more money the big food producers make, so no wonder the government has been ineffective. They wouldn't want to cut those profits would they? Food waste is a crime and the fact that food cannot easily be given to the poor because of over-zealous health and safety legislation is a travesty. It could be so different, but where would the profits come from?

CHAPTER 20

Greed

'There is no calamity greater than lavish desires. There is no greater guilt than discontentment. And there is no greater disaster than greed'. - Lao-tzu

This massive subject was aired in my Gazette article as follows:-

I think we all agree that greed is an unacceptable thing, especially when there is not enough to go around. Our parents rightly taught us to share didn't they? Not to eat all the cake? This is a very simple philosophy and, as we are teaching it to our kids, how come we let the adults get away with such selfish actions? The world is no longer capable of sustaining the ravages of corporations that seek huge profits at the cost of just about everything else around them so things have to change.

Further, when you boil every problem we have down to its true cause, the endless search for wealth and greed are the stains left at the bottom of just about every pot. There is a limited amount of wealth in the world, you can imagine it as a bucket full of cash, and some people are grabbing huge hand-fulls, leaving the majority to fight over the loose change in the bottom

In answer to this I would propose two things. One would be to introduce complete and utter transparency on profits and earnings so that the people who are stashing away disproportionately huge sums of money would not be able to hide the fact. Everyone could see how much everyone around them earned so there could be no hiding disparity by any employer.

Second would be to introduce a maximum wage. I would propose to do this by setting an annual earnings limit of, say, £1 million, which I consider to be plenty to get by on, and after that the rate of taxation would rise above 100% to, say, 110%, meaning that the more someone earned after that the more it would cost them. Now of course they could carry on working and losing money but I think this would slow the big earners down and encourage them to take a holiday or two thereby leaving a better slice of the cake for the rest of us.

As defined in the Oxford English Dictionary - Greed, grēd, noun:- intense and selfish desire for something, especially wealth, power, or food. At the bottom of every government/corporation co-operation that does not serve the people, is that nasty little thing called greed. Avarice. While being one of the 'deadly sins', there is no law preventing, discouraging, or protecting us from it. Even though it is something that should be frowned upon, our tabloids would have us believe that those who are earning gazillions and buying fleets of Ferraris or super-yachts and living it up at the expense of our planet are simply 'glamourous' and well deserving of their disproportionate wealth that is killing us all. Earning money is fine. Earning a lot of money is also fine but limitless wealth breeds poor behaviour and disconnects many of those with it with issues that are affecting everyone, and that is unacceptable behaviour, that incredibly is not punishable.

There is a finite amount of money to go around and when the elite 1% are grabbing 98% of the available wealth of a country or a planet, it is obvious that the less fortunate are going to suffer. The government are not interested in improving the lot of the lowest in our society and only pay enough lip service to the problems to avoid accusations of inaction.

An example was when there was uproar about the vast bankers bonuses that were paid even as the institutions collapsed. Later the government made a public statement in the press saying that the bonuses had been capped and that the problem had therefore been addressed. We were, however, never told the details of the deal they had come to. A year on the E.U. passed legislation saying that bonuses could not exceed a whole years pay, and the UK bankers went ballistic, saying they were going to massively lose out. Which begs the question, what the heck was the deal our government agreed to if the doubling of bankers salaries at a stroke was seen as a devastating pay cut?

In a later similar article I wrote: Do you ever get the feeling that whenever you are due a bit of fun or have something going your way for a change there is always someone waiting in the wings to take advantage of it? Example - New Years Eve. Once a year, lots of fun, so let's go and celebrate, except my local pub wanted £12.50 to get in. What for? Nothing. Just cashing in on a captive audience (we elected not to give them our money and went elsewhere). What miseries.

Private pensions were no different. The Government gave us tax breaks (hoo-bloomin-rah) as an incentive to save, what did the finance companies do? Took so much commission that, while it was still just in our favour to go ahead with their outrageous rip-off (they stole the first two years contributions which are the most important, savings wise and champagned it up at our expense) we were clearly paying way more in commissions than we should have been. Then, when the bubble burst, they suddenly reviewed the rules but sadly too late for most of us. Never mind, it's only our pension that someone has nicked to cover their massive end of year bonus. We shall just have to work longer, like a worn out pit pony that might never get to see that green field, that's all.

And how about a couple of stories I read in the Advertiser recently starting with Purbeck District Councils decision to hit planning applicants for an additional £950 per bedroom to generate £9.1 million for road improvements? Is that legal? Can they just wallop in a ruling like that out of line with the rest of the country? Where are they expecting people to magic that money from? Very dubious. I would love it for someone to put up a legal challenge. To my mind this is no more than them cashing in on your good fortune of happening to own a property in a buoyant market (mostly as a result of the city boys snapping up all the property with their bonuses - which of course is really your money in the first place! Neat trick huh?)

Well there are a few anomalies about this. One, I don't see a direct correlation between an extra bedroom and more road use and two, don't we already pay road tax? Personally I don't much like the sound of all that road building going on in Purbeck. What are they planning I wonder? A dual carriageway to Wareham? Another shrewd and visionary decision taken by our Council at a time when our thrust should be away from the motor car. I heard Jim Knight MP happily chirping on about getting a dual carriageway to Weymouth in time for the Olympics (which, after all, only goes on for a month). Great! More tarmac and one of the most scenic approaches to a Victorian seaside town gone forever. Thanks Jim, good work.

The second story was about the Dorset Wildlife Trust (of whom I am a member and monthly donator) cashing in by selling a property donated to them. That doesn't sound all that shocking until you understand that the house, gardens and woodland were left to them in a will to be kept as a nature reserve. Imagine, the dying wishes of someone who obviously loved that space and simply wanted to preserve a little safe haven for the creatures that frequented it, trusted it to the DWT and they flogged it off to developers. Worse, they then tried to justify the decision because only 4 houses can be built there. How absolutely sickening. And they are supposed to be the good guys! If you can't trust the Trust where else can you go?

Do you watch sport? (Or rather would you watch it if you could afford to?!) The England and Wales Cricket Board let everyone down by selling the rights for us to watch our national team on terrestrial television, and the reason they gave? So they can encourage more kids to play. Really? Well tell me ECB, what is the first thing Coca Cola and McDonalds do if they want more kids to buy junk food? Stick it on the telly! And I tell you, one thing those boys really know about is marketing.

Question. Which country is the only one you have to pay to watch play rugby on TV if you live in England? Answer. England! Hold on - I think I am seeing a pattern here! Football is even worse. How do top players sleep at night knowing that they earn so much that lots of kids can't afford to go and see them anymore? Talk about taking financial advantage of a little popularity. And these guys are looked upon as heroes? I would have thought that helping yourself to a kids' pocket money would make you a villain.

Of course all this means that underprivileged kids, who I am sure we can all agree need the healthy stimulus of sport most of all, are the ones who are most deprived - again. No wonder the bus shelters are getting smashed up.

The only way to get multinational corporations to consider the impacts of climate change is to get them to think about how much it would cost them. For example, getting them to consider the cost should they have to pollinate plants by hand, instead of having a free army of insects to do it for them. Man! Does there have to be a pound sign on everything before it has any value? They would charge us for watching sunsets if they could find a way to sell the tickets!

So where am I going with all this? Well, it seems to me that there are plenty of people out there who are less focused on money doing demanding jobs simply because the work is rewarding in itself. Now for some reason this ethic isn't echoed at the top. Corporations, Government bodies and wealthy individuals are solely focused on generating cash. This wouldn't be quite so bad if it wasn't your and my labours they were generating it from.

But do you want to know a secret? We actually are the power base here. If we can be bothered, we can steer these things by just not complying. We can shun corporations who make unethical decisions, challenge unreasonable costs imposed by local government and stop buying if we are not happy with the terms. Until we do this things are going to get tighter and tighter. So next time you reach for your wallet or purse have a real good think about it and, even if it means going without for a while, if you are not completely happy with the deal, save your money (in an ethical bank!)

Years later Nigel Morris of the Independent wrote on Tuesday, 10th March 2015: *"Britain's divided decade: rich are 64% richer, and the poor are 57% poorer.*

The gap between richest and poorest has dramatically widened in the past decade as wealthy households paid off their debts and piled up savings following the financial crisis, a report warns today."

He goes on to say that by contrast, the worst-off families are far less financially secure than before the recession, triggered by the near-collapse of several major banks. They have an average of less than a week's pay set aside and are more often in the red.

Adding that younger workers have fallen behind older people, while homeowners – particularly those who have paid off their mortgages – have become increasingly affluent compared with their neighbours who are paying rent.

He said that there were 18 million people who cannot afford adequate housing, and evidence of Britain's rapidly growing wealth gap was revealed by the Social Market Foundation (SMF), which analysed the changing incomes and savings of thousands of people.

It found that the average wealth of the best-off one-fifth of families rose by 64 per cent between 2005 and 2012-13 as they put more money aside as a buffer against future shocks. They have average savings and investments of around £10,000 compared with £6,000 seven years earlier.

Nigel goes on to note that the inter-generational gap in incomes and wealth has widened significantly. The wages of those aged 26 to 35 fell steeply and they are far less likely to be property owners, with the proportion in this age bracket who are buying a home falling from nearly three-quarters in 2005 to just over half in 2012-13. On average, they have less than a week's income in savings, owe 45 per cent more money than they did in 2005 and are increasingly running up overdrafts to pay their bills.

The SMF say in their report titled 'Wealth in the Downturn: Winner and losers', that there is a need to support those on the lower incomes and younger age groups to save more. But this will be challenging, especially for those with little income to spare once necessities have been paid for. The process of repairing personal finances will most likely only begin once the expected growth in wages materialises.

'The number of children in relative income poverty is currently 2.3 million in the UK.

The declining financial health of younger workers and people on low incomes limited the economy's ability to rely for growth on consumer spending among all income levels. And it warned that these groups are ill-prepared for future financial shocks or rises in interest rates."

Need I say more?

CHAPTER 21

Animal Testing

'Mankind's true moral test, its fundamental test (which lies deeply buried from view), consists of its attitude towards those who are at its mercy: animals. And in this respect mankind has suffered a fundamental debacle, a debacle so fundamental that all others stem from it.' - Milan Kundera

In an attempt to awaken people from their apathy toward this vile subject I wrote:-

What I should like to know is: who amongst us is truly in favour of animal testing? If you shot your hand up then I suggest you try keeping it up while reading the rest of this article out loud to your friends.

Did you know, for example, that in the U.K. alone about 2.5 million unfortunate creatures are tested upon each year, with a further 8 million 'luckier' ones being bred and destroyed as 'surplus to requirements'? And what do these hapless innocents endure at our hand? Well, a real favourite is vivisection 'cutting while alive'. Other experiments 'likely to cause pain suffering distress and lasting harm' include delights such as poisoning, disease and mutilation. The incarceration alone causes intense psychological distress, and we are not just talking about mice and rats here. Live pigs, cows, monkeys, cats, dogs and horses are all regularly experimented upon. Think you could happily cut up a horse while it is still alive? Then keep that hand up!

Government Minister, Caroline Flint, says that they 'permit only essential research with clear medical benefits'. I am sorry Caroline, but that is not true. Ever heard of the Draize test? This is when a product is dripped onto the skin, or into the eyes, of a creature for some considerable time (weeks), to see what happens. Most household products are tested this way, bleach, polish, air fresheners, oven cleaner...nice! I tell you, that mild green washing liquid does not seem so very mild after it has been squirted into your eyes every hour for a couple of days. Hand still up?

If so, maybe you should consider the LD50 test, which used to be mandatory and is still considered a valid experiment. The LD stands for lethal dose, and the 50 stands for 50%, and this is how it works. All you have to do is take a sample of, say, 200 rabbits, dose them with a known quantity of some toxic product, say, weed killer, and when 50% of them have died you can calculate a figure to show just how toxic your weed killer really is. How useful! Now if your hand is still up maybe you should have a go at this fun experiment at home with your neighbours rabbits and see what opinion your family and friends form of you!.

But Andy! Think of all the benefits to mankind! Well here is the catch, testing on animals is not beneficial because animal physiology is different from our own. For example, dogs don't need to intake vitamin C - do your own test by trying to tempt one with a strawberry - and as a result harmful drugs regularly get through the net. Thalidomide was just one particularly graphic animal testing success story. Another thing, animals are not great at giving feedback, 'well I was a bit lethargic when I was on my wheel this morning and had a bit of nausea after my seeds'. It just doesn't work.

In the British Medical Journal way back in December 1979 it was concluded that 'today's main killing diseases are due to the way we live' and according to an epidemiological study undertaken by recognised researchers Doll and Peto, 85% of cancers are avoidable. 85%! In short, we mostly bring about our own health problems by self-imposed toxins (e.g. deodorants), poor diet, stress and unhealthy living habits. And by the way, just 0.33% of the Governments health budget is dedicated to health education. Hmmmm...0.33% of budget to allay 85% of cancers - work that one out if you can.

So why is our Government so behind animal testing? Because it big business and good for the economy and they don't want to upset the pharmaceutical companies (even though many of the drugs produced are unaffordable by the NHS.) Check this out. The MoD tested vile chemical and biological weapons on animals at Porton Down for decades, but when they decided that they had enough information did they close it and end the suffering? No! They turned to the cosmetics industry to earn a bit of extras cash! And where did the money come from for that new controversial Biomedical Research Laboratory being built at Oxford University? A company called Technikos handed over £12million to O.U. in the hope that they can get a good return, and there we have it, it's official, money really is the root of all evil. Oxford University - shame on you!

By the way did you know that Justice Grigson ruled that protests about the lab at O.U. can now only be carried out by up to 25 people, in a designated area, between 1 and 5 pm on a thursday - phew! And I thought free speech was dead! No wonder animal rights activists are tearing their hair out (like, no doubt, some of the animal experiments that will go on). In my opinion, anyone who risks their freedom by striving for justice for those less fortunate than themselves, with no hope of personal reward, should be applauded.

But even if there were clear benefits, there is an overriding moral issue to consider here. Our society rightly supports the philosophy of caring for the weak. We are comparatively good at extending that to the elderly, the young, the infirm and the disabled, but are less good at extending this thinking beyond our own species. Mind you, it wasn't so very long ago that we didn't even extend it beyond our own race, with endless wars, the enslaving of Africans and Nazi experimentation on the Jews being some recent examples, so what hope do animals have?

A greater understanding that humans are not at the top of the evolutionary tree, but are only an animal representing one tiny branch of it would pave the way to a more compassionate society, and this lesson has to be learnt in school. Animals are too often treated with apathy, but they seek to survive, engage in what brings them pleasure and avoid what brings them pain, they love, and will sacrifice everything for the survival of their young - as we humans do.

Consider this, a new born child has less interaction with its surroundings than does, say, an adult cat but can you imagine the furore if someone did a little Draize testing on it! Or how about testing chemicals on your pet dog? Or the robin in your garden? My point is most of us cannot ignore senseless suffering when we have the slightest emotional involvement, and would put an end to it if there were greater transparency for witnessing the experiments first hand. Perhaps a laboratory version of

Big Brother, where we get to watch a defenceless dumb animal getting a bucket of diseased material thrown over its head is needed. Well....no change there then.

If you read this article, you can no longer pretend you do not know what is going on, and, if you care then please DO something about it! For more information on how to avoid supporting the bad guys, by not purchasing animal tested products, and other opportunities to be more pro-active in the fight to end needless animal laboratory suffering, log on to, among others, www.uncaged.co.uk.

And ten years since then? The Telegraph reported on 20th July 2016:-

"Thousands of pigs, rabbits and monkeys have been mutilated in tests at the Ministry of Defence laboratory Porton Down, it was revealed on Wednesday.

Figures show 7,373 experiments have been carried out since 2014 at the controversial government-run complex in Wiltshire. These included 124 on primates, 158 on pigs and 439 on guinea pigs.'

They add that in one Public Health England procedure, 21 long-tailed macaques were forced to inhale a version of the smallpox virus and observed for 12 days before being killed and dissected.

We were told that animal rights campaigners have called for the 'disturbing' experiments at Porton Down to stop. Another test meant four rhesus macaques being infected with TB before being observed for two weeks. Two became so violently ill they had to be killed after one week. In other experiments, carried out by the MoD, it was reported pigs were shot, rabbits blown up and guinea pigs injected with a toxic nerve agent invented by the Nazis.

We were told that Dr Katy Taylor, director of science at Cruelty Free International said that the level of suffering animals endure in military experiments conducted at Porton Down is completely unacceptable. Cruelty Free International Animal rights campaigners have called for the "disturbing" experiments to stop.

She added *'We all want to ensure the safety of soldiers and civilians, but we do not believe that animals need to be butchered or poisoned, or subjected to such cruel and disturbing experiments in order to achieve this. The level of suffering animals endure in military experiments conducted at Porton Down is completely unacceptable.*

"There used to be additional parliamentary oversight of the experiments conducted at Porton Down, but shockingly this has been disbanded. Some of these controversial experiments appear only to be demonstrating the usefulness of techniques that are already being used on the battlefield."

Animals tortured in their thousands to feed the corporate war machines and big pharmaceutical companies? Government oversight of the hideous and disturbing torture disbanded, giving Porton Down a free reign? Just business as usual then. Keep voting them in.

CHAPTER 22

Beaches and Climate Change

'Climate change is a terrible problem, and it absolutely needs to be solved. It deserves to be a huge priority'. - Bill Gates

You may have to bear with me a little here. Climate change and rising sea levels are my number one passion, being, I believe, the most significant threat to us all. The articles I wrote were months apart, and when read in succession may overlap information, but they have all been included, for whilst there is some repetition of information I had attempted to get this desperately important message across in as many different ways as I could think of and that gives each merit. I hope you find the discussions both interesting and entertaining.

My first article read:-

So the regeneration of Swanage beach is soon to start and while I, like everyone else, would dearly love to see a beach for everyone to enjoy, I am sad to say that the 'solution' - and I use the term incorrectly, shall be short lived.

The truth is that Swanage is not the only place in the world to have a beach with desperate erosion problems. What the 'experts' don't seem to have noticed is that every beach in the world is disappearing. Indeed beaches are soon to be a thing of the past and putting sand down, groynes or not, will be as effective as putting a sticky plaster on a melanoma.

In my time I have done quite a bit of beach research - (15 years and 60 countries - well some-one had to – and I can hear you now – oh great Andy – no wonder the planet is in trouble – but many of those countries were travelled to overland and I have personally planted 200 trees to offset my emissions so I hope we can move on here) and it does not make for happy viewing. Every revisited beach was, year on year, seen to be a fraction of its former width. But what was particularly puzzling was that in every instance the local community believed that the problem was theirs alone, and were quick to conjure up some scapegoat or other. In Swanage the wrongly accused villain is the Banjo Jetty, and no doubt if the marina had come to pass it would have taken a share of the blame as well.

So what is causing the problem I hear you ask? Well it is our old enemy global warming. I guess everyone knows about the meltdown of the polar regions and how that is adding water to our seas (in quantities large enough to make the sea in southern Australia almost fresh enough to drink - I have tasted it.) But the factor that is less aired is that as water heats up it expands, so higher temperatures mean more water volume.

Yep - every little bit of fossil fuel each of us burns as we go about our daily business melts a little more ice and heats the water of the seas a little more causing a little more expansion, and both of these effects combine to creates a little rise in sea levels. And where is all that water going to go? Well it will flood over the land. Sorry - did I say 'will'? What I meant to say was 'will continue to' because you see it has already started, the lowest lying land typically being the beach, and that is why Swanage beach has eroded away.

So how much will the seas rise? Well conservative estimates predict 10 meters, other schools of thought say 70 meters - and soon. In a few years the battle for the beaches will be lost and the fight will turn to keeping Shore Road open, then to saving coastal towns, then to saving valleys and cities. Ultimately there will be nowhere to run to.

Now I am very sorry if this all sounds a bit gloomy and has taken the fun out planning your next motoring holiday but, as anyone who has read one of my articles will know, I do not air and expand on a problem without providing a real and feasible solution.

I can hear your jeering even as I write - go on then - make the seas go back down 'King Cnut of Swanage'. O.K. I will! Now I know there are several parts to the solution but number one on the list is in obtaining our energy from another source, burning fossil fuels has to stop - and that source is - (drum roll) - hydroelectricity!

But Andy! - I hear you shout - are you crazy? Where are the mountain lakes in Dorset? Well actually building dams is just one way to move water past an impeller, but another way is by tapping into the infinite power of the gravitational pull of the sun and moon in the form of tidal currents.

Think about this for a moment. The spin of the earth through these gravitational pulls shifts all the waters of the world around four times a day. Just imagine how big a machine you would need to pump the Atlantic about like that?! The even better news is that the currents at the bottom of the oceans are even stronger than at the top because there are underwater mountains and valleys to channel them. Placing turbines strategically on the sea bed would provide endless, out of sight out of mind, predictable and permanent, CO_2 free power - for ever and ever - Amen

Imagine how easy and clean obtaining energy from that source would be and how archaic the whole concept of digging up, transporting, refining and burning barrels of black gloop would become!

And do you want to know the really clever bit? These turbines would be extracting energy from the seas - but in what form would the seas relinquish that energy (as energy is neither created nor destroyed - remember your physics laws of thermodynamics?) Well it is heat!! So the more energy we extracted the cooler the seas would become, reducing, then reversing not only the expansion effect of the water, but reforming the polar ice caps, resetting the weather patterns and saving us all - as well as the beaches!

Yes it is a huge task - we would need quite a few of these things - but hey! - did you count the number of cars out there recently? Why not set up a treaty for every country to have to put one of these things into the water for every car made?

And as usual Britain is perfectly placed to take the lead. We already have a couple of companies building these things and have the engineering design expertise to make them super-efficient and reliable. We have lots of tidal currents and shipyards that don't have a lot to do at the moment, that could knock them out by the thousand. Wouldn't it have been great if we had a thinking Government who had seen the opportunity to commission MG Rover to design and build these things, instead of letting the Chinese get hold of it to build their crummy cars? British racing green turbines! And what about the shipyards? Standing empty with unemployment until the MoD allocate the next frigate update, so why not get them on it? Save the dole money and get the community working on something worthwhile for a change!

What is needed right now are pilot projects to show the world how to do it and where better than Dorset? We have plenty of coast and tidal currents. So if you find yourself nodding approval of this article and want to save yourself and your children then please take 10 minutes to write to Jim Knight urging him to pressure the concept with the Government. In a few years you may be really happy that you did!

In April 2006, on the same subject, I wrote:

This month I was fully planning on writing on another subject altogether but I am so incensed by the ill-informed press about the reinstatement of the beach at Swanage and the disappearance of it at Studland that I just couldn't control myself!

If, for example, I hear one more time that the good old 'Banjo Jetty' at Swanage is responsible for the erosion of the north end of the beach I shall scream. Just go and have a look yourself at the sand beside the new breakwaters and it is absolutely transparent that it is already deeper on the south (or town) side, showing that they, and the jetty, are saving sand on the southern side. Now if this weren't beneficial why would the engineers have bothered to go to the expanse of putting in the breakwaters at all?

And while we are at it I think it truly disgusting that the Council should heave elected to form the breakwaters from hardwood, shipped in from British Guyana. This is an indisputable truth as I have read the shipping labels myself. How much Orinoco rain forest had to be cut down and transported half way around the world? Well I reckon that the 18 groynes each with about 20 300mm square posts plus around 2 miles of hefty planking equates to the destruction of at least 200 huge ancient trees. Given that these plants are critical in the fight against the global warming by locking up CO_2, the increased levels of which are responsible for the beach disappearing in the first place, I think this was an extremely poor and thoughtless decision.

We are told that the new beach will be in place for about 25 years but if you take the time to go and have a look at it toward the northern end you will see right away that major erosion has already started. Sand has been washed away forming steep ridges half way up the beach and up to three feet of it has disappeared from the north side of the breakwaters. Personally

I give it 5 years. [5 years later. I was absolutely on the money. The beach had already all gone.]

And then let's see what's happening at Studland. Well the beach huts are going to be washed away and the café and car park are under threat but ....the National Trust 'expert' is extremely economical with the truth, saying the beach is 'altering shape' as it has always done. Well I am sorry but this is utter and complete rubbish. Take a wander yourself and keep an eye open for the high water mark shown by the highest line of deposited sea weed (the sand between high and low water doesn't count as beach as it is foreshore) and you will see that the beach is actually only a few meters wide and in places there is none at all.

At Plettenburg Bay in South Africa (with not a 'Banjo Jetty' in sight!) the loss of the huge beach to a postage stamp size has been so alarming that they have erected a board explaining what might be the cause. What was truly worrying was that the effects of man's activities on sea levels was relegated to a post script in the bottom right hand corner. Incredibly many people still believe that we are only witnessing natural cyclical changes in sea levels and that it will all sort itself out. A huge part of the problem is that there are plenty of multinational corporations that have such a massive financial interest in us continuing with our damaging consumer habits that they actually fund bogus 'research' to 'prove' that we need not panic. (Like they are still 'proving' that cigarettes do not cause cancer).

Now I have written before about how we can start to solve sea level problems by extracting energy from it (thus cooling and contracting it) in the form impellers driven by deep sea tidal streams generating hydroelectricity and I do not want to become a bore, (never! I hear you shout) but this is such an important issue.

Since writing last time on this subject the Dti have given £50 million pounds for tubines to be installed around Aldeny and schemes have started around Barbados and Vancouver Island, so I am thankful that other people have come to the same, and to my mind obvious, conclusion. And to the gentleman who wrote in to the Gazette poo pooing the idea quoting laws of thermal dynamics, I am quite aware that one cannot extract energy from nowhere and that there is no such thing as perpetual motion, but I am suggesting harnessing the gravitational energy of the earth rotates respective to sun and the moon which has to be a pretty plentiful source!!

CHAPTER 23

The writing on the wall

'When the writing is on the wall you know you are in trouble.
When it is on every wall, the floor, the ceiling, the doors
and the windows you'd do well to get off your arse and do
something about it' – Andy Kirkwood

A later article on my personal passion read:-

You awaken one morning and your head is splitting. Well, it could be that couple of pints in the Globe last night couldn't it? Let's ignore it. But then the nausea and the vomiting starts but that might just be a bug? Mmmm, you never had a seizure before, this is becoming a bit of a worry but hopefully it will all be ok. Wow, you keep losing your balance and your thinking is getting kinda muddled. Must be stress. Today you were paralysed all down the left side of your body, there has to be a simple explanation. You make a note that you really ought to see a doctor. And all the time those headaches.... Sorry sir, but you have a brain tumour. If only you had come in earlier we would have had a much better chance of dealing with it.

The question here is when would you have gone to the doctors? Sooner? I hope so. In which case how many symptoms of a planet in plight do you need to witness before you start demanding that a cure is sought. You see I have been doing a little survey out there and the feedback I get is not encouraging. There is just too much 'keep my fingers crossed and with a bit of luck it will happen after my lifetime' by really smart and educated people, going on for my liking.

'Oh but Andy, this has all happened before in the middle ages and anyway, scientific opinion is divided on the subject. Oh really? Well let me tell you. Opinion is not divided, it is corrupted and you can trust me when I tell you that there are plenty of people out there who would risk even the world that supports them if they can generate more money. You do not need to be a historian to understand history, and you do not need to be a scientist to understand science. So why don't we all do a few little first principles observations and see what we come up with?

Do you ever get sun burnt in March or April? Does a tan no longer offer proper protection against burning? Are trees with broad leaves scorched on the sunny side by June? Is the light harsher, the shadows starker and colours washed out on sunny days? Have burn warnings appeared in our weather forecasts? Have off the shelf sun screen factors doubled and redoubled? Now was it like this ten years ago? No? So can we agree then that something has changed and that in all probability that something is ozone depletion? Good. Er - well not good at all because this tiny layer of O3 molecules which at surface pressure would only be a few millimetres thick - is our best defence against UVB which is very effective at breaking down DNA. Sunburn? Scorched leaves? Well that appears to fit.

And how about the sea levels? Walk down the beach and look for the high tide mark as shown by the sea weed. Yep - there it is right up at the top of the beach. Wow! And look, all those dunes are being washed away! Doesn't matter where in the world you go it's the same story. Hmmmm...the water must be rising. Now why would that be?

And while we are at it lets check the weather. Lovely! Hot and sunny! Not a hint of rain. Wonderful....if this were August. As I said, you don't have to be a scientist. All you need is a thermometer and a calendar to see that something very wrong is going on here. Complete this well-known saying - April s-----s. Here is a clue. This year we didn't get one. Not too obvious I hope? You never saw the African images when the rains failed three years in a row and the family forlornly look over the oxen skeleton lying on the cracked mud? Are you absolutely sure that that couldn't happen here? Soon? Well as it stands no-one is. [Note – in 2018 it did happen when the ground at my pitch and putt in Swanage burnt and cracked with gaping tears up to six inches wide due to lack of rain.]

So why am I banging on about this again? Well, the first step to dealing with a problem is awareness and raising it is what I am trying to achieve, although from my research I seem to be failing miserably. The next stage is to filter out misinformation and excuses. There are plenty out there. For example, the other day an electrical shop keeper tried to persuade me that energy saving bulbs were not effective unless they were left on for at least four hours at a time. It transpires that the pay back starts in less than a millisecond . Still, that is only a margin of error of nearly 1.5 million times. But imagine if I were an elderly person asking advice? Another tiny nail in the Earths coffin.

The third is to seek a cure. Just like the tumour patient the sooner this is done the better success rate we can expect, although right now it appears very touch and go. Agitate your Council to stop hacking down perfectly good trees in the name of health and safety. We make enough fuss about the Amazon but in the end a tree is a tree. Demand better public transport. Request that hideous all night street lighting is turned off. Think about how to cut your journeys and heating bills. Feel guilty when you fill your car. I do which is why I have a railcard. Turn off your TV and computer at the socket. Unplug phone chargers. Canvass for renewable energy. Get a heat exchanger, solar panels, wind turbine and ground pump. Pray.

In your heart you know all the arguments and most of you really know the truth, which as Al Gore so eloquently pointed out is 'inconvenient'. I agree - it is, but as it stands the headaches have been going on for about 30 years, the vomiting for 10 and the paralysis is about to set in. Are you sure you don't want to seek the doctors advice yet?

In yet another attempt to awaken a seemingly complacent sleepwalking population I wrote:-

I am going to say something that I think shall make me unpopular. (I know what you are thinking. 'Oh really Andy? That wouldn't be a first would it?') Most of us do not have the slightest intention of doing anything to help this wonderful but ailing world that gives us life, unless there is a short term gain in it for ourselves.

As a single small example. In April, when we had blistering hot days and not a drop of rain, everyone was out on the beach saying 'well...if this is global warming bring it on!! (Who cares about mass starvation elsewhere?)' But when we got dumped on by record rainfall in July suddenly there was a switch to 'this isn't fair! Someone has to do something!' Well - if you don't want more of the same (or much, much, worse) then that someone who has to do something (and you have probably held this truth in your heart for quite a while) is you.

So does that mean that collectively we can be viewed as uncaring? Self-interested? Ignorant? Shallow? Thoughtless? Lazy? Unwilling to help? It that us? I don't think that describes anyone I know - so what is going wrong here?

Well - there is still a surprising amount of 'Oh I don't believe in any of that nonsense' about. Given the massive amount of compelling evidence I would say that holding on to that opinion is as bright as saying that you still don't believe in Italy. If you are still thinking like this, for all of our sakes you have to wake up! Use your senses. Do some reading. Watch a bit of Al Gores' movie. Do anything, but please get up to speed because our collective CO2 emissions can be thought of as one big communal bank account and a single selfish act squandering a million makes a mockery of any of us diligently saving pennies.

I realise it really doesn't help when BBC weatherman John Kettley, who you would think would have done his homework, glibly says that we have only been experiencing 'just another old-style British summer'. Hmmmm... Warmest winter, driest April and wettest July on record. And if you are still not convinced, how about 50 degrees C in a southern Europe that is ablaze, snow in the lowlands of Argentina and South Africa, 20 days of continuous rain drowning 500 villages and displacing 20 million people in India or droughts in Florida so severe that the Everglades have shrunk to small ponds stuffed with alligators that are now having to resort to eating each other. South-east Australia is enduring such an epic drought (thought to be the worst for a thousand years) that, because the mighty Murray River has dried up completely, 'a 'garden of Eden' of hundreds of thousands of red gum trees, some 400 years old, has 'become a graveyard' . O.K. - just your regular global weather patterns then John?

'Oh, but the Government are just using global warming as an excuse to raise taxes!' I agree. Their flat footed thinking and complete lack of correlation between additional taxes and active measures is disheartening and sends out a poor message. We are not dealing with alcohol and tobacco here! 'In this Budget we are going to put a penny on carbon'. No, no, no! This is not helping and is turning people away for the wrong reasons. If we are to solve this then we have to pull together - and that means that we shall all have to make sacrifices of some sort, however that doesn't have

to mean returning to the stone age. Ask any 12 year old and they will tell
you that we just need to change our habits to cycling, walking, using public
transport, sharing, fitting energy saving bulbs, cutting out excesses, plant a
tree or two and generally considering and balancing the consequences of
our actions. That wouldn't be so bad would it?

I have friends who think nothing of driving to an away football match two
hundred miles away, even though it shall be televised. How about tumble
drying on sunny days!? It is this kind of thoughtlessness that, should we
come to a sticky end, really takes away any excuses. Patio heaters! Did you
know there are 2.3 million of them in Britain alone?! Oh yes! Let's heat up
the great out-doors! Much comfier - well - until the sea comes swirling in! I
am utterly dismayed by the number of electric heaters popping up outside
pubs in Swanage. Man! If you are cold put a jumper on! Or how about the
Swanage Co-op's recent re-fit? No thought of introducing natural light and
the chillers are on so hard that the staff are blowing on their fingers! Right
above the chillers are about 7 kilowatts of hot old incandescent light bulbs
to make the produce look attractive. In today's world this sort of energy
waste is utterly unacceptable but I hear the Co-op wins environmental
awards! How??!

Another favourite excuse I hear to avoid doing anything positive is 'Oh
but what about the Chinese and the Indians expanding their economies.'
Well I agree that third world development, in terms of consumption smacks
of the beginning of the end, but surely we all can understand that someone
has to lead the way? We have had the luxury of enjoying endless energy
before most nations on this planet, coal fueled the creation of our Empire,
and as such we have higher levels of wealth, health, education and
infrastructure than most. Harnessing deep sea tidal currents (and there has
been a sudden proliferation of companies investing in the development of
just such schemes - so yah-boo to all you doubters when I mooted this idea
a couple of years ago) is the painfully obvious answer to clean, predictable,
free, and CO2-less energy.

Wouldn't it just be great if Britain lead the way showing the rest of the
world just how easy it is to do! When was the last time we did that? And if
we did, imagine the implications for developing nations seeing that wealthy
Britain was setting itself up for endless, harmless, free energy. Maybe they
would start to consider the obvious advantages and re-think their disastrous

outdated coal fueled power station plans, and our extinction might still be averted.

We know that a threshold where we can no longer save ourselves is approaching fast. How far off it is nobody knows but the estimates get ever closer. Ten? Five? Two years? And when that moment has passed, and it becomes clear that we cannot survive the onslaught of a world out of balance, what will you tell your kids when they ask you 'what did you do to help save the world, mummy?'

And since then? Andrew Griffin of the Independent on Tuesday 31 October 2017 wrote:- *"UN releases warning about 'catastrophic' lack of action on climate change*

Donald Trump might be about to make a decision that would make the situation 'even bleaker', the report warns.

There is a "catastrophic" gap between what needs to be done on climate change and what governments and companies are actually doing, the UN has warned.

Andrew tells us that despite pledges to work to mitigate and deal with climate change, current plans still lead to a 3-degree Celsius rise in temperatures by the end of the decade, a major new report warns. If that happens, it will not only break through the 2-degrees target set in the Paris agreement, but also lead to deadly changes in the climate across the world.

He adds that in its latest "Emissions Gap" report issued ahead of an important climate conference in Germany next week, the program takes aim at coal-fired electricity plants being built in developing economies and says investment in renewable energies will pay for itself — and even make money — over the long term.

Climate change might be worse than thought after scientists find major mistake in water temperature readings. Tuesday's report comes as U.N. officials are making a renewed push to maintain momentum generated by the Paris climate accord of 2015. It aims to cap global temperature increases to 2 degrees Celsius by the year 2100 compared to average world temperatures at the start of the industrial era.

But that agreement has come under threat after Donald Trump suggested he might opt to pull out of it. The new report doesn't include any impact from the US withdrawing, and if it did then the picture would become "even bleaker", the UN said."

Here we have the ultimate inconvenient truth. Climate change that is being created by man's selfish activity is causing mayhem on our planet and risks life for all of us and the creatures that we share this magnificent rock with. Any changes to alleviate climate change will bring about a loss of profits on the oil, gas and automotive industries, who control the government so guess what? Nothing that will upset those money making machines will be done, and Trump even wants to go further, the corporate puppet that he is.

CHAPTER 24

Alcohol and those 'other' drugs

'An alcoholic is someone you don't like who drinks as much as you do.' - **Dylan Thomas**

In June 2006 I wrote:-

Stop me if I sound a little out of touch but isn't the European Union an extension of the Common Market, set up to allow for the free passage of people and goods, leading to greater freedoms and prosperity for all? So why am I thinking that all we got is another fat layer of bureaucracy sucking up our cash and justifying its existence by creating reams of daft legislation (which our Government, more than most, just loves to enforce). Surely we would have at least got the free movement of goods between the countries as some form of compensation, right?

I am going to ask you a question about Cornish smugglers. What were they smuggling from where to where, and when? Wasn't it alcohol and tobacco from Europe to Britain in the 18th Century because, in Britain, the taxes on the stuff were too high? So here's another question: has much really changed in 200 years?

Thankfully last year someone finally stood up to our over-zealous customs guys and you can now bring back personal amounts of contraband, but how about that brilliant idea of internet shopping for that stuff in Latvia? Excellent! Low cost booze and fags in the U.K. at last - and we don't have to drive over personally to get them, saving heaps of fuel and saving the planet! It's is E.U. duty paid so it must be legal! Wow! What a saving! Something good to come out of the zillions we have been investing in Brussels at last! Let's raise our glasses! 'Er - no. Sorry guys. Stop anticipating having some affordable fun and go back to work and generate more taxes.' As usual, the party is over before it even started.

So tell me pray, all wise and knowing government would you make a decision like this? 'Er - well - er - it is because we know better than you, even though you are an educated adult that we try to make you believe are free to choose. You are clearly unable to make any sensible decisions for yourself when it comes to the very serious matter of alcohol or cigarettes.'

Hey! Listen you morons, even when alcohol is free most people can say 'when.' Go to a Sandals resort (I have never officially gone to one - only gate-crashed) and the guests, while they love having free drinks, aren't drunk off their tits first thing in the morning - and they are on holiday. They go to the gym, sail, cycle and play volleyball not spending all day vomiting into the pool.

'Oh but then we wouldn't have any taxes to pay for - (wait for it) - The NHS.' Now when the Government is pleading poverty why is it always the NHS that is going to lose out? Any emotional blackmail going on there perhaps? 'Oh O.K. then - if it's the NHS losing out I'll just keep being ripped off when I buy a beer – thanks.' Well here is a suggestion Gordon - how about losing the tax money out of the £100 billion you are currently setting aside for 3 new nuclear submarines (that are to be built abroad. Still at least we still might get all that business for a load of jet fighters from the corrupt and torturing Saudis, so it's not all bad!)

Personally, I would much rather have a good stiff affordable whisky (which incidentally in Argentina costs just £4.50 a bottle) than know I had personally contributed to building evil menacing machines of war designed to wipe out millions of innocent civilians most of whom, if you met them at a dinner party would, in all likelihood, become your friends.

And while you are at it, stop faffing about with incomprehensible legislation and wasting police time. Legalise marijuana, take the profits out of the hands of the underworld and separate a harmless drug from those that are less so (remembering of course that alcohol, tobacco, tea, coffee and aspirin are all also drugs.) How about that mad 'marijuana use always leads on to other drugs' propaganda they feed us? They do that so that then they can talk about the dangers of 'other drugs' while marijuana is in fact much safer than alcohol and tobacco (deaths due to drug abuse states 240,000 deaths annually compared with none ever from marijuana), however the government being unable to tax it is one of the most compelling reasons why we are being lied to.

Think about it. Other than canals and Rembrandt what have the Dutch got to offer other than pot? And did you try to get hotel room in Holland without booking recently? Legalised marijuana, cheap booze and Buckingham Palace - well it would certainly get the tourist industry buzzing!

If you are dead set against this idea can I suggest you stop repeating the propaganda you have been fed, go to Amsterdam on a sunny summers day and have a few puffs on a big fat one. Sit by a canal, have a good think about your life and see what is revealed to you. When was the last time you discovered something new about yourself anyway?

My personal experiences helped me to open my heart and listen to my soul. I understood with lasting clarity what my desires truly were. I felt spiritually enriched, closer to God and wow that chocolate cake sure tasted good! Aggression and running around making money flew right out of the window, which of course is another thing the government is afraid of. This I can promise you. If M.P.s were to have a doobie and as a result voted with their hearts on nuclear submarines or jet fighters, neither of these projects would stand a chance. I believe the world would be a better place as a result.

So in the meantime, enjoy the festive season and while you are knocking back your beer (which is 95% water and 600% more expensive than petrol) try not to think too hard about all the nuclear warheads you are inadvertently helping to make. Happy New Year?

CHAPTER 25

More drugs? Well why not?

'Herb is the healing of a nation, alcohol is the destruction.' -
Bob Marley

Another article I wrote on this thorny subject read:

This month I would like to talk a little about drugs. Now I know this will have some of you clutching your pearls in horror but did you know that, without exception, we are all drug users? 'Me Andy? Not on your life! You must be mistaken!' Really? So you never had a cup of tea then? A glass of wine? A cigar? Aspirin? Or how about a bit of the really hard stuff. Never? Are you sure? Because, receiving any anaesthetic, local or general, makes you an appreciative recipient of an opium derivative. Yep, those Afghan poppies that get so much bad press save us all an awful lot of screaming in our hospitals and dental surgeries. So can we at least start by agreeing that, in certain circumstances, there can be an upside to drug taking?

Now I am not promoting the recreational use of drugs, not at all, but it is time for us to stop pretending that this doesn't go on in every crevice of our society. Because it does. So surely any law that attempts to make criminals of huge numbers of otherwise upstanding, tax paying and reliable individuals, many of whom you happily interact with on a daily basis, can't be right. If someone should choose to involve some narcotic intake as part of their social and personal lives, and if this isn't harming anyone else, then I really struggle to see what business that is of anyone else's, or even how a crime is being committed at all. Isn't this simply a freedom of choice? (Which is something our Government seems focussed on eroding).

Oh but Andy, how can you talk about drugs like this when they kill so many people? Well let's put it this way. Alcohol and tobacco are drugs (oh yes they are!) and between them they kill about 240,000 people in Britain each year. All the other drugs put together nail only about 1,500 of us, with about half of those deaths being caused by prescribed methadone. By the way, did you know that over half of us adults have tried marijuana at least once in our lives? And just how many deaths are attributed to its use each year? Well.... it's none. Nada! Zilch! Zippo! Diddelysquat! So, on that basis, which of the above would you think a responsible Government would decide to make legal? Of course! It's obvious! The deadly ones they can tax! It's true. Hypocrisy reigns supreme.

So let's focus for a moment on the only safe recreational drug there is. If you pay attention to the 'against' lobby, most of whom have never even had a go and therefore really don't know what they are talking about, they just can't stop telling us how evil marijuana is. For example, 'it always leads on to other drugs'. Sorry but that is a lie. It's like saying that lager always leads on to methylated spirits. The reason that point is bandied about with such exuberance is to widen the discussion to those 'other drugs' because on its own there simply isn't enough wrong with marijuana. 'It is more carcinogenic than tobacco'. Well who cares? I mean, you are hardly going to do forty a day are you? 'It causes schizophrenia'. Well, even with all the research this is still a supposition, and anyway, are you telling me that the aggressive behaviour caused by legal alcohol consumption is not a personality altering phenomenon? Do you know what I find hilarious? When an athlete is banned because they have traces of it in their blood. So what? Like that's really going to help cut their 110 meter hurdle time!

While I accept that over indulgence in anything, even gateaux, is not to be recommended, what bothers me is that if you talk to someone who does use this weed they will happily tell you all about the good stuff, and there appears to be quite a bit of it that we never get to hear about. Now I don't want this to sound like a commercial and I am certainly NOT promoting anything, but I think we should all open our minds and understand that we are only talking about a naturally occurring plant placed on Gods own earth – by God. If I were then to take away the labels that we have been taught and simply describe this herbal remedy as I have been told, that when ingested invoked feelings of love, peace, generosity, and calm; encourages one to put the heart and soul before the mind; increases spiritual awareness, creativity and appreciation for ones surroundings, wouldn't you think that that sounds like a good thing?

What do you think the Native American Indians were putting in their peace pipes? And it was called the peace pipe because....? What was at the centre of the 'ban the bomb' anti-war love and peace movement of the 60's? Sure it slows one down for a while, but looking at the rate at which we are tearing our world apart that surely can be no bad thing!

No, marijuana is illegal because of Governmental financial issues and the health arguments are (no pun intended) just a smoke screen. Apart from loss of taxation revenue from alcohol consumption they know for sure that there would be droves of people leaving their meaningless jobs at the ball bearing factory in search of a fuller life and enlightenment, and that would be bad for their all important economy. (Although did you try to get a weekend hotel room in Holland without booking recently?)

In my opinion marijuana should be legalised thus separating it totally from other drugs and enabling proper controls, such as in age of purchase and where it is sold, to be put in place and it would remove the profits from the hands of the underworld. By the way, I am far from alone with this way of thinking. The Scottish Socialist Party, the Greens and the Lib Dems (although they have backtracked a little) agree with me. Even the police keep pleading with the Government for a change in the law as it would free up time wasted in what is clearly an un-winnable battle. Each arrest for possession takes about 5 hours of police time and costs about £10,000 to bring to court. Is that really how you want the police to use up their precious resources?

If it were up to me I would go further by making it mandatory for M.P.'s to have a quick puff before voting. At least then we might get to hear a little honesty coming from the heart instead of the capitalist rhetoric we mostly have to put up with. 'O.K., listen up you guys! The next vote is about those new billion pound Trident nuclear submarines - so light up now!'(...thinks... well... it would provide employment... and maybe we could hide behind it...but wow... if we ever used those weapons they would kill millions of blameless innocents ... and herald the end of civilisation as we know it... poison our planet beyond repair... they undermine our arguments against other people having weapons of mass destruction... and get in the way of making friends from our enemies...soak up money that could be used to combat world poverty...so my heart says... NO WAY!). 'We vote against!

Hey!... can we all go out and watch the sunset for a while before we come back and vote to put a trade embargo on Japan until they stop illegal whaling?' If only.

So what have we learnt in the decade since writing this? *Alcohol-related liver disease accounted for nearly two-thirds of the 6,830 deaths in 2014.'* James Meikle of the Guardian, on the 20th of September 2017 wrote. He continues: *'Alcohol-related deaths in England up 4% in one year. Local government body shocked by figures that show almost 1.1m diseases or injuries linked to drinking were recorded between 2013-14 and 2014-15*

James expanded by saying that alcohol-related deaths in England had risen by 4% in a year and by 13% in a decade. Alcohol-related liver disease accounted for nearly two-thirds, 63%, of the 6,830 deaths in 2014, a total described by local councils as "shocking". Admissions to hospital where alcohol-linked disease or injury was the primary reason increased by 32%, to 333,000, between 2004-05 and 2014-15, said the Health and Social Care Information Centre.

He says that in its new report, Statistics on Alcohol: England, 2016, pulled together data from various sources to give a picture of the changing impact of alcohol consumption on health over time. It revealed that diseases or injuries linked to drinking either as a primary reason or secondary diagnosis went up by 30,000, from 1.06m to 1.09m, between 2013-14 and 2014-15, with men accounting for 65% of the total. This broad measure is regarded as the best indicator of the total strain alcohol places on national health.

The report also said prescriptions for medicines to tackle alcohol dependence rose from 109,000 in 2005 to 196,000 in 2015.

The Local Government Association said the figures were shocking. Izzi Seccombe, who holds its community wellbeing portfolio, said the figure of almost 1.1m for the broader measure covering alcohol-related admissions indicated a large number were from middle-aged and older age groups.

"Despite drinking comparatively little, older people consume alcohol far more often," said Seccombe. *"These figures warn of the dangers of regular drinking over a long period of time and the impact this can have on the body of an older person, which is less able to handle the same level of alcohol as in previous years."*

So surely this begs the question why, oh why, is it illegal to use marijuana? No known instances of any direct link to a single death, so surely it has to be better than this? I love a pint or two, and sometimes have had a great deal more and it doesn't appear to have done me much harm however it would appear that the massive tax generation through alcohol is blurring the governments thoughts on this. Each pint we drink in the UK generates them 80p in tax plus the 20% vat, so about £1.50 altogether, for each pint consumed. Of course the brewers are mostly big corporations and the government won't be upsetting them any time soon.

As written in the following government report:-

Cannabis legalisation worth millions. By Nick Hopkins, Investigations correspondent, BBC Newsnight, 13th October 2015

"Legalising cannabis could generate hundreds of millions of pounds a year in tax and cut costs for the police and prisons, a government study has found.

The internal Treasury report, obtained by BBC Newsnight, said regulating the market would "generate notable tax revenue" and "lead to overall savings to the criminal justice system".

Nick tells us that MPs debated the issue on Monday, after a petition calling for legalisation drew more than 220,000 signatures, however Ministers do not plan to alter the law. The Home Office said it had "no plans" to change the law on cannabis, which is currently classified as a Class B illegal drug, adding that cannabis use was falling gradually.

He adds that the Treasury study was undertaken earlier this year at the behest of the Liberal Democrats when they were in coalition, but was not published. Civil servants were asked to consider the "potential fiscal impacts of introducing a regulated cannabis market in the UK".

The study notes that 2.2 million people aged 16 to 59 are thought to have used cannabis last year - smoking a total of 216 tonnes.

Government analysts reviewed the work of the Institute for Social and Economic Research, which has estimated that licensing cannabis could help reduce the UK budget deficit by up to £1.25bn a year - from taxes raised and cost reductions."

220,000 sign the petition forcing the debate but still no movement on freeing the use of a naturally growing herb. It's interesting to note that the discussion isn't about the freedom of people being able to enjoy their chosen lifestyle without fear of prosecution but about how much money could be made from it. Typical.

CHAPTER 26

Wildlife

'Plans to protect air and water, wilderness and wildlife are in fact plans to protect man.' - Stewart Udall

Another Gazette article I wrote for Octover 2005 read:-

A couple of weeks ago an amazing thing happened. I saw a wasp. So what was so amazing about that you might ask? Well, it was the first and only one I had seen this year. Did you know that last year the Council were called out to exterminate over 200 nests in Dorset? And by the way do you know one of the methods of disposing of pesky wasps? They put the nest into a black bin bag with some petrol and burn them all alive - now isn't that nice? And now it would seem that there are not too many left, and this lead me to counting up some of the notable insects, as a lay, but active, insect observer, that I had seen this year. Maybe you can fill in your own numbers.

Grasshoppers - three, ladybirds - two, Peacock butterflies - one, Dragon flies – four. When was the last time you saw a real cloud of moths at night around a light? And we live in rural Dorset! And this is the bottom of the food chain with lots of creatures relying on it for their own survival. O.K. lets go a little bigger. Slo-worms - one, Hedgehogs - none, people - twenty six million three hundred and forty two thousand nine hundred and seventy two - although I might have counted my neighbour twice. Clearly something very bad is going on here.

So what? Who cares? Well sadly that does seem to be the general consensus - but the truth is that I do care. And I believe that, if the time is taken to pay attention to it, underneath it all and in private we all care.

Doesn't everyone get a sense of well-being from gently blowing that ladybird from your hand or watching that mad looking shield bug on the picnic table? And when they are finally gone won't we just miss them a little bit?

So where are they going? Well as usual there are a number of factors to give everyone a convenient smokescreen to hide behind, but the problem lies pretty fairly and squarely with farming practices. Now don't get me wrong, some farmers, and I can think of one or two fine local examples, really care about the conservation of their land, but by and large it is intensive farming with over-zealous use of herbicides. pesticides and fertilizers that is wiping out plant diversity and the insect population.

It is not unusual for a field to receive upwards of 10 doses of various chemicals and I have seen quad bikes go around the outside of the field armed with sprayers to make sure it gets right in under the hedgerows. Yep - if you happen to be a weed or have six legs you are pretty much doomed.

Of course we have all heard of how the farmer is caught in the middle of the dictate of ruthless supermarkets and bizarre European laws, and there is truth in that. However blaming someone else for your own shortcomings and removing yourself from the responsibility of your own decisions is a culture reaching epidemic proportions in Britain, and I believe this is a fine example. If there is a passion to improve things then there is always a way. If farmers truly wanted to put insect populations over a new 4x4 with aircon they could, and they would, do it.

Now I noticed in the Independent on Sunday that Jim Knight, our local M.P. and Minister of Nature Conservation has popped down to the Congo to look at the plight of the mountain gorillas (incidentally isn't it interesting that Jim didn't say one word about Nature Conservation at the Q & A's leading up to the election - in fact I was the only one to bring up issues of the environment - not that I am bitter or anything!) and his findings were? 'It is difficult to stop African people eating monkeys.' Well, that was a good use of time and public money then!

So can I make a suggestion or two here Jim? Of course it is commendable to fight the cause of any of these beleaguered creatures, the world is sadly brimming over with those problems, but surely that can be done from here? So how about putting forward a couple of schemes that would truly make a difference in Dorset.

How about changing the land set aside rules so that farmers are no longer paid for leaving whole fields untended but the cash is shared out to every farmer in return for them compulsorily leaving a three meter margin free from herbicides and pesticides around every field?

How about strictly licensing agricultural chemicals, or placing a huge tax on them to discourage their over use and encourage organic farming practices?

How about getting your health colleagues to run a campaign revealing how pesticides on our shiny perfect looking vegetables is causing massive health problems not least of which is the rapid increase in cases of Alzheimer's where studies suggest that the brain is damaged by years of consumption of insecticide. I can see Jamie Oliver on the telly right now - 'If it's good enough for the maggot it's good enough for me!'

And since then? Damian Carrington of the Guardian on Wednesday 14 September 2016 wrote:-

"State of Nature reveals the destructive impact of intensive farming, urbanisation and climate change on plants, animals and habitats. More than one in 10 of the UK's wildlife species are threatened with extinction and the numbers of the nation's most endangered creatures have plummeted by two-thirds since 1970, according to a major report.

Damian adds that the study found that abundance of all wildlife has also fallen, with one in six animals, birds, fish and plants having been lost, the State of Nature report found.

It said that together with historical deforestation and industrialisation, these trends have left the UK "among the most nature-depleted countries in the world", with most of the country having gone past the threshold at which "ecosystems may no longer reliably meet society's needs".

He states that the comprehensive scientific report, compiled by more than 50 conservation organisations, spells out the destructive impact of intensive farming, urbanisation and climate change on habitats from farmland and hills to rivers and the coast. It found that the fall in wildlife over the last four decades cannot be blamed on past harm, but has continued in recent years.

"It wasn't just all back in 70s and 80s, it is still happening now," said Mark Eaton, at RSPB and the lead author of the report.

Eaton said that there were good examples of wildlife and habitat recovery, but with public funding for biodiversity having fallen by 32% from 2008 to 2015. "The ability to do it is within our grasp, it is just about resources and the willingness."

Sir David Attenborough, who wrote the foreword to the report, said: *"The natural world is in serious trouble and it needs our help as never before. We continue to lose the precious wildlife that enriches our lives and is essential to the health and well-being of those who live in the UK."*

In pure monetary terms nature provides economic and health benefits of about £30bn a year, according to a 2011 government analysis.

The report added that insects and other invertebrates, which make up 97% of all animal species, are particularly struggling, with 59% in decline since 1970. These provide vital services such as pollination and keep soils healthy. Eaton said *"The work they do for us is just immense. If they were to disappear, I think we'd see environmental breakdown very quickly. They are about the most important things out there."*

We were told that among the species in decline, great crested newts, hedgehogs and corn marigolds have suffered from changes in farming practices. The draining of bogs has harmed the large marsh grasshopper, while the degradation of heaths has caused the sand lizard population to fall. Urbanisation is a cause of falling water vole numbers, while bottom trawling offshore has harmed the ocean quahog, a bivalve which can live for 500 years.

Damien went on to say that the report included a new "biodiversity intactness index", which analysed the loss of species over centuries, showing the UK had lost significantly more nature over the long term than the global average, with the UK the 29th lowest out of 218 countries.

"It is quite shocking where we stand compared to the rest of the world", said Eaton. *"The index gives an idea of where we have got to over the centuries, and we are pretty knackered."*

In summary Damien tells us that the government's own assessment, published in August, found that much of England's best-loved wildlife remains in serious decline, with 75% of over 200 "priority" species across the country falling in number."

Well, why should we care? Wildlife doesn't earn us money does it? So why bother? And we aren't. The corporations keep raping the countryside and the government condones it, while a spokeswoman from DEFRA is trying to convince us that things are actually improving for our wildlife. A typical whitewash of the truth. And the government analysis of the situation? 'Nature provides economic and health benefits of about £30bn a year,' they just can't stop thinking about the money can they?

CHAPTER 27

Energy Waste

'Don't get me wrong: I love nuclear energy! It's just that I prefer fusion to fission. And it just so happens that there's an enormous fusion reactor safely banked a few million miles from us. It delivers more than we could ever use in just about 8 minutes. And it's wireless!' - William McDonough,

For November 2006 I wrote:-

Imagine you are blindfolded and knowingly walking toward a cliffs edge, what would you do? Stop? Shuffle gently along feeling with your feet? Crawl? Try to turn around? Or would you march along with a big glazed grin on your face? Because, when it comes to climate change that is what I see most people doing.

Jim Hansen, renowned climatologist and thorn in the side of the Bush administration now predicts that we, (and that means you and I) have less than ten years to act before global warming becomes an unstoppable process. The Jet Propulsion Laboratory in California has shown from satellite images that Arctic perennial ice shrunk by 14% (280,000 square miles) in a single year and this, I promise you, is not a good thing.

You can be sure that a devastating and irreversible chain reaction shall be unleashed any moment now, and we are causing it. As we heat the earth, all that nice shiny white ice melts and it is replaced by dark sea which speeds the process by absorbing even more of the suns heat. Next the tundra shall continue to melt (yes - it has already started) at an ever increasing rate releasing sqillions of tons of methane (which is a much worse greenhouse gas than co2) into the atmosphere. Next the rainforests shall start to die and rot, turning our best friend, who we have abused for decades, into our worst enemy and just a few years down the line the lucky ones amongst us shall find themselves hanging on to a plank with no hope of rescue wondering why they were so blasé about it all. Still, it's not all bad. At least you won't have to worry about what happened to your pension any more.

I have been openly predicting this turn of events for about 20 years and have picked up a fair amount of ridicule over it. When the first scientist predictions came out they were wildly optimistic, stating 'by the end of the century some parts of Bangladesh will experience flooding' - well, with respect, who cared about that? Too far away both geographically and chronologically, especially when it seems that no-one is willing to change their convenience habits to even save themselves today! But since then the predictions have been reigned in over and over and only now, in the form of Mr. Hansen, have I heard someone agree with what I have been saying all along. Unusually for me, however, in this instance I take no pleasure in being right. I truly wish that I wasn't.

Now there is a simple solution. that I have written of before. Really? Simple? Affordable? Yes!! You could still be saved! Now I am not going to go through the whole process as I wouldn't want to bore my regular readers, but when you know you have a solution that can save the planet it is hard not to repeat yourself! So, in case you missed it, turbines harnessing tidal (not wave) power is the answer. Predicable, clean and infinite energy which, by extracting energy from the seas in the form of heat, have a cooling effect on the oceans which, luckily, is just what we need to do to reverse global warming.

However, CO_2 emissions can be thought of like the balance in your bank account. Yes we need to start putting CO_2 free energy in but we also need to stop spending. I think everyone knows what the big problems are with transport, domestic and manufacturing energy expenditure headlining the bill, by why aren't we even tightening up on the little things?

It is all very well the Government running commercials telling us, quite rightly, not to fill the kettle right up and turn our lights off, but what sort of example are they setting? Have you been out on your street at 3am recently? Try it. It is so illuminated that you could invite your friends around for a game of 5-a-side! And empty! (well except for you now of course). 'Oh but Andy the streets would be so dangerous if they weren't lit!' Well leave every 5th one on until midnight then. Stay in. Carry a torch. How about the motorways? Not a great deal of muggings going on there are there? Hands up everyone who's car doesn't have headlights. Exactly.

Putting aircon (which eats up about 10% of your fuel) in modern cars shows just how much a cynical automotive industry really cares. What happened to winding down the window and sunroofs? People who leave their parked car engines ticking over shows that they are either not paying attention or are so self centred that they simply don't care. Wakey wakey! The monster is upon you! Even worse perhaps is that trains and busses do it too, which, as I take the train when possible to save emissions, I find particularly galling. (And if you do take the train don't, whatever you do, have a cup of tea - plastic cup, plastic lid, plastic stirrer, plastic milk pot with foil top, paper sugar sachets, paper napkins and you MUST have a brown carrier for health and safety reasons - and they DON'T recycle. But then again the Council don't even bother! All their litter bins? Straight into the ground . That is of course until those two new incinerators are build in Dorset. I caught the end of the Councillor spokes lady on the radio justifying this insanity by saying 'well we generate so much rubbish, we have to do something with it.' Aaaaaaagh! Recycle it! You mad blinkered people! You are going to kill us all! However, I digress.

The introduction of tighter control over building insulation is a good thing, (even if there is no balance taken into account for the high toxicity of new insulating products, a proportion of which shall inevitably end up as landfill) but then anyone can go and buy as many patio heaters as they like. How does that compute? Wasteful use of energy is all around us and I think it a great shame that, with a little thought and enlightened leadership this part of the problem at least could be rectified without us even having to encounter a downside to our unnaturally extravagant life styles. It would be a start, if only one small step away from the cliffs edge.

You may consider this a little presumptuous, but I liken my position with that of Churchill in the run up to WWII, desperately trying to persuade a reluctant Government to avoid disaster by urgently building Spitfires. Today, however, the enemy is far more fearsome, but the weapons we need are only wind and water turbines. Lots of them. Mother Nature has issued us with warning after warning that she is preparing to wipe us from the planet. The big difference here, of course, is that we are the ones who have declared war on her. All we have to do now, by putting some love back into this planet of ours, is make peace, and soon.

And since then? The 'Help Save Nature' website tells us: *""Crisis" seems to be the buzzword of the 21st century. After the water and food crisis, it is the time of financial and energy crisis. The industrial revolution of the 18th century, offered mankind the luxuries that were never experienced before. Since then, we have been busy indulging in the comfort that came with the advent of technology. We barely have time to notice the rapidly depleting energy resources. The more we choose to ignore this issue, it becomes more difficult to solve it. The only way to combat this problem is by conservation of energy. However, this may not be as easy as it sounds. There are several problems that need to be addressed before this undertaking such steps.*

It goes on to tell us that the uncontrolled and unreasonable use of energy resources in the past few decades has led to the depletion of conventional type of resources. Although, measures are taken at the government levels to control the energy consumption, these attempts only meet with little success and public awareness is the only way to successfully deal with this problem.

It points out that wastage of energy is the biggest culprit of energy crisis. Unnecessary illumination, running the appliances even when no one is using them, using two or more devices for achieving the same purpose, etc., can all lead to wastage of valuable energy. Self-discipline is the only way to resolve this issue.

And sums up by saying that mindful use of resources is different from wasting energy, but it yields the same result. This includes choosing the wrong appliances that consume more electricity, or buying luxury cars that are extremely inefficient regarding fuel consumption. Choosing your options wisely can solve this problem. Public awareness can be generated, in order to educate people regarding the intelligent usage of energy.

'Although, measures are taken at the government levels to control the energy consumption, these attempts only meet with little success.'

Yes I bet they do. There is no way our government would be given the authority to cut any of those pound creating uses of burning oil and gas. A bit of solar has appeared along with a puff of wind but nothing to dent the profits of the big boys. 'Wastage of energy is the biggest culprit of energy crisis including unnecessary illumination', which of course is why there has been hardly a jot done to get unnecessary street lighting turned off. Cynical and unworthy of the name, our government continues to be the ineffective puppet of the energy corporations.

CHAPTER 28

Middle East

'I have been to the Occupied Palestinian Territory, and I have witnessed the racially segregated roads and housing that reminded me so much of the conditions we experienced in South Africa under the racist system of Apartheid.' - Desmond Tutu

For December 2006 I wrote:-

Q. Imagine you live in a nice part of town where everyone gets along pretty well, but then the Council, without your approval, decide to move a new family, who likes to do things a little differently, into the bottom of your garden. Understandably you make a bit of a fuss about this turn of events, but things slowly settle down until one day you see that they have put a shed up on your side of the fence. So you go round and ask if they would be kind enough to move it but, because they know a couple of big tough families on the other side of town, they slam the door in your face. So then the whole town gets involved, asking for the shed to be moved, but instead more sheds get put up across the road.

Now everyone naturally gets quite frustrated about this and, while you are trying to get the new family to do something about it, some of your kids start throwing stones at the new neighbours windows so show how upset they are. The next thing you know your new neighbour comes around, supported by the tough families, and starts smashing up your house. Now everyone is pretty angry and a few more stones get chucked so the neighbour decides to build a really big strong fence between you, but deliberately puts it in the wrong place, stealing a chunk of your garden, and putting the shed that was in your garden on his side. Then things get really bad. All the other neighbours are now upset and can't resist being rude to the new neighbours, but every time one chucks a rotten apple at them, the new neighbour comes around smashing the place up, chopping down your trees and demolishing your home. Now, how would YOU put an end to this downward spiral?

A. By curtailing the help of the strong friends, putting the fence back where it belongs and removing the sheds in return for an agreement from the kids to stop throwing stones. I guess you all got that one right? Then give yourself a pat on the back because you have just solved the Middle East crisis. Not really difficult is it? (And if you came up with a different answer then I truly hope you never move in next to me!!)

Now the real problem is that the U.S. are massively aligned with Israel because the Israelis don't mind being used as an unsinkable aircraft carrier for them, partly because of the plethora of Zionists in high position in the American government, and, as there is lots of oil to be had in the Middle East the Americans, as we know, have quite an interest in the region. So to keep this relationship sweet the Yanks have a Foreign Military Financing (FMF) fund, which gives Israel nearly 3 billion dollars, (that's three thousand millions by the way) to spend on American military hardware (meaning some innocent teacher in Iowa is going about their job, duly paying their taxes and unwittingly funding death and misery on the other side of the planet, which I find pretty disturbing).

But even the U.S. have legislation in place to try and prevent unnecessary suffering called the Arms Export Control Act. Section 4 of this states that 'military items transferred to foreign governments by the United States are to be used solely for internal security and legitimate self defence.' Well what we are witnessing clearly isn't internal security, so all this smashing up of the infrastructure, bombing of apartment buildings and turning of hundreds of thousands of innocent people into refugees must be their idea of self defence. Of course! Well Tony Blair must think so. That's why he's so happy for Britain to help with the transporting of all those bombs! It's no better than saying he wants to break up a pub brawl while slipping one of the geezers a broken bottle. My, when I see him walking hand in hand with Bush up to those lecterns to spout time wasting rhetoric while innocent people are being slaughtered it makes me so proud to be

British! If his inaction doesn't spark a fresh round of bombings in London I shall be pretty surprised.

Anyway, Israel actually annually spends about 15 billion dollars on military hardware, mostly with America, which of course is very good for business, (as long as you don't mind having children's blood on your hands, which it would appear they do not.) And while we are on the subject, did you know that the Americans export more arms annually than the total sold by the next 14 countries in the sales league table put together?

Of course all this expenditure makes the Israelis so much more powerful than their neighbours that they really don't have to give a damn about getting along with anybody else, which, by the way they conduct themselves, seems to be how they like it. The trouble with that policy is that every time they take a life or displace a peaceful hard working family (whether by mistake or design it makes no difference in the end) they generate another aggrieved follower for Hammas or Hizballah, thereby making their existence less secure, which in turn leads them to purchase even more arms.

Considering this is all happening in Jesus' Biblical Holy Land there really seems to be very little evidence of forgiveness going on, so to my mind, if the Israelis really want to sleep soundly in their beds they only need do two things. One is to permanently pull out of all currently occupied territories without exception, (you don't even need a map to know that the Sinai Desert, the Gaza Strip, the West Bank the Golan Heights and Southern Lebanon are all the bits of land next door to Israel because you hear about them on the news every time the Israeli's pop round for tea without an invitation) and two is to invest a proportion of their massive arms budget in sweetening relationships with their Arab neighbours. Now I don't know for sure how much a medical centre or a school costs in Palestine or Lebanon but I am guessing that a million dollars would make a pretty big dent in setting one up. If they dared to donate even half their defence budget into, say, the health and education of those around them (and that would generate enough to create 7,000 'million dollar 'establishments annually and still break even!) then I think attitudes would rapidly change for the better, and forever. Peace at last.

Mind you, here in Britain we are hardly setting a good example. Recently Gordon Brown has threatened to drag us into a new era of uncertainty for the whole of mankind by pledging untold amounts of your money toward a new nuclear 'deterrent' should he become P.M. Well, if you only need one single reason not to vote Labour at the next election then that is it. In my opinion the man appears as a presumptuous, egotistical overgrown schoolboy who's only concern is getting into the history books at any cost.

Nuclear weapons are not a deterrent for attacks if they manifest themselves as suicide bombings in the subway, but we could protect ourselves very simply by listening for a change. Various factions are clearly upset with us and it is time we tried to understand why. Let's just start being nice! I mean, who plots to attack Canada or Brazil or Thailand? Why don't we set an example to the rest of the world by spending Gordon's holocaustic budget helping those that don't like us! Let's make friends by sharing the wealth that we are currently prepared to waste on war and spend it on fighting starvation and investing in education and health in countries less fortunate than ourselves, and see who gets upset about that!!

So why, you may ask, do our leaders still act in such a primitive manner? Well it's all about living in the fear of losing what is ours, rather than living with the joy of giving. Ina word, greed. Replacing that fear with love, which is a lesson I think we all, myself included, need reminding of from time to time is all we have to do. And wouldn't it be wonderful when aliens finally arrive on Earth for us to receive a real James T. Kirk moment in their assessment of mankind with 'you have come far, Earthlings, there is hope for your kind yet.'

And since then: Perter Baker and Julie Davis of the New York Times on September 13th, 2016 wrote:-

U.S. Finalizes Deal to Give Israel $38 Billion in Military Aid

"President Obama and Prime Minister Benjamin Netanyahu of Israel in the Oval Office last year. The agreement represents a major American commitment to Israel's security after years of fractious relations.

JERUSALEM — The United States has finalized a $38 billion package of military aid for Israel over the next 10 years, the largest of its kind ever, and the two allies plan to sign the agreement on Wednesday, American and Israeli officials said.

They went on to tell us that the State Department had scheduled a ceremony to formally announce the pact, to be signed by Jacob Nagel, the acting national security adviser to Prime Minister Benjamin Netanyahu of Israel, and Thomas A. Shannon Jr., the under-secretary of state for political affairs, and Susan E. Rice, President Obama's national security adviser who handled negotiations, plans to be on hand.

We were told that the package will provide an average of $3.8 billion a year over the next decade to Israel, already the largest recipient of American aid, including financing for missile defense systems that defend against rockets fired by groups like Hezbollah and Hamas. Under a previous 10-year agreement that expires in 2018, the United States provides about $3 billion a year, but lately Congress has added up to $500 million a year for missile defense."

And. . .

On 14ᵗʰ December 2017 Al-Jazeera wrote

'The decision of US President Donald Trump to recognise Jerusalem as the capital of Israel has generated a series of reactions in Palestine and around the world.'

Al- Jazeera told us Pakistani Prime Minsiter Shahid Khaqan Abbasi on Wednesday at the OIC summit asked, *"the key question is - what should be our response?"*. *"Should we accept this as fait accompli? We hope that a few demonstrations of rage will not dissipate in passive acceptance of the status quo. Our response should be a clear expression and renewal of our solidarity and unity,"* Abbasi said, stressing a need to *"overcome political differences"*.

We were told that Saudi Arabian King Salman delivered an annual speech outlining his government's priorities for the coming year, reiterating the Kingdom's stated commitment to a Palestinian state with East Jerusalem as its capital.

He said *"I repeat the Kingdom's condemnation and strong regret over the US decision on Jerusalem and for its relinquishment of the historic rights of the Palestinian people in Jerusalem."*

We were also told that, in seeking a united stance against Trump's decision, leaders from the Organisation of Islamic Cooperation (OIC) gathered in Istanbul on Wednesday for an extraordinary session where Palestinian President Mahmoud Abbas said the Palestinians won't accept any role for the United States in a peace process with Israel "from now on" and called on countries who have not recognized Palestine as a state to do so. Abbas also urged those who recognize

Israel to reconsider, saying the Jewish state has not committed to any international resolution.

What possible chance of peace can there be? The Americans fuel Isreal to the tune of $3.8 billion ($3,800,000,000 longhand) every year to be spent exclusively on American weapons and at a stroke unilaterally recognizes Jerusalem, that is half run by the Palestinians, as Israel's capital. Hardly surprising really, congress is awash with Zionists in powerful positions and of course the Jewish owned banks who control governmental decisions have their own patriotic agendas too.

However it has to be the arms manufacturers who are rubbing their hands by getting vast orders for weapons to be used on the other side of the planet (and not just for defence) paid for exclusively with public taxes. So sad, and they are *still* covering their tracks by talking about the peace process. Cynical or who?

CHAPTER 29

Misinformation

'The lowest form of popular culture - lack of information, misinformation, disinformation, and a contempt for the truth or the reality of most people's lives - has overrun real journalism. Today, ordinary Americans are being stuffed with garbage.' - Carl Bernstein

October 2006 saw me writing:-

A year back I caught the tail end of a news item on radio 4 in which some mad lady was claiming that the ozone layer had miraculously repaired itself largely due to refrigerators being built to a better specification so that the refrigerants no longer escaped. What?! How did that crazy lady get onto the news spouting inane gibberish like that? Sure, like we are always going to the fridge to find our food all mushy and a puddle of evaporating CFC's on the floor, right? And anyway, these days I understand they use HFC-134a (1,1,1,2-Tetrafluoroethane) these days as that doesn't harm the ozone layer.

But do you want to know what was really scary about this? During the next week or so I had a dozen people, intelligent informed acquaintances of mine, tell me not to worry about the ozone layer anymore as it had repaired itself. Ring the bells! The war is over! No need to concern ourselves with all that air pollution nonsense anymore! I knew it was all going to be alright in the end! Let's build a bonfire to celebrate! Wrong.

How do I know? Well you don't need a scientist, or to be a scientist, to work it out for yourself as you are already equipped with all the sensors and data you need. Try doing these simple tests. What colour did you draw the sun when you were a child? Yellow? Well glance at it on the next clear day and what colour is it now? Polar white. This is because more blue light is getting through adding to the red and green (which combines to form yellow), making white. And what is next to blue in the electromagnetic spectrum? Ultraviolet. And what filters all that short wavelength light like blue and ultraviolet? Ozone. Less ozone = more blue = whiter sun. Fact.

Feel the sun on your skin. Is it nice and balmy or hash and caustic? Is a sun tan alone, which is how nature protects you, enough to stop your skin burning these days? Has your face got burnt in March or October recently? Look at the colours of the world about you on a sunny day. Hey! Who has been fiddling with the controls? The contrast and brightness have been turned right up and the colours down! Is the picture all washed out and the shadows too stark and black? Are more people wearing sunglasses? Incidentally I even heard the results of a 'scientific study' that concluded that more people were wearing sunglasses because they wanted to emulate movie stars like Tom Cruise. Oh yeah! Of course! How stupid of me! And I thought it was because you couldn't drive without squinting! Are skin melanomas on the increase? Are sun screen factors still increasing? Did they even make a factor 60 when you were a kid? Are the leaves on the sunny side of broadleaf trees all burnt up by June? But hey, don't worry too much because, apparently, the O3 layer is fine and this is all a figment of your imagination.

I should just mention here that the ozone layer is pretty precious (no life on earth can survive without it) and pretty vulnerable (just a few centimetres thick at ground level pressure) and very tricky to regenerate. So armed with this knowledge wouldn't you think it worthwhile preserving what we have left?

But surprisingly perhaps this article is not just about the ozone layer, it is about the multimillion pound 'disinformation' industry that is busy feeding us bogus findings via the media to confuse the issues thus ensuring that the multinationals can go on making money unhindered, and the potential harm is massive.

Another example. A company called International Policy Network, who are incidentally funded in part by Exxon-Mobil, have been so successful at disinformation that they have helped to delay action against global warming by years, which is of course is exactly what a giant oil company would want.

The only intsy wintsy snagette is that the ultimate cost is likely to be counted in millions, if not billions, of lives says Phil Thornhill of Against Climate Change. IPN's director, Professor Julian Morris tells us 'the way to combat pollution is to encourage respect for the free market and private property because property owners have a vested interest in a clean environment'. Oh yeah! Now you mention it Phil, why didn't I think of that before?

He also says 'the question is whether global warming is actually a good thing or a bad thing. In certain parts of the world an increase in temperature will enable larger levels of crop production.' Shame on you Phil. That's like telling a kid that having leukaemia is good thing because they get to eat more ice cream.

So multinationals simply pay for the services of (bribe) someone with recognised qualifications in their field of interest to feed tosh to the public thus muddying the waters and slowing down, or halting all together, positive action. And because this comes from the mouth of an 'expert' their argument carries more weight with the media and in a court of law than any crisp, logical discussion put forward by some genuinely concerned, intelligent, thinking person like - er - well - like me!

Sadly anyone who purposely misinforms cannot ultimately be held accountable, because they can argue that they were only expressing an opinion. However, much in the same way that councilors are not allowed to vote on issues that they have a vested interest in, I think the same should apply here. But then again, why not make people accountable for misinformation that causes harm? The Bush administration censored their own report on global warming to suit their oil producing wants (not needs) so ultimately, when their actions lead to death and destruction shouldn't they be accountable for manslaughter and pay compensation for damage attributed to climate change weather chaos? Maybe then you would hear an honest discussion for a change.

In the meantime, smoking doesn't cause cancer, pesticides are O.K. to eat, mobile phones are safe, hunting deer with dogs doesn't cause stress, the ozone layer is fine and global warming is being caused by an ice age. However, disinformation only works if you allow it to. So all I ask is the next time you read something in the press take a little time to consider if there might be a financial or power agenda behind the discussion and, for your children's sakes, filter out the substantial amount of male bovine excrement you are being fed. Of course some people write simply because they have a passion for the truth. You be the judge.

Since then Matt Drake of the Express on Mon, Nov 27th, 2017 had this to say:-

"UK lives in danger because of Russian propaganda and fake news over MMR jabs British citizens are at risks from deadly diseases because of Russian lies, propaganda and misinformation, it has been claimed.

Matt told us that it is feared the Kremlin is using misinformation over flu jabs and the MMR vaccine. He said that experts have previously warned that Russian President Vladimir Putin's government has been trying to erode trust in US and European Governments by spreading lies on social media and "fake news".

He added that Chris Phillips, former head of National Counter Terrorism Security Office, said it has become a threat to daily life, and that *"This is all about destabilisation by external forces. War is ever changing and becoming much more cyber-based. For generations, governments in the UK and the West have been extremely worried about destabilisation from external forces. The Russians have long felt that the UK, America and the European Union is a major threat to them so have developed major strategies in how to interfere with politics, policy, and now it seems the interference is impacting on vital decisions in our daily lives."*

Matt went on to tell us that the art of being able to exert control over a society is arguably one of the most powerful weapons in modern warfare. *"If the Russian government, or whoever, wishes to exert this kind of influence, is able to cause difficulty in decisions, in trusting the government of the day in that country, or otherwise trusted media and news organisations, then so much the better for them."*

This is tricky line to walk, I know, but bear with me. I recognize that I have been pulling news stories from the press to demonstrate the relationship of government, banks and corporations, and to expose how it is only the money that these people are interested in, however that doesn't mean that we should be taking every story that we read in the papers or hear on the TV news as verbatim gospel truth. Not at all.

The papers can be a good source of information, of course, as they have a responsibility to report the truth. However, many stories that should be written are not and there is massive room for interpretation of the facts. From the research of the MMR jab that I have personally undertaken I believe it to have significant and undeniable health risks. There is a compelling school of thought that the government wants this jab in place as a standard part of the birth process to smoothly pave the way for the future implementation of a microchip to be injected into all new-born babies.

Now if that were indeed the case (and I certainly do believe that) our government would vehemently oppose any suggestion that it weren't safe. They can say that all they like of course, but how about if they make it sound like it's all a subversive plot by the Russians. Really? Is this really how Russia hopes to undermine our society? Breaking news! The Russians are telling us not to eat an apple a day to bring down the western capitalist system. Hum, it would take a while.

But if we look at the paper on the research undertaken to evaluate the risks of the MMR jab, which is available on line with a big red 'RETRACTED' stamp across it, anyone can rapidly see that this is no fabrication or half measure. It is not undertaken by a single deluded individual, as has been widely reported, but by a team of highly qualified professionals, which included: A J Wakefield, S H Murch, A Anthony, J Linnell, D M Casson, M Malik, M Berelowitz, A P Dhillon, M A Thomson, P Harvey, A Valentine, S E Davies, J A Walker-Smith.

Between them they compiled the exceedingly detailed and thorough research paper that was published in the Lancet, and later retracted, due to government pressure and threats. These academics had spent a great deal of effort on this, as you can read below (I have only included the introduction and conclusion of a detailed five page document containing graphs and charts and statistics.)

'Background. We investigated a consecutive series of children with chronic enterocolitis and regressive developmental disorder.

Findings. Onset of behavioral symptoms was associated, by the parents, with measles, mumps, and rubella vaccination in eight of the 12 children, with measles infection in one child, and otitis media in another. All 12 children had intestinal abnormalities, ranging from lymphoid nodular hyperplasia to aphthoid ulceration. Histology showed patchy chronic inflammation in the colon in 11 children and reactive ileal lymphoid hyperplasia in seven, but no granulomas. Behavioural disorders included autism (nine), disintegrative psychosis (one), and possible postviral or vaccinal encephalitis (two).'

Well that sounds pretty clear to me, and if you want to look further there are five pages crammed with method and results with placebos and everything in order as per any dedicated research. They did a pretty comprehensive job. So it would seem that the information being spread by Russia is perhaps not mis-information at all, (and almost certainly the Russians never even said a word) but this paper is an inconvenient source of a truth that our government does not want to gain any popularity, so it has to be discredited and nipped in the bud by their own counter-mis-information. I should think just the headline of 'UK lives in danger from Russian propaganda' should do the job pretty well if you want the people of Britain to form an opinion without looking further.

What is very important to note is while the claim that there *are* health issues associated with the MMR jab has been supported by an extensive piece of research carried out by 13 medical professionals who specialise in the subject, the argument that this is mis-information carries no more qualification than a newspaper headline and a statement by an unqualified government official. There is no counter proof paper or any consultation document ever produced to prove it's 'unworthiness.' Hmmmmmmm.....

Further, if we can believe that the Russian government are indeed capable of mis-information, then surely *every* government is capable of that. Why wouldn't they be? So could this not be UK based mis-information about something that they don't want the public to discuss that is in itself just sane information, Russian or otherwise? We all know they will say anything they want can think of to keep the man in the street working and paying tax while harvesting off the cream for themselves and their corporate masters. And who profits in a mass immunisation programme, even if it were safe and needed? Oh yes, those big pharmaceutical companies - again.

A final word on mass immunisation. They tell us that it only works if everyone is immunised. But if the immunisation works then surely it doesn't matter if some aren't for, should someone contract a disease, others that they came into contact with would be safe. Because they are immunised! This means it should never be mandatory, but a matter of personal preference.

CHAPTER 30

Nuclear Folly

'For 50 years, nuclear power stations have produced three products which only a lunatic could want: bomb-explosive plutonium, lethal radioactive waste and electricity so dear it has to be heavily subsidised. They leave to future generations the task, and most of the cost, of making safe sites that have been polluted half-way to eternity.' - James Buchan

For May 2006 I wrote:- Hands up everyone who believes that, while we all make mistakes on our journey through life, poor decisions provide an invaluable gift of learning so that next time around your greater experience gives you the wisdom to do things differently, and better.

So why is it that an authority, like our Government, bristling with overpaid consultants, is transparently unable to do the same? For example, why are we having to listen to these ludicrous discussions about building nuclear power stations AGAIN when we haven't even started to solve the problems left over from the last time we went down this precarious road?

And why, you may ask, has a solution not been found yet? Is it because nobody has ever bothered to think about it? No! It is because the problem of dealing with nuclear waste can never, EVER, be resolved.

Consider this. All nuclear materials have a half-life, which is the time taken for half the stuff to change to something else - which is normally also radioactive. Now the trouble with half-lives is that they can be pretty long. In the case of depleted Uranium 238 (which the military love to spray all over the place as a tough armour piercing layer on bullets) is about 4.5

billion years - that's 4,500,000,000 years to you and I. It then still has to alter through 13 different radioactive elements, emitting various lethal rays at each stage, before eventually turning to lead.

Even nastier is manmade plutonium which has a comparatively measly half-life of only 24,000 years. Yep - that is how long you have to keep it tucked away safely if you don't want monsters in the family or terrorists holding you to ransom. But in that time still only half of it will have changed - and into Cesium-137 and Strontium-90 both of which, trust me, are not things you would wish to find in your sandwiches. And if that isn't enough, these latter elements are 'pyrophoric' which means they combust spontaneously with air, and, if you put too big a dollop together (any more than about a cricket balls worth) it cascades into an uncontrolled nuclear chain reaction - mmmmmm - nice!

It wasn't so very long ago that our Governments 'solution' to the problem was to bung the whole lot into standard oil barrels and ditch them off the side of a boat into the Atlantic. I wonder how much the consultants got paid for that piece of advice?! And if you want my opinion not much has moved on from there. Burying at sea or in mountains (for at least 40,000 years mind!) or blasting into space are the ONLY options available. Gives a whole new meaning to 'light blue touch paper and retire' don't you think? Ex-members of the committee concerned with nuclear disposal recently quoted the Government's plans as 'shambolic'. That's comforting then!

And do you want to know something else about radiation? Your body cannot detect it. There is no smell, feeling, heat, taste, sound or touch, and normally the particles would be so small that you would be unable to see them. It gets into your food, your water and the air that you breathe. And once inside you, most of it just hangs around radiating your bones and delicate organs and altering your DNA - permanently. And there is no such thing as a safe level - it is all a game of mathematical odds.

Now we all know that lots of radiation is a very bad thing with tumours, lesions and a nice variety of cancers taking the lead in what will probably terminate your life horribly and very early, but I think that even this is belittled by the example of a service man exposed during the Christmas Island experiments in the early 50's. His unfortunate wife endured six horrific and still born child births, his surviving daughter suffered brain, heart and spinal problems. But here is the really terrible bit. Even his two grand-children, who, like their mother, had never been anywhere near any radiation, were deformed with one having a double row of teeth and the other raised veins all over her body. God alone knows what delights the next generation will bring. What a legacy to leave your descendants!

Reactors do go wrong (and it is not just the Russians that make mistakes!). They might appear pretty reliable by vacuum cleaner standards but, as with all machines, if you multiply the chances of a failure occurring by the time it is running then eventually the odds begin to err on the side of an accident happening. (Not to mention that nuclear material is transported by train (through our city centres!) and on aeroplanes - and they never crash do they!?) Put a meltdown in a country the size of Russia and you have a huge problem, but put it in a country as tiny as Britain and you can turn the whole place into an uninhabitable desert - forever.

Greenpeace has estimated that the cost of decommissioning the worn out existing reactors (but not 'disposal' of the radioactive waste) is going to be about £60 billion - £1,000 for each of us - and that building the new generation of reactors, if it were to come about, will make this cost look like peanuts.

So what is the answer? Well anyone who regularly reads my column knows my feelings about renewable energy, and wouldn't you rather have the Government spend their nuclear budget on providing every household with their own energy generation equipment? A small windmill and a patch of solar panels on the roof of each house, perhaps a heat exchanger in the garden and that would pretty much solve the whole domestic energy problem. Your own clean co2 free electricity for ever - and no bills!

Now you may be concerned about the aesthetics of these devices appearing on your neighbours house, but if so maybe you would prefer to move in next to a nice new shiny reactor with all those yummy fringe benefits that I have pointed out?

After all - if our Government are unable to recall the mistakes that they made in the 50's and 60's and so have no greater wisdom now than they did then, then sadly most of us, whether we like it or not, will end up having to do just that.

On May 17th 2019, Olivier Bonhommeor of The Washington Post published an article written by Gregory Jaczko, who served on the Nuclear Regulatory Commission in the U.S.A. from 2005 to 2009, and as its chairman from 2009 to 2012.

"Nuclear power was supposed to save the planet. The plants that used this technology could produce enormous amounts of electricity without the pollution caused by burning coal, oil or natural gas, which would help slow the catastrophic changes humans have forced on the Earth's climate," said Gregory

"But fission reactors have a dark side, too: If the energy they produce is not closely controlled, they can fail in catastrophic ways that kill people and render large tracts of land uninhabitable. Nuclear power is also the path to nuclear weapons, themselves an existential threat.

As the certainty of climate change grew clearer, nuclear power presented a dilemma for environmentalists: Was the risk of accidents or further spread of nuclear weapons greater than the hazard of climate change?"

He then went on to tell us that the Fukushima Daiichi crisis reversed that momentum. This involved a massive release of radiation from that plant as its four reactors failed that lasted for months. The world watched as hydrogen explosions sent huge chunks of concrete into the air — a reminder that radiation was streaming, unseen, from the reactor core. More than 100,000 people were evacuated from their homes and their communities, and most have not returned.

Gregory added that after Fukushima, people all over the world demanded a different approach to nuclear safety. Germany closed several older plants and required the rest to shut down by 2022. Japan closed most of its plants. Even France, which gets about 80 percent of its electricity from nuclear power, proposed reducing that figure to 50 percent by 2035, all because safety could not be guaranteed. Trying to make accidents unlikely wasn't enough.

When a reactor incident occurs, the plant should not release any harmful radiation outside the plant itself. I was not yet antinuclear, just pro-public-safety. But nuclear proponents still see this as "antinuclear" although they know that most plants operating today do not meet the "no off-site release" test.

Gregory summarises, *"I think a reasonable standard for any source of electricity should be that it doesn't contaminate your community for decades."*

Since then Adam Vaughan of the Guardian had this to say about the building of new Chinese reactors in Britain on Sunday 1st October 2017:-

"Chinese firm behind Essex nuclear plant refuses to reveal security information."

State-owned company refused disclosure of security arrangements for Chinese plant the Bradwell nuclear station could be modelled on.

Adam told us that the Chinese state-owned company planning a nuclear power station in Essex refused to share the security arrangements for a Chinese nuclear plant with the British authorities, it has been revealed. Inspectors from the UK nuclear regulator visited the China General Nuclear Power Corporation (CGN) in Shenzhen earlier this year, as part of the four-year approval process for the reactor the company wants to build at Bradwell.

He adds that a green light from the Office for Nuclear Regulation (ONR) would be a huge boost for China's aspirations for exporting nuclear technology and Bradwell would be the first Chinese reactor to be built in a developed country. However CGN said it could not share material about security measures to protect its nuclear plant in Fangchenggang, China, which Bradwell could be modelled on.

"With regard to the sharing of information, such as the security plans for FCG [Fangchenggang] Unit 3, CGN stated that these were protected documents under Chinese regulations," the UK authorities wrote, in a glimpse of UK nuclear regulation rubbing up against Chinese state secrecy.

Adam said that during the visit, the regulator told the Chinese that the UK's formal assessment of the reactor would be a "long journey" and would require China to be forthcoming with a "sufficient description of the design" so nuclear safety claims could be checked.

We heard that Antony Froggatt, a nuclear expert at the Chatham House thinktank, said: *"The ONR clearly highlight to the Chinese partners that there are resource adequacy implications and risks, and I would be more blunt and say their ability to adequately do their job, if not being provided with sufficient material."*

We were informed by Adam that CGN put up a third of £18bn cost towards EDF's project to build French-designed reactors at Hinkley Point C in Somerset, in return for developing its own plant at Bradwell in Essex. The Bradwell B project is two thirds owned by CGN and one third EDF.

In summary Adam told us that the government paused approval for Hinkley for several months last year, because of concerns over China's stake. CGN is becoming an increasing central player in Britain's atomic plans, having recently confirmed it is considering buying Toshiba's troubled NuGen project to build a nuclear power station in Cumbria."

Well, it is full steam ahead with Chinese nuclear reactors then. I have a question. If you want to buy a really reliable product which country would you turn to first? The Germans are pretty good at getting things right, the Scandinavians have a good record, even us Brits can do a good job when pushed, but China? Really? Reactors all over our green and pleasant land? Chinese products that I have accidentally purchased include footballs that went flat after the first kick, lighters that fell apart or exploded in three turns of the cog, camping chairs that buckle in an hour, tents that the zip has broken in a day or two, exterior grade metal fittings that immediately rust and that came with screws that were as strong as tin and. . . . and. . . .and. . . I'm sure you have your own failures you could add. It's possibly not such a huge thing that they won't tell us what is going on with their own reactor at home, but failures look pretty likely and if they are not transparent now, how can we count on them ever being so?

And what are they going to do with the residue? Well, as there is nothing you can do with it, and as there is no mention of that anywhere in the press. They might opt for the same solution as the French, putting it into a shipping container and not letting anyone close for a billion years (as we have also done at Windscale). There is evidence that the U.K. might follow the U.S. initiative to stuff it down old fracking holes, thereby tempting it to leach into our drinking water supplies (creating a great opportunity for Nestle to sell us non-raido-active water. Great!!)

To go down this road you surely would either have to be insane, or controlled by the corporate giants who plan to make a fortune and really don't give a hoot about the well-being of the people. Sadly, much as they like to use that smoke screen, they are not insane. Thanks for that government.

CHAPTER 31

Terror

'We simply cannot afford to allow our government to go unscrutinised, most of all in amid the bleak seeming imperatives of the 'war on terror'.' - Nick Harkaway

October 2007 I wrote:-

So another anniversary of 9/11 has come and gone and it was with no surprise to any of us that our old mate Osama Bin Laden, the 'Evil Doer' made another timely appearance. Only there wasn't one, but two utterly conflicting broadcasts made just days apart. Now that's strange isn't it Andy? Why would he do that? Well the simple answer is of course that...... he didn't.

The first came on 6th September and here are a couple of exerts. It's long but worth the read. . . .

"And with that, it has become clear to all that they [western governments] are the real tyrannical terrorists. In fact, the life of all of mankind is in danger because of the global warming resulting to a large degree from the emissions of the factories of the major corporations, yet despite that, the representative of these corporations in the White House insists on not observing the Kyoto accord, with the knowledge that the statistic speaks of the death and displacement of the millions of human beings because of that, especially in Africa. This greatest of plagues and most dangerous of threats to the lives of humans is taking place in an accelerating fashion as the world is being dominated by the democratic system, which confirms its massive failure to protect humans and their interests from the greed and avarice of the major corporations and their representatives."

"And despite this brazen attack on the people, the leaders of the West - especially Bush, Blair, Sarkozy and Brown - still talk about freedom and human rights with a flagrant disregard for the intellects of human beings. So is there a form of terrorism stronger, clearer and more dangerous than this? This is why I tell you: as you liberated yourselves before from the slavery of monks, kings, and feudalism, you should liberate yourselves from the deception, shackles and attrition of the capitalist system."

"If you were to ponder it well, you would find that in the end, it is a system harsher and fiercer than your systems in the Middle Ages. The capitalist system seeks to turn the entire world into a fiefdom of the major corporations under the label of "globalization" in order to protect democracy. And Iraq and Afghanistan and their tragedies; and the reeling of many of you under the burden of interest-related debts, insane taxes and real estate mortgages; global warming and its woes; and the abject poverty and tragic hunger in Africa: all of this is but one side of the grim face of this global system."

"So it is imperative that you free yourselves from all of that and search for an alternative, upright methodology in which it is not the business of any class of humanity to lay down its own laws to its own advantage at the expense of the other classes as is the case with you, since the essence of man-made positive laws is that they serve the interests of those with the capital and thus make the rich richer and the poor poorer."

"There are no taxes in Islam, but rather there is a limited Zakaat [alms] totalling only 2.5%. So beware of the deception of those with the capital. And with your earnest reading about Islam from its pristine sources, you will arrive at an important truth, which is that the religion of all of the Prophets (peace and blessings of Allah be upon them) is one, and that its essence is submission to the orders of Allah Alone in all aspects of life, even if their Shari'ahs [Laws] differ."

"And did you know that the name of the Prophet of Allah Jesus and his mother (peace and blessings of Allah be on them both) are mentioned in the Noble Quran dozens of times, and that in the Quran there is a chapter whose name is "Maryam," i.e. Mary, daughter of 'Imran and mother of Jesus (peace and blessings of Allah be upon them both)? It tells the story of her becoming pregnant with the Prophet of Allah Jesus (peace and blessings of

Allah be upon them both), and in its confirmation of her chastity and purity, in contrast to the fabrications of the Jews against her. Whoever wishes to find that out for himself must listen to the verse of this magnificent chapter: one of the just kings of the Christians - the Negus - listened to some of its verses and his eyes welled up with tears and he said something which should be reflected on for a long time by those sincere in their search for the truth."

"He said, "verily, this and what Jesus brought come from one lantern": i.e., that the magnificent Quran and the Evangel are both from Allah, the Most High; and every just and intelligent one of you who reflects on the Quran will definitely arrive at this truth. It also must be noted that Allah has preserved the Quran from the alterations of men. And reading in order to become acquainted with Islam only requires a little effort, and those of you who are guided will profit greatly. And peace be upon he who follows the Guidance."

Not a single threat. Not one promise of violence, and I don't think any of us could argue against any of what he has to say can we? Corporate greed supported by our capitalist system IS the ravaging monster feeding the heart of the whole climate change and wealth disparity problems. Right on! Re-cycle Bin Laden is talking sense!

The second broadcast was transmitted on the actual day of the anniversary 9/11 and only has 'Osama's' voice introducing one of the hijackers, Waleed Al-Shehri's last testament before supposedly flying a plane into the twin towers in which he threatens the U.S. of more terror to come, and ....is a piece of bullshit fiction from start to finish. How can I be so sure about this? Well, among other things, a clue would have to be that Waleed Al-Shehri isn't dead! He is alive and well and living in Morocco! (BBC news 23rd Sept 2001). Yep - call me picky here, but that kind of discrepancy makes me just a little bit suspicious! So, Mr Al-Shehri was either very, VERY lucky to escape (!) - or someone is trying to deceive us. Someone with a vested interest in making us all fearful. Now I wonder who that could possibly be?

Let's now have a quick look at an American Government web site and read what they have to say, which is plenty. "We continue to see a very determined enemy who wants to plot, plan and kill Americans and act against American interests," says White House Homeland Security adviser Fran Townsend. Russ Knocke a spokesman of Homeland Security states "we are in a period of increased risk". The National Terror Alert Response Centre speaks of "unprecedented attacks on schools". "Fear grows in the dark and enjoys the company of the unprepared" "We shall tell you what you can do to keep you and your family safe". Does any of that have anything to do with Osama's real broadcast? No. This is transparently all about gaining control through fear.

But what have those crazy Yanks got to do with us Andy? Well, I feel we should make ourselves aware of what is going on over there because our Government is doing the exact same thing over here. Did you know that at the moment the Terror Warning Level (which is downloadable free onto your own website - just to help you spread the hysteria) is down from critical to severe, which (apparently) means an attack is 'highly likely'. Is that how you feel when you leave your front door? No? Neither do I.

Dame Eliza Manningham-Buller, Director-General of MI5, repeatedly issued apocalyptic warnings, starting in 2002 (without presenting any substantiation) of imminent terrorist attacks. Amongst other things she claimed that despite increased funding and manpower, MI5 are overwhelmed by the vast scale of the problem. She warned of 30 "Priority 1" ongoing "mass casualty" terror plots in Britain, identifying 200 terrorist networks involving at least 1,600 people and spoke of the use of chemical, bacteriological and nuclear technology. So in the six years since 9/11 how many arrests for terrorism by Muslims have there been? 9. That's NINE. And the weapon of choice? Plutonium? Anthrax? No - fertiliser and petrol. Hum...can I just ask you then Eliza - who told you to say all that stuff? And what was their agenda? Maybe it's the justification of the continuance of the war on terror? Keeping our troops in Iraq and Afghanistan? The bringing in of I.D. cards (which now seems to have subsided as by carrying a smart phone you pretty much have one that tracks you with you anyway)? To increase the DNA database? To move toward micro-chipping children as soon as they are born? Or is it, as I suspect, all of the above?

So maybe you think I am getting carried away here? Well this week Sir Ian Blair Chief of the Metropolitan Police said 'the number of terrorist plots in the UK is 'mounting' and their ambitions are 'growing' - and what is he after? A 90 days detention period - not without trial, mind – but without charge! Do you want to live in a country that can lock up you or your family perfectly legitimately for three months without levelling a charge or even giving a reason? With no course of redress? I don't! But at least Sir Ian had the decency to link the threat and the desired reaction for us.

David Icke's compelling DVD's of his seminars (yes, he of 'son of God' fame but don't comment until you've seen it - and you should) goes a step further and makes a mind numbing but utterly convincing argument that the 9/11 and 7/7 atrocities were inflicted upon us not by Muslim Terrorists, but by our own Governments. I have to say it is deeply worrying how compelling his arguments are and how well his proofs fit together.

If you are in doubt about the American government's involvement in 9/11 maybe research and answer the following. Why did building 7, a steel structured building which was never hit by a plane, collapsed ten minutes after the BBC reported it already had? (You can see it in the background behind the reporter.) How was it an incriminating passport came to be found in all that rubble? How was it that some of the supposed hijackers turned up alive and well and living in Morocco having never been to the USA? Was it just a bit convenient that a discarded Koran was found in the back of a taxi? How come there was no plane wreckage found at the pentagon, or even any video footage of a plane hitting it. Why was there no wing damage to the building (the hole is too narrow), no fuel incendiary damage (there are intact books on desks in photographs taken of the open damaged building), and no damage to the grass out the front, even? Why was there no plane wreckage either at the Pentagon (the whole plane, including the several ton engines were, we were told, combusted to nothing) and absolutely nothing to be seen other than smoke at the supposed crash site of flight 93? No luggage strewn about, no bodies and no wreckage.

How were calls supposedly made from flight 93 on people's mobiles, which is impossible, (United Airlines even brought out a system enabling mobile phone calls to be used on their flights some years later heralding it as a breakthrough in passenger convenience) where some callers spoke to their mothers but addressed themselves using their family name? When was the last time you used your surname when saying hello to your mother?

What were the reasons for the eye witness reports by fire officers saying they heard rapid multiple explosions occurring in both towers to trigger the collapse? Explosions that can be seen on Youtube footage to this day. Why did George Bush go into a two minute coma, caught on film, when he was told of the event, and didn't react with any surprise or alarm or issue any orders? Why did a long string of eye witnesses disparaging the official story die in sudden and suspicious circumstances? Why were the jet fighters from Andrews Air Force base, down the road, not alerted? And when they were alerted too late, why did they fly out to the Atlantic?

Could it really be a coincidence that there was an ongoing terror flight simulation exercise, which confused air traffic controllers who couldn't tell exercise from reality, going on at that very hour on that very day which dramatically, and purposefully, slowed their response to the alert. And how can anyone believe that a few hours training in a Cessna is enough preparation to steer jet into a direct hit with the tiny target of a building. Three times and no misses? Buildings look pretty big from the ground but from the air they are tiny All of these anomalies are freely available to view on line, and if you can answer them all, or even any of them, then please just let me know.

7/7 is even easier – and this is how it was probably done. First you assemble a few Muslim lads, pay them well and tell them that you are doing a security test. Tell them that all they have to do is carry a backpack each onto the tube to test if the staff will stop them. While they are out doing the job you put some bomb making stuff in their homes, detonate the backpacks and tip off the police with their home addresses and voila! The police do the story for you. That is why the lads were recorded on CCTV joking and laughing and not stressed at all, and why they bought return tickets and paid for their parking. They weren't planning not to come back.

Now why would the government do this? So that we will run to them in fear and plead for them to remove our liberties as a 'protection' against 'terrorists.' They did exactly that in the U.S. with the deceptively named Patriot Act, (which resulted directly from the 9/11 attack.) This dictated that a slew of human rights were immediately binned with the government awarding itself rights to snoop, pry, and to go into your home without ever letting you know. Hey! They found a whole barn full of fertiliser! Quick give me an I.D. card! Please hold me for 90 days without giving a reason! Please take my DNA! Please microchip my car and my kids! Please keep our army in Afghanistan!

No-one wants to hear this, but at the very least you should look for yourself at future events and see if you can spot any 'coincidental' correlations between terrorist threats, bombings and subsequent Government liberty removing actions or electioneering. I listen to the continual rhetoric of our Home Secretary Jacqui Smith with horror. It seems highly likely our civil liberties, that we so take for granted, are about to be seriously eroded and once gone they shall never be back. If we should be fearful of anything for ourselves and the sakes of our children, it is that. My advice? Speak now or forever hold your peace. This choice may soon be gone.

As George Bush said "We all live in a dangerous world". As Bill Hicks replied "Yeah. Thanks to you, you fucker."

Now that is not to say that every bombing is our government. Sometimes people have genuine grievances and are extreme with their methods, but you just have to look at each case and it seems the government are complicit much of the time.

In a following article I wrote:-

Here's a question for you...how on earth can Jack Straw be Foreign Secretary when he says that Britain having an army of occupation in a Muslim country has nothing to do with the spate of suicide bombings, by Muslims, in London? Er - like did we have these problems before Iraq? No? So must just be a coincidence then eh Jack? Just a bunch of crazy fanatics who didn't have much on that week is that it? I guess having an army of occupation in Ireland didn't have much to do with the IRA bombings either?

Like any thinking person I cannot condone these horrific acts but I do believe that there is a genuine grievance behind them. Tony Blair was bang on when he said that we, as a Nation, cannot properly protect ourselves, even through ever tightening security - and anyway who wants compromise our civil liberties for all time? The key of course is in trying to understand these grievances and doing what can reasonably be done to put them right. Friends and relatives of those that carried out these terrible crimes said what perfectly normal people they seemed to be. We can assume therefore that we are not dealing with fanatical lunatics, but highly principled people passionate enough about a cause that they are willing to give their lives for it.

If it is difficult to understand this then we must do some role reversals and imagine ourselves in the other persons position.

Imagine for a moment that it was the Iraqi army that invaded us for some trumped up reason. Upset? Now imagine that it was your daughter who's wedding was bombed killing 30 odd guests (yes I know it was the yanks that messed up (again) but we are pretty aligned with them at the moment – sadly.) So, happiest day of her life? Hardly. And by now do you think that you would have forgiven your invaders? Well you tell me.

How about Northern Ireland? Make Ireland England and slap a German flag on 5 of the counties - including Dorset. Put up a little German flag flying over St. Mary's church and a nice oompah band marching up and down Station Road every year just to really rub our noses in it. Time for a bit of action I wonder?

French Resistance. Freedom fighters or fanatical terrorists? Goodies or baddies, it is all a matter of perspective. The only thing in common with extreme violent action is that rightly or wrongly those carrying it out believe they have no voice and a just cause. Start listening and understanding and the problem goes away.

After 9/11 the Americans had a golden opportunity to finally understand that their overseas military policies were not making them popular. Here was a chance to have learnt, understood and start putting things right but oh no - not baby Bush. No, he had to UP the punishment the U.S.A. was dishing out. Fight fire with fire the old Testament way! What a statesman!

It is no coincidence that this attack was not on the CNN tower in Toronto, after all what do the Canadians do to upset the world other than club a load of seals to death each year and mine tar sands? Think of any country that does not attract terrorist activities and you find that they are the ones not trying to tell everyone else what to do. The Scandanavians seem to have it right. Iceland, Sweden, Denmark, Norway, Finland, none of which seem to suffer much in the way of terror.

If two kids have a fight in a playground a good teacher will sit them down and find out what it is all about. With the grievances resolved often those kids will become best friends, (I have been there!) and this is how our leaders should be acting. Not by working out violent ways to get even. Justice, understanding, compromise, reconciliation, giving and loving. This is what we teach our children. If only we could teach our leaders the same lessons, the world would quickly become a much better and safer place.

Maybe what is needed to pull mankind together is a common enemy. One more terrible that anything we have ever seen. One that threatens our very existence, and actually that enemy is right upon us. Even as we sit here our lives are in danger. From what? No, it's not aliens, but climate change. Again Tony is bang on, even if he isn't telling the whole truth so we don't panic. He knows that mothership earth is sinking and there are no life boats. Sooner or later mankind will have no choice other than to put aside out petty squabbles and man the pumps. Let us pray that somehow we can find the collective wisdom to transform the fictitious 'War on Terror' into the real war, the 'War on Warming' - and soon.

Since then Victoria Ward of the Telegraph told us on 15th of September 2017: *"The UK terror threat level has been raised from severe to critical, the highest possible level, meaning an attack is "expected imminently". The Prime Minister announced the threat level had been raised after the Parsons Green tube bomb attack.*

Vitoria went on to tell us that this means that troops will patrol the streets and security will also be stepped up at major public events and terrorist targets such as railway stations and airports, and that Isil have claimed responsibility for the London attack.

She adds that Prime Minister Theresa May said military personnel would replace police officers *"on guard duties at certain protected sites which are not accessible to the public who will see more armed police on the transport network and on our streets, providing extra protection. This is a proportionate and sensible step which will provide extra reassurance and protection while the investigation progresses."*

Vitoria said that the last time the threat level was raised to critical was in May, in the direct aftermath of the Manchester bombing, but it was reduced again three days later. That was the first time in ten years the UK was on its highest alert.

She reported that a manhunt is under way after the improvised explosive device (IED) sent a fireball through a packed London Underground train carriage in south west London, during the Friday morning rush-hour. Met Assistant Commissioner, Mark Rowley, said the police were making "excellent progress" in the hunt for the terrorist.

He added that officers were trawling through hundreds of hours of CCTV footage and 77 images and videos taken by members of the public at the scene were also being examined. Mr Rowley said the IED had now been made safe and was being examined by specialist forensic scientists.

The Joint Terrorism Analysis Centre, which was established in 2003 and is based at MI5's London headquarters, decides the threat level.

A number of factors may be taken into account, including available intelligence, terrorist capability, terrorist intentions and timescale.

We were told that Rita Katz, the director of US-based Site Intelligence, said IS claimed the bombing was the work of a "detachment" rather than simply a "soldier", which she said implied it was a coordinated attack. According to her, the terror group has frequently declared that it was behind terrorist incidents in recent years but experts have warned their claims should be treated with caution, and this was the fifth terror attack on British soil in six months.

Images taken by commuters caught up in the atrocity appeared to show that fairy lights had been used as a detonator in the bomb made inside a bucket and carried inside a plastic Lidl carrier bag. It is believed the device had a timer but detonated unexpectedly as the bomber fled the carriage.

A total of 29 patients needed hospital treatment, many of whom suffered burns. Others were injured in the panicked stampede to flee the station."

Hmmmm…..well there are questions to be asked all over the place here. I looked into pictures of this 'bomb' and it didn't even look like a firework had gone off. Fairy lights in a bucket in a carrier bag – so not really a huge bucket then. At least the report admits that injuries were from burns and from the stampede. There are plenty of images from the Manchester bombing that would suggest that possibly the horror was not quite how it was reported. Happy party goers with loose bandages over their heads, or sporting a ripped pair of jeans, was what the papers had to show of the carnage.

I wasn't there so can't comment for sure but what I can say absolutely is that terror is very good for controlling a frightened population, cutting liberties and getting huge defence contracts approved. It stands to reason that normally the ones who benefit most from an event are likely to be the ones behind it, and the corporations and government seem to be doing very well from the suffering. Obviously.

CHAPTER 32

Crime and Punishment

'Punishment is the last and the least effective instrument in the hands of the legislator for the prevention of crime.' - John Ruskin

Another Gazette article I wrote read:-

Should you happen to live in Purbeck and hear a bump in the night, how many police officers do you think are ready to rush to your aid? Twenty? Ten? Try two - in one car. And if you are in Swanage and they are in Wareham? Time to hide under the covers!

In East Devon, where I used to live, the situation is the same. Three towns, a hundred square miles to cover and just two officers on duty. I know this as I happen to be friends with one of them. In his own words - the public have got no idea just how thin the blue line has become - and I suspect the situation is similar in semi-rural areas the country over.

Now if you want to find out what the officer on the beat has to say about this you had better go and ask them, which is exactly what I have done. The message that comes back is one of over stretched officers with understandably deflated morale working with the near impossible manacles of a country gone PC mad (that's politically correct not police constable!) inundated with paperwork and overburdened with management.

Now I wont bore you with talking about fixing this as just about any officer on the force will tell you how to do that, and they would be right, as could any nurse sort out their hospital or any teacher their school, if they didn't have to keep wasting time absorbing bureaucratic lunacy dressed up as 'bright ideas' descending from 'the top'.

Incidentally isn't Jim Knight MP Minister of Schools these days? But wasn't he Minister of Biodiversity a couple of months ago? Wow! What a wide range of specialist subjects he must be a leading expert in! I had no idea.....and now I think about it, probably, neither did he.

But anyway I digress. In my opinion we all put plenty of funding into the Police but the cover we are receiving is dwindling before our eyes, so where is all that money going? Well, restructuring the Force nationally with all it's associated paperwork and re-badging will waste huge amounts of man-power and soak up quite a few millions (as probably did the 'consultants' that advised the Government on the plan in the first place) but let's look at a couple of my favourite recent cases that I think might help us solve the rest of the puzzle!

In January 2004, 83 year old Lieutenant Colonel Riley Workman was shot dead at his home in the village of Furneux Pelham. What followed was a two year investigation that took officers 'around the world' (!) conducting interviews with more than 3,000 people (!). Detective Inspector Sparrow who heads up the operation is still determined to catch the killer, even though neighbours agree that there is no undue threat to their safety. (Independent 7th Jan '06)

In March this year Lin Liang Ren was sentenced for his part in causing the accidental death of his cockle pickers. To solve this 'mystery' - and I use the term loosely - 200 officers were allocated to the case, a team of 30 officers travelled to China, Spain And France, 1,500,000 (!!) pages of evidence was prepared and over 20,000 (!!) phone calls on 5,100 phones were listened to, all at a cost of about £3,000,000 (!!!). And this doesn't even take into account the public borne costs of the £5,000,000 (!!!!) trial, with each defendant being represented by an eminent QC, a new £400,000 computer for Preston Crown Court no.1 and every item of evidence being translated into Mandarin (!!!!!!) by interpreters (Times 25th March '06) all for a conviction of 14 years in jail, the cost of which shall also be paid for by you.

Now let's think about this for a moment. On the one hand we are unable to find funding for proper manning of our local police station or for a regular Bobby on the beat, and on the other hand vast resources are being gobbled up at an incredible rate with the police have little choice about doing otherwise because of the remit that they are working under.

Now of course it is all very worthy that a murder case is never closed and that utterly damning evidence is accumulated before a trial, but actually most murderers are one off offenders and are normally rounded up pretty quickly. So given the decline of funding to our local police stations I question the 'solving out of date murders at any cost' ethic which can suck money up like a sponge.

And in the case of Mr Rens personal £10,000,000 cost to the British tax payer, if you made the losing defence lawyers, at least in part, responsible for the trial costs then I think you would see a much speedier, lower cost trial that would, without an army of barristers trying to muddy the waters, have a higher chance of providing a sound judgement. I mean, it would have been cheaper to PAY him £5million just to plead guilty! Personally I think a one way economy ticket back to Beijing with a note in his pocket for the Chinese authorities explaining what a naughty boy he has been would have done the trick. That would send out a message to would be non-British offenders wouldn't it?

Now, taking just these two cases, and there are hundreds like them going on every week, the public money spent would have been enough to fund about 220 police officers in Britain for a whole year - and that is only these two! Now multiply it up by each painfully expensive investigation or lengthy trial you hear about and there is the cash you need for proper police staffing levels countrywide.

But amazingly all of this pales to insignificance when compared with the dreaded Identity Cards. Not only is their concept an infringement upon your freedom (by storing details of your every move from what bread you eat to where you go on holiday - frankly I think they shall make the KGB look like raw amateurs by comparison) but how about that £14.5 Billion (!!!!!!!!!) cost - plus annual running expenses of nearly £600 million. That equates to about 290,000 police officer years. Enough to put out 3,000 additional officers in every county in Britain for the next ten years AND provide proper manning at the local stations, which I think is what the vast majority of the British public would truly would wish to see.

So which would you prefer and which would make you feel safer? A proper round the clock police presence on the streets of your town, or a plastic card that you shall be forced to carry, even when taking the kids to the beach, that shall almost certainly have no effect on the over-hyped fears of terrorist attacks? Your choice. Get writing!

Since then Mark Piggott of the International Business Times, on May 17, 2014 wrote:-

"Crime doesn't pay, so the saying goes – but the costs to society are high.

Marks said that according to The Times, HM Treasury calculates that the total cost of each murder committed in Britain is a staggering £1.8 million. The figure was reached by adding together the physical, social and economic costs of the average murder. These included the cost of a transcript to a murder trial, which according to the report costs £700.

We were told that although the emotional costs of murder are incalculable, other costs can be estimated. According to the Treasury, an average murder costs more than £1 million in social costs, £530,000 in economic costs – including "lost output" – and £174,000 in direct costs to the NHS, police and criminal justice agencies, making a total of £1,778,000.

Mark expanded with: although the average figure is shocking, some murders – particularly ones which go unsolved for years – can cost much more. In the UK no unsolved murder is ever closed, and according to the most recent statistics there are still 1,143 unsolved killings on the books dating back to the brutal slaying of Janet Rogers (also known as Henderson) in Scotland in 1866. Even when murders are solved the costs can be huge: keeping Moors Murderer Ian Brady incarcerated for the last 50 years has cost the tax-payer some £14m. Last year a report by the Institute for Economics and Peace revealed that violent crime costs the economy around £124 billion a year – 7.7% of GDP."

So let's think about a few things in this article here. One, your life, if it lost is, is viewed by government as 'lost output' is it? So is that how you are viewed when you are alive? As potential 'output?' That is a worrying thought. And then 1,143 murders remain unsolved and so are never closed, meaning that they must periodically be revisited and worked on, including one dating back to 1866. 1866? Really? Are they planning to dig up a bit of evidence, and what punishment were they thinking of putting on the perpetrator if they worked out who it was, considering that person would now be approximately 180 years old. Then there is the cost of keeping Ian Brady in a high security prison, which we are told was £14 million for the 50 years, that equates to £280,000 each year, or if you prefer, over

£750 a night. That equates to a pretty good suite in a London hotel paid for every day by the tax payer. And the total cost of all this pursuit of crime and punishment that we pay for is £124 billion every year. 7.7% of gross domestic product, so £7.7% of your yearly effort, or the profit from a whole month of your years' efforts annually is squandered in the pursuit of justice. I'm not saying that the control of crime is a bad thing, only can we really keep affording to throw so much money at this? And who is it who receives the money? Well the police and hospital services are publicly run and end up shouldering a large amount of the responsibility. But prison services are starting to be privatised, lawyers receive their considerable fees as do the courts. Money and jobs for the boys, and here we are picking up the tab, as ususal.

CHAPTER 33

Council Recycling

'Waste does not exist in nature because ecosystems reuse everything that grows in a never-ending cycle of efficiency and purpose.' - Frans van Houten

July 2007's article read:-

I see that the Council have at last planned to do something pro-active about recycling with their scheme to alternate weekly between recycle pick-ups and traditional refuse ones, but am mortified that they plan to give everyone a wheelie-bin. I understand their muddled thinking about fortnightly rubbish pick ups but what sort of mixed message does that give? 'We really urge you to re-cycle so hey! - have a bigger dustbin!!' Come on Council think it through!

I also noticed from that informative leaflet that they sent round (printed on recycled paper I see - nice touch!! - by the way is all the Council stationary recycled I wonder?) that plastics are not on the list as being 'un-economical' to collect. Well I shall let you all into a little secret here. The Governments targets and thus the Councils performance on recycling is not measured in environmental impact, it is measured in weight. Sadly all those pesky bits of plastic wrapping that are chucked away, that we know are loaded with toxic carcinogens and poisons, and that we know gets in to the water that you drink - and into the animals and plants you eat, that we know accounts for premature deaths, cancers and allergies just don't weigh much. So to look good on paper (recycled?) the Council have plumped for nice heavy inert glass, paper and cans. That way they have a better chance of hitting their weight target and it will look like we are doing a really good job! No problem that the burning health issues aren't dealt with. Yep - that sounds about right.

O.K. - enough whining, so how about a real solution? Do you want to know how to bring recycling up to the high nineties percent almost overnight? How to cut right back on unnecessary packaging? How to stop littering? How to remove the threat of incinerators being built in your back yard? How to clean up the air we breathe? How to clean up the water we drink? How to clean up our seas and rivers? How to cut down on costs of raw materials? How to slice down your council tax? How to persuade even the most ardent chuck away-ers (like good old Ronald 'I don't care about utilisng rain forest for packaging even though a thousand year old tree might only be used for half a minute - I simply don't want to waste a dime washing up' McDonald)? And do you want to know how to do all this at almost no cost?! O.K. - here's how....

Deposits. Remember those Corona bottles we used to spend the afternoon cleaning and taking back for the sixpence - or was that just me?

Like a happy swimmer oblivious to the shadow of the shark 20ft below them it seems that a lot of people still haven't worked out the health threat that landfill creates for themselves and those they love. So to really get their attention all you gotta do is to involve money!

Every product has a bar code that makes it unique. Get a panel together to look at each product and assign a deposit based on how recyclable the packaging is. So, for example, an environmentally sound rinse and return bottle of juice might only carry a deposit of 10p, whereas a Tetrapak carton constructed of card, plastic, foil and toxic ink might attract a deposit of 80p because it is an environmental nightmare. The consumer can always get every penny of the deposit back, but most shoppers would lean toward taking a bottle of juice at 80p compared with a carton of the same product for £1.50. This would put pressure on the suppliers to re-think packaging strategies so as not to lose market share (it's all about money again), and encourage them to thin it down on all those wrapping which would solve half the problem right away.

Every consumer would end up with a bin full of rubbish that would have a significant value - say about £20, that today is worth nothing and would just be thrown away. This provides financial incentive (money) to return every item back to the shop, have the bar codes read and get a credit to purchase items from that shop. This would provide an incentive for shops to take back the packaging as the credit would only be useable in their store (more money!)

And the arguments against? 'I wouldn't have the time to bring the stuff back', or in other words 'I just can't be bothered', which is where we are today. First, everyone finds time to buy the food when they are hungry, then take it home, cook it and eat it. They even have time to do the washing up! So probably you have time to take the packaging back - but if not HEY! - don't worry at all!! Your garbage is worth £20!! Simply get on the phone and donate your rubbish to your favourite charity! Or just leave it outside your door and some entrepreneurial person will gladly whisk it away for you. Go ahead, throw that cigarette package on the pavement and see how long it would stay around if it were worth 50p. No more littering! Clean countryside! Clean water! Clean cities! No incinerators! No landfill! Vast savings of natural resources! Healthy water, healthy air and healthier people! Garbage collection replaced overnight by 98% profitable sustainable recycling! All of which would save all of us LOTS of money! Free! Today! Next?

Since then Adam Vaughan of the Guardian on Thursday 15 December 2016 told us *"Recycling rates in England have fallen for the first time ever, prompting calls for a tax on packaging and meaning EU targets are now almost certain to be missed.*

Adam says that the amount of rubbish sent to recycling plants by householders had been steadily increasing for more than a decade, but more recently flatlined for three years. Now new government figures published on Thursday show that the recycling rate in England has dropped from 44.8% in 2014 to 43.9% in 2015.

Apparently, the fall back to levels not seen since before 2012 will be an embarrassment for ministers, who have pledged to lead the first government to leave the environment better than they found it.

According to Adam the waste company Suez, which operates more than a thousand rubbish trucks in the UK, called for a tax on packaging manufacturers that would pay to drive up recycling rates again. It said the tax could operate on a sliding scale depending on how much of a product was recyclable and non-recyclable.

"The UK is at a tipping point and without radical change to improve England's household recycling rates the UK will not meet its EU agreed

target of 50% recycling rates by 2020," said David Palmer-Jones, CEO for Suez recycling and recovery in the UK."

The truth is that recycling, while infinitely better than dumping is in itself a fudge. When it was first realised that plastics were non-biodegradable there should have been, right then and there, a re-think in its use. Oh yes, I get the appeal, nice and shiny, cheap and airtight, but the problem of generating mountains of it that was going to pollute our environment to the point of collapse was always going to happen at some stage. Surely any thinking caring government would have taken vigorous action to divert this disaster in the 1960's, unless of course the corporate hold over government would make such a stance untenable.

So we face a future where packaging is being created by corporations without any fear of reprisals by government and over half of all our waste is still being burnt or put into the ground. It all adds up to a death sentence for our beautiful planet, when there are so many easy alternatives available to us. Unacceptable, and all in the name of profiteering for the corporations.

Since then there has been a shift in awareness about plastics and how they are choking our seas, destroying marine life and causing illnesses like cancer. But sadly the situation continues to get worse as Sandra Laville and Matthew Taylor of the Guardian point out in their article written on the 28th June 2017. *"A million plastic bottles are bought around the world every minute and the number will jump another 20% by 2021, creating an environmental crisis some campaigners predict will be as serious as climate change.*

They say that new figures obtained by the Guardian reveal the surge in usage of plastic bottles, trending toward more than half a trillion that shall be sold annually by the end of the decade.

Adding that the demand, equivalent to about 20,000 bottles being bought every second, is driven by an apparently insatiable desire for bottled water and the spread of a western, urbanised "on the go" culture to China and the Asia Pacific region.

They tell us the insane news that more than 480bn plastic drinking bottles were sold in 2016 across the world, up from about 300bn a decade ago. If placed end to end, they would extend more than halfway to the sun. By 2021 this will increase to 583.3bn, according to the most up-to-date estimates from Euromonitor International's global packaging trends report.

They embellish the story with the facts that most plastic bottles used for soft drinks and water are made from polyethylene terephthalate (Pet), which is highly recyclable. But as their use soars across the globe, efforts to collect and recycle the bottles to keep them from polluting the oceans, are failing to keep up. Fewer than half of the bottles bought in 2016 were collected for recycling and just 7% of those collected were turned into new bottles. Instead most plastic bottles produced end up in landfill or in the ocean.

We were told that between 5m and 13m tonnes of plastic leaks into the world's oceans each year to be ingested by sea birds, fish and other organisms, and by 2050 the ocean will contain more plastic by weight than fish, according to research by the Ellen MacArthur Foundation, and that experts warn that some of it is already finding its way into the human food chain.

They said that scientists at Ghent University in Belgium recently calculated people who eat seafood ingest up to 11,000 tiny pieces of plastic every year. Last August, the results of a study by Plymouth University reported plastic was found in a third of UK-caught fish, including cod, haddock, mackerel and shellfish. Last year, the European Food Safety Authority called for urgent research, citing increasing concern for human health and food safety "given the potential for microplastic pollution in edible tissues of commercial fish".

Hugo Tagholm, of the marine conservation and campaigning group Surfers Against Sewage, said the figures were devastating. "The plastic pollution crisis rivals the threat of climate change as it pollutes every natural system and an increasing number of organisms on planet Earth.

"Current science shows that plastics cannot be usefully assimilated into the food chain. Where they are ingested they carry toxins that work their way on to our dinner plates." Surfers Against Sewage are campaigning for a refundable deposit scheme to be introduced in the UK as a way of encouraging reuse.

Tagholm added: "Whilst the production of throwaway plastics has grown dramatically over the last 20 years, the systems to contain, control, reuse and recycle them just haven't kept pace."

We were told that in the UK 38.5m plastic bottles are used every day – only just over half make it to recycling, while more than 16m are put into landfill, burnt or leak into the environment and oceans each day.

"Plastic production is set to double in the next 20 years and quadruple by 2050 so the time to act is now," said Tagholm.

As a summary we were told that *'there has been growing concern about the impact of plastics pollution in oceans around the world. Last month scientists found nearly 18 tonnes of plastic on one of the world's most remote islands, an uninhabited coral atoll in the South Pacific.'*

How terrible is that? And how utterly obvious was this disaster? The moment it was discovered in the 1960's that plastics were non-biodegradable, production of them, unless there was a clear recycling or re-use path should have been outlawed. Of course that wouldn't have helped the corporations make mountains of money so there, yet again, lies the problem.

CHAPTER 34

Sport

'Hunting is not a sport. In a sport, both sides should know they're in the game.' - Paul Rodriguez

In April 2007 I wrote a flippant article on sport. This was largely because my previous one, which made the case of George Bush and America being a far bigger terror threat than Osama Bin Laden was censored. It read:-

After my censoring from the March edition of the Gazette (no hard feelings by the way) I thought I might take a break from tackling the important issues and write a piece on something safe - like sport - after all it is just a game - right?

It would seem that many of us are so fixated on these 21st century equivalents of the gladiatorial games, (which of course are designed to go on perpetually, thereby distracting us from how mundane and controlled our modern lives have become) that sport has become big business, monopolised and homogenised by corporations to such an extent that it too has become farcically dull.

Take football. Before the disastrous 2006 campaign I watched several of England's players being interviewed and they all said that a good result was more important than an entertaining game. Huh? So what they were really saying is that they were preparing to dish up a load of mundane rubbish (which they did), but if they won we should all be happy because we would have the opportunity to be bored senseless again in the next round? Sorry, but I think they are missing the point. Entertainment and distraction from a dull reality surely are what we, the public get out of it. In every sport the essence of spectator enjoyment is skillful, daring play and a close nail bighting finish. If this is not what you regularly get then the formula needs tweeking.

In football a scoring system like ice skating, with the teams being awarded up to ten goals for entertainment and technical merit (verve and panache) by a panel of judges, with the goals they score being just a bonus, would certainly get the teams motivated to entertain. I mean, anything has to be better than when Greece won Euro 2004 by boring us all to death. What a yawn! And while I am at it, the penalty spot is clearly too close to the goal and plays too big a part in the game. Fine for those wet heavy pig-skin balls of 1908 but didn't anyone notice that things have moved on? Who wants to pay good money to watch a game when it (or even a whole tournament) is decided by a single (and often poor) decision from the referee? And the penalty box is the wrong shape. It should be an ellipse which faithfully encompassing the most goal threatening areas. Don't tell me a player right down in the corner with his back to goal who gets a tap on the ankles was imminently going to score. It's all most unsatisfactory.

About half of all World Cup tournament tickets now go directly to sponsoring multinationals like Coca Cola and MacDonald's (explain to me if you can what those two American Corporate giants who supply unhealthy food products to our kids have got to do with football? Oh - er - other than just cashing in of course!) As a result real fans can't get in (I know, I have tried), and are replaced by disinterested freeloaders. And if you do watch, how about those horrible new moving signs? What a distraction and hideous invention they are! I personally make a note of the advertisers so that I can avoid buying their products just to get even. And even if you are 'lucky enough' to get in, the grounds are so sterile and the crowd so controlled that the atmosphere has all but vanished. To my mind watching football sitting down is every bit as enjoyable as watching opera standing up.

So let's move on to cricket. Did you see how many spectators there were at the world cup in the Caribbean? Not many. At all. Now why is that? Simple. They tried to rip everyone off and priced themselves out of the market. Good! I hope someone lost a packet and learnt a lesson. The flights leapt up in price, as did the hotel beds and the tickets were always overpriced. In a word, greed. If you watch it on the TV it's Sky only because the ECB sold us out on the flimsiest of pretexts. (They said the money they got from SKY could be invested to get kids interested in the sport. Well if you want a kid to be interested in anything just put it on the telly, which is where it was. It's what McDonalds does.) To my mind all National teams are public domain and nobody should have the right to any exclusivity at all and everybody should have the right to view them on terrestrial TV.

If you do elect to pay through the nose and tune in (and Sky hits the pubs for up to £20k for the privilege) there can be up to six different advertisements squeezed on to the screen at any one time. What are they trying to do? Hypnotise dumb animals? Well, now you mention it.... So how about the games themselves? Other than the astonishing (and possibly fixed) win by the Irish over Pakistan, mostly it has been a procession of predictable one sided affairs, especially when the second division no hopers play one of the big guns. So why not introduce a handicapping system like a 100 run start, at least we might get a close finish from time to time. I mean, where is the fun in watching Australia beat Bangladesh by 10 wickets? Well actually, where is the fun in watching Australia beating anyone, full stop.

Formula 1. Now there is something I don't understand. A game of who has got the most money. Couldn't they decide who wins by seeing who can donate the most to a children's charity, and then race last year's cars? As it is they can't overtake anymore (oh, actually I think someone did manage that once the season before last), so what is the most exciting bit? When they change their tyres! Wow! Let's all go down to ATS for some thrills! Now if they introduced a few surprise variables, like a reversing furniture van on lap three, or a couple of hundredweight of ball bearings on the track and each car was fitted with a bazooka then I might start watching! Answer me this. Why does the fastest car start at the front? If you were racing a hare and a tortoise which would you give a head start? So why don't they line up the grid in the reverse order of the Championship placings so that we actually get to see a race instead of a procession? Because there is too much money at stake and the sponsors wouldn't be happy. Corporate control.....again.

And that leaves me with the Olympics. Wow! Someone ran a thousanth of a second faster than four years ago! Let's all celebrate! After all it only cost us 10 thousand million pounds of tax payers money awarded to wealthy big businesses to find out! Now I'm sorry if I sound a little cynical here, and believe me I am an ardent sports fan, I just don't like to be taken for a fool. When 'we won' the Olympic bid all the Government talked about was how good it will be for the economy, not about how good it would be for the sport, and that should tell you all you need to know. If they swapped the baton in the 4x400m and 4X100m relays for a BigMac or a Coke bottle it wouldn't surprise me for a moment.

Since then Kevin Mathews of Care2 had this to say on February 2nd, 2013

"I used to get fairly worked up about my favorite sports teams; after one particularly distressing loss, I finally asked myself: why do I care? As a spectator, I realized that the importance of the game extends no further than the value I choose to assign to it. From then on, I devoted less of my time to sports and made a conscious effort to prioritize pursuits that seemed more worthwhile.

Noam Chomsky said that sports are used as a distraction for the masses. The renowned intellectual, activist and linguist believes that spectator sports are a form of propaganda designed to divert society's attention. In his book *"Understanding Power,"* Chomsky says:

"In our society, we have things that you might use your intelligence on, like politics, but people really can't get involved in them in a very serious way—so what they do is they put their minds into other things, such as sports. You're trained to be obedient; you don't have an interesting job; there's no work around for you that's creative; in the cultural environment you're a passive observer of usually pretty tawdry stuff; political and social life are out of your range, they're in the hands of the rich folk. So what's left? Well one thing that's left is sports—so you put a lot of the intelligence and the thought and the self-confidence into that. And I suppose that's also one of the basic functions it serves in the society in general: it occupies the population, and keeps them from trying to get involved with things that really matter."

Kevin summarises with, *"whether or not the diversionary tactics are intentional, they do seem to be working: more people can identify football player Peyton Manning than the sitting Vice President. Sporting events earned a higher combined rating than one of last year's Presidential debates. And newspapers don't make room for a number of critical international affairs, yet devote a whole section to sports. While global warming will have a much bigger impact on our lives than the outcome of any baseball game, inevitably exponentially more people will show up to a stadium to shout and hold signs than to a rally supporting climate change reform."*

Have you noticed the endless conveyor belt of sport today? Cricket tournaments that play a best out of five final instead of just the one game. And how long is it between the World Cup football final and the start of the next world cup? A month. And how many countries participate? 180. How many winners? 1? So how many losers are there? 179. All acting as a distraction and a pre-programing for a life without success.

Famously, as the Holy Roman Empire collapsed Caesar and the Senate gave the people 'the games' and the Coliseum, where the slaughter was in such massive proportions that it even made the people of Rome gasp, was born. This kept the eyes of the people away from what was really going on, the collapse of the Roman Empire. Football and cricket similarly appear about keeping the peoples' eyes on the ball that doesn't matter and *off* the ball that does. Not much has changed really has it?

CHAPTER 35

Tax

'The best way to teach your kids about taxes is by eating 30% of their ice cream.' - Bill Murray

On this emotive issue I wrote:-

I read recently that, according to a poll taken by the Guardian newspaper, one in five of us has seriously looked into leaving the country - permanently. Now Britain as we all know is (potentially) a green and pleasant land, comparatively safe and disease free, steeped in heritage and tradition. So what did they say was the main reason for this dreamed of exodus? Over taxation.

Now while I agree that onerous taxation has a major influence in making life unnecessarily difficult for many of us, I would say that a simple lack of ability to easily make ends meet is the core problem. It is not unusual in today's British working family for both partners to be taking on long hours, often with multiple jobs, slotting quality life in where they can and still having to budget and utilise food banks to get through the week. In a country with such obvious wealth as Britain, this, transparently is unacceptable.

At the heart of the problem is, of course, ludicrously priced housing. Now I know that I have written on this before but it is so simple to resolve this it just drives me nuts! We all need somewhere to live - housing is a necessity - so how can it be acceptable for the wealthy to speculate on homes just to generate more income? I meet people all the time who are celebrating their fourth (empty) flat in Swanage. Well whoopee doo for you! A nice little bonus in the city means that another local working family will have to go without, and that is unacceptable. A very simple answer is to phase in an annual country wide levy (yes, tax if you like) of, say, ten thousand pounds on any second home, twenty on a third and so on, to take the fun out of owning one. Or treble rates on a second home, or simply outlaw the practice. This would lead to plenty of properties becoming available to live in all over the U.K., thus lowering prices (to perhaps half) making mortgages affordable to everyone with no need for further building on our precious and disappearing countryside. Less work, easier lives and less financial stress for all of us. Well, that would be a start anyway.

Here is another thing. The Government encourages everyone who can, to have children by providing tax breaks. They do this because of course they know that once you have a family in place you shall pretty much be working flat out for the rest of your days, behaving yourself and paying them lots of nice taxes. (48 weeks on 4 weeks off!? How else would they get us to agree to that one!?) Now I totally understand that many of us have a strong urge to breed, and I readily support (admire almost) that free choice. But shouldn't a little more balance be put into the decision process these days? After all it is transparent that there are too many people living in a world groaning under the weight of mankind with, what is increasingly becoming, a very uncertain future. Kids are an expensive hobby and not everyone I know relishes the experience. Personally I think that if the Government really cared about free choice they should point out that an awful lot of fun in the form of holidays is a valid alternative. Having free time to get in touch with your soul and truly discover yourself is rare, but should be a given. School uniform or skiing holiday? Mmmmmm....let me think about that for a moment! And tax breaks for having kids? I never did get that one. Sure, go ahead, but surely you don't expect everyone else to help you out with your life choice? I mean, I love curries but....

Now I think we can agree that none of us really love paying taxes, after all the Government are in reality just a third party helping themselves to your hard earnt cash (legally because they also made up the rules, pity I missed that meeting!) However, money spent wisely and carefully, as a trustworthy guardian might, by providing health, education, upholding a free society and so on is no bad thing. But sadly I also witness vast and escalating sums frittered away on 'clever' innovations, that cost the earth and provide no advantage to us. Consultants, war, and so forth. When it all goes wrong no-one seems to take responsibility for any losses.

For example, let's look at the failed NHS computer system. Can anyone explain the up side of that £6.2 billion (six thousand millions before you let that amount wash over you) piece of software that never worked in an attempt to centralize our medical records?

You are, apparently, allowed to view your own medical file, so why not just scan your details (with the help of a school leaver at your local medical center) onto your chosen e-mail address and give your doctor and yourself the password? Job done. G-mail gives each of us unlimited of space for free. Then the money could be spent on keeping those health centres open that local communities are always having to campaign for, and bake cakes to raise funds for, because there are 'no funds available'. And here is the question – who got that £6.3 billion of our money for doing nothing, because somebody did!

They are thinking of tracking every one of the 60 million cars on our roads every second of the day - imagine the database! Now there is a financial black hole if ever I saw one. And just so they can keep tabs on us and punish us more easily for speeding, that is not how I want my money spent thatnkyou!

Are you comfortable about spending £30 billion of your money each year on 'defence'? When exactly was it the last time we were attacked? Er - 1940 wasn't it? Because I don't think other people retaliating against us for occupying their country really counts as 'attacked.' So it's not really about defence at all. Naughty old Gordon also wants some new nuclear bombs to play with. By the same token will he give his kids a gun when they go to school to act as a 'deterrent'? Because in both cases if you use it, you have had it! By the way, have you ever seen a nuclear missile? No, me neither. So how about just putting up a few huge empty concrete bunkers, surrounding them with barbed wire and writing 'Nuclear Deterrent' on the side? Oh well - don't worry too much, it will only set you and I back another £25 billion. I saw a good fridge magnet once which said 'wouldn't it be great if schools got all the funding they needed and the army had to hold fetes to raise the money to buy bombs?' I wish.

How do you feel about spending £90 billion (that's £1,300 for each man woman and child) cleaning up our old nuclear reactors (although the problem will never be truly dealt with of course). Now there is a necessary expenditure that once was an avoidable cost. And they say they want to go and build 10 more?! - at countless billions a pop - are they nuts!? (you don't need to answer that one). What they seem to have missed is that we already have a nuclear reactor that is a safe distance away providing us with more energy than we could ever need. It is called the sun, and harnessing its power is safe, clean and easy, but not so very good for prospective shareholders, and there lies another problem.

Well that is just the tip of the 'wanton waste' iceberg. Luckily for you I am running out of space here. I think it is very sad to see our money being squandered and directed away from the places you and I would choose to spend it. So what to do about this? Well, demanding accountability would be a start. If one person were publicly responsible for the success of any project then we would know who to throw in jail if we felt we didn't get great value for money. That would shut up a few wannabe history makers!

Lastly, so as to give this piece a little balance, Britain, for all its problems, is still a fine place to live. It's just that it could so easily be a whole lot better. The best even. Like they say, there is no place like home, even if it does needs a little financial spring cleaning.

Since then a Newsmax article put it like this for the U.S.: *'Cost of Government Day in 2013 fell on July 13 for the average American, who worked more than half of the year just to pay for taxes plus government regulations.*

After more than 100 years on the progressive road to serfdom, the average American now labors more than half his or her working life just to pay what the political ruling elite demands. In effect, we have created a new kind of slavery in pursuit of failed progressive ideology.'

In the UK it is actually closer to seven and a half months labour out of the twelve that is stolen in taxes, and it's not over then. You still have your mortgage to pay, which is interest on money that never existed in the first place, and should you happen to drink beer a further third of everything you spend on it vanishes as tax. That, and doing arduous work that they do not want to undertake themselves, are the two reasons why we are tolerated by the elite.

CHAPTER 36

Tree Damage

'Global warming is a scientific fact as much as the hole in the ozone layer or Earth's orbit around the sun.' - Johan Rockstrom

In July 2003, as an exercise in bringing worrying ultra-violet damage to trees to attention I wrote a description of the problem accompanied by pictures from several countries, and sent the file to every authority and non-governmental organisation and newspaper I could find who may have had an interest, but received no discernible thanks or positive feedback. It read:-

It has been noted for the last three years that certain varieties of trees are suffering from damage to leaves. This damage starts to occur early in the spring, almost as soon as the leaves appear, and carries on throughout the summer.

The damage appears as a brown crisp edge that spreads across the leaf from all sides until the leaf turns completely brown and is discarded by the tree. The only leaves to be affected are those in direct sunlight, while those in shade appear much healthier.

The damage was first noted on an avenue of horse chestnut trees on Victoria Avenue, in Swanage. These trees were seen to suffer considerable damage with many of the trees losing most leaves on the south facing side of the tree by the end of the summer. The loss was so dramatic in spring of 2002 that the trees put out fresh young leaves in June, but these too were rapidly damaged and lost. It was also noted that these trees did not flower or produce seeds on the south facing sides for the first time this year.

As this is a fairly recent phenomena, it is reasonable to assume that some new factor is affecting these trees. And as the only foliage to be affected is in direct sunlight, it is logical to assume that sunlight is a contributing, or perhaps the only, factor causing the problem. It is also well documented that ultra violet radiation levels have been increasing and so it is not unreasonable to suspect that these two events are linked. The horse chestnut trees have exceptionally broad leaves and so it is also plausible that, with their larger surface area and their longer leaf veins, these leaves might be more susceptible than most trees to burning due to increased levels of ultra violet.

The scientific community has been contacted and lengthy conversations held with bodies whose principle concerns are in the fields of conservation, environmental protection, trees and research. The results were virtually unanimous. Not one expert made any examination of the trees, and all experts, from the confines of their offices, threw up an instant and unverified cause. To date not one consultant has dared to consider that the damage to the foliage might simply be the result of increased levels of ultraviolet due to ozone depletion.

Interestingly, and frustratingly, if a consultants field of expertise is acid rain, then acid rain is the problem, if their field was root damage, then it is root damage, and if they have expertise in many fields then the problems, naturally, would be a combination many factors.

The suggested causes of the problem (without any examination of the trees) were mooted to be: Root damage due to walking pressure on the ground around the trees, wind damage due to passing vehicles, poor pollarding practices, natural ageing of the trees, frost damage, the rapid change in temperature between winter and summer, fungal infections, bacterial infection, insect attack, moths, damage to xylem and phloem in the trunk or branches, acid rain, salt spray damage, infra-red radiation, drought, prevailing wind damage. Not one person agreed with increased ultra-violet content in the sun rays due to ozone layer thinning.

However, since that first discovery, it has been noted that the damage is not limited to horse chestnut trees in one location but in many locations. Further and importantly, it has been seen that lime trees and maple trees, both of which also have a broad leaf structure, are exhibiting the exact same problem.

With the knowledge that these trees are not suffering in isolation, and that the damage is not confined to one species it doesn't take much application of logic to conclude that most of the above arguments could carry little or no weight.

To each of the suggested 'causes' above apply the model of a relatively small sample of "At least three varieties in at least three locations" and see how many might really be a plausible cause. Bearing in mind all the time that the damage is only happening to foliage in direct sunlight and that the shady side of the tree is in perfect health.

Of all of the above only infra-red and drought provide any other likely point worthy of discussion. A lack of ability for proper transpiration through the leaves due to excessive sunlight hours, heat and lack of water may well be considered to be a significant factor.

However, if drought were the only cause of the problem, why hasn't there always been these problems with these trees before now? There have been plenty of drought conditions in Britain over the past forty years and, of course, at times, trees do completely die due to drought. But until very recently it has not been noted for the whole of the sunny side of the tree only to be damaged. Even leaves on the same branch, if one is sheltered by another, then the more shaded leaf is healthier. Further, the leaves on the shady side are comparatively healthy, which is not a typical symptom of a tree distressed by drought. The fact that the damaged foliage can be seen in the spring when the ground is saturated with moisture is also a significant factor not consistent with a drought theory. It should also be considered that horse chestnut trees are not a native species in Britain but originate from Italy. It would therefore be reasonable to assume that of all the tree species in Britain the horse chestnut would be one of the better ones survive a hotter more arid climate.

So is infra-red light the problem? The levels of the infra-red end of the light spectrum have not markedly increased, but this foliage damage is a new and recent phenomena. If nothing has changed with that part of the light content, then how would it follow that that was the cause of this relatively recent problem? It is also understood that recent research on oak trees has shown that their leaves are producing a greater level of red pigment, which is an indication that the leaves are trying to absorb less 'blue', or ultra voilet light. If infra-red were the problem, the oaks, by producing greater levels of red pigment, would simply be creating a larger problem for themselves. Mother Nature does not make such mistakes.

In conlusion. Of course it is recognised that the systems involved can be complex, that one factor can lead to another and that one event can create an unexpected result. However, by the same token, it must also be recognised that sometimes the cause and effect can be simple and straightforward. It is not always difficult for a doctor to make a diagnosis or for a detective to spot the murder weapon. The damage to the leaves on these trees is recent, real and simple to see. The only common factor is the sunlight. The only new factor related to the sunlight is the increase in ultra violet radiation. Surely the link at least merits investigation? The scientific community so far have refuted this argument, without even examining the evidence, and have put forward, at times, utterly implausible explanations. This would almost be comical if it were not for the seriousness of the situation. What is needed is some proper investigation. Qualified results are the first step to understanding. Understanding is the first step to awareness, and awareness is the first step to change. The question really is who can open their mind enough to take some initiative?

NASA had this to say about UV in 2011.

"NASA scientists analyzing 30 years of satellite data have found that the amount of ultraviolet (UV) radiation reaching Earth's surface has increased markedly over the last three decades. Most of the increase has occurred in the mid-and-high latitudes, and there's been little or no increase in tropical regions.

The new analysis shows, for example, that at one line of latitude — 32.5 degrees — a line that runs through central Texas in the northern hemisphere and the country of Uruguay in the southern hemisphere, 305 nanometer UV levels have gone up by some 6 percent on average since 1979.

Longer wavelengths (from 320 to 400 nanometers) — called UV-A — cause sunburn and cataracts. Yet, UV-A can also improve health by spurring the production of Vitamin D, a substance that's critical for calcium absorption in bones and that helps stave off a variety of chronic diseases.

UV-B, which has slightly shorter wavelengths (from 320 to 290 nanometers), damages DNA by tangling and distorting its ladder-like structure, causing a range of health problems such as skin cancer and diseases affecting the immune system."

Yep – and plants get sunburnt just like us as they also have DNA, but they can't reach for the factor 50 or put a hat on.

CHAPTER 37

Another Election

'Elections are won by men and women chiefly because most people vote against somebody rather than for somebody'. - Franklin P. Adams

So, what can we deduce from coming up with these simple and common sense solutions to the plethora of problems facing the country and the planet, which our government refuses to see or implement? After all, they certainly spend plenty of money on 'consultants' so you could be forgiven for thinking that the government might have come up with at least one fix out of that lot in ten years. Not too much to ask, don't you think?

Christopher Hope, Chief Political Correspondent for the Telegraph on 13th Jan 2016 told us: *'Spending on consultants in Whitehall has nearly doubled to £1.3billion, the public spending watchdog has found, with nearly 50 paid more than £1,000 a day.*

The National Audit Office found that spending on consultants was increasing again after being cut back as a result of austerity measures imposed in 2010.

MPs accused ministers of playing "fast and loose" by allowing spending on consultants to jump by up to £600million in three years.

The only conclusion that can be drawn from this is that the government is so controlled by the banks and corporations that want to carry on profiteering, that they will never implement any good sense policies that will help either the people or the planet if it loses those people profits.

I realise that forcing my ideas on the people would only be substituting one authoritarian paradigm for another, even if they were indeed much needed solutions. People might reject any mandate for all sorts of reasons, and so the fairest answer would be to initiate a true democracy where people were free participate in the decision process. At the very least, if we collectively got it wrong we would only have ourselves to blame.

The time duly arrived for me to embark on another election merry-go-round. I was feeling better equipped and was putting in more work than with the Party Party. The Movement for Active Democracy website looked pretty good and could be found on MovementForActiveDemocracy.com and VoteForYourself.co.uk, (incredibly a guy I knew, Von, who had similar views had already taken VoteforYourself.com. We had a pretty interesting conversation when I rang the number on his site and found we knew each other.) My site was loaded with clips exposing the ludicrous way things were being done, and informing people that a true, one person, one vote society on issues and not candidates was now possible due to the advent of the internet.

I was interviewed by BBC radio live news outside Swanage Railway station, along with the other candidates. As usual I was allotted a third of the time that South Dorset's MP, Jim Knight got, but I was able to say, 'a thousand years ago we had to send the Squire up to London to represent us because he was the only one with a horse and it took three days, but guess what, we can now all travel to Westminster in the blink of an eye as we have the technology for us to easily and regularly participate in referendums from the comfort of our own homes. M.P.s are an outdated concept. Who can represent your views better than you can? The time has come for Britain to lead the world by creating the first true democracy. I see myself as a Trojan horse standing at the gates of Westminster and if I were to get inside, my mission would be to stealthily open those gates and allow forty million voting adults to come flooding in.' I thought it was a reasonable thirty second sound bite and was encouraged when a friend of mine from Brighton, who I used to do hospital radio with, texted me to say he had enjoyed hearing it.

A friend of mine, Lorna, who I had met as a result of my writings in the Gazette, and who was fully into' Chem trail' and 'UFO' theories, dropped by and showed me a picture that a guy in Swanage, David, had done for her. It was a stunning montage of Cleopatra stroking a cat in a blue gloaming evening with the great pyramids behind. Cleopatras' face was unmistakeably Lorna's. It was a gorgeously fantastical image and I was so intrigued I asked her for the David's details and went to see him the next day.

David was an easy going guy, you know the sort, glasses, beard, softly spoken, and he was a genius at making up these montages using photo-shop. He could transport in any background, add any detail and your face, blend it all together like an airbrushed painting, and the results were brilliant. I told him that I wanted to show the Illuminati pyramid in the background and wanted my own logo, the pyramid upside down with the people dancing on the top celebrating their new found freedom, in a crystal ball suggesting it as a vision of the future. He asked me who I wanted to be in the image and I told him 'Aragorn from Lord of the Rings.' I mean, every guy wants to be Aragorn right?' That old ego of mine.

He took a couple photos of me holding an opaque ball from one of his lounge side lamps and set to work and the result was simply breath-taking. To give it the link to an election I had the front of the election cards printed with *Living in a true democracy need no longer be a fantasy*', and 'Go M.A.D.! Cut out your M.P. middleman and Vote for Yourself!' at the bottom. On the flip side it read:

'Who can decide what you want better than you?
If you can't decide between parties it is probably because you realise
there are no good choices. I am offering you a real alternative – to
move away from our 800 year old political system which encourages
frustration, corruption, control and greed, to a fresh, new, fair
and equal democracy giving each of us our say on everything.
We have the technology now for us all to join in
'X-factor' type referendums from home!
This is your democratic birth-right that is being withheld from you.
Andy Kirkwood – South Dorset Candidate

Movement for Active Democracy (M.A.D.)
Please lend me your power by voting for me and I promise
to fight to give it right back to you, turning the pyramid of
power on its head and placing the people above and in control
of the government where it is our democratic right to be.
See www.voteforyourself.co.uk as to how.
YOU are an adult, it is YOUR country, so isn't it time
YOU decided how YOUR taxes are spent?

When you stand in an election you are given free delivery of your election material to every household in your constituency. South Dorset has fifty-six thousand homes but I went with sixty to have some to hand out in pubs and hustings debates. Before printing it is essential to get approval from a committee who look at everyone's material and provides a verification number to qualify you for the free delivery, and they are very fussy about what you can and cannot put on there.

I had a window of four weeks to get the proof approved which sounded plenty of time, but was shocked to find the turnaround from the committee was at least a fortnight. You can take the chance, but if they aren't happy then all your efforts are in vain. Mine came back as not approved, and the reason? We had put my address as the candidate together with the printers details, but we hadn't included the publishers details. I was confused. Who was the publisher? I called them but no-one at their end knew either, so I just put my name to it and with a day to spare got the go ahead. It was a tense time.

I had decided to print onto a post-card and Mark, my printer, did a great job getting them run out in double quick time. Next, I had to bundle them into packs of one hundred. The thought of counting out five hundred piles seemed pretty arduous but actually once one pile had been counted the rest could be just levelled off and elastic banded. Once done they had to be boxed with a particular number of bundles being placed into each with postcodes on the outside to make life easy for the post office.

A call had to be made to the sorting office to arrange a drop off date as they didn't want more than one candidates leaflets at a time and I was aghast to find out that nearly all the days were already taken. Finally, I was given a date and time and duly set off with my car stacked with thirty heavy boxes to drive to Fareham, and hour and a half away.

I was at a loss to find the office, but after several passes up and down the busy, and lengthy, main road, I spotted a supermarket trolley on the pavement outside a scruffy large shed with a bit of cardboard box sellotaped to it with 'Election' scrawled on it in felt tip pen. 'Blimey', I thought, 'all the fiery hoops I have to jump through and that's the best they can do?' The guys inside were helpful and we had a bit of a laugh. They were clearly thinking 'hello! Here's another one of them Monster Raving Loonies!'

A few days later someone called me and suggested I look at the Observer Guardian on line. I Googled it up and found a 'respected blogger' had posted my election card out to his readers. The Guardian had picked it up and had it on their on line publication with the strapline 'Is this the best election leaflet ever?' I was gobsmacked. There was a problem with the article as it made out there were no policy behind the graphics, and talked about rolling a hexagonal dice and playing dungeons and dragons, which was misleading and disappointing.

It disturbingly also only showed the top half of the card with the evil eyed pyramid in the background so, without clicking the small link to see the whole card it looked like that I was actually supporting that, not fighting it. I couldn't help thinking how controlling that was. The reporter had obviously been told not to have the anti-masonic, anti-illuminati, anti-establishment logo that I had thought up open to immediate viewing. Yet more evidence that they are controlling, fearful and holding back the people from free thought against the system. Still, like they say there's no such thing as bad publicity.

The next breakthrough was a minor T.V. channel had decided to produce a documentary about small parties standing in the elections and they gave me a call asking if I would like to participate. I told them that I most certainly would, and to ensure they understood the level of my sincerity took the train to their Tottenham Court Road offices to chat it over. They were to visit six minor parties, of which mine was one, and do a documentary about why each was standing and what we were doing in the run up to the election.

The day came and the guys arrived loaded with their kit and we had a relaxed look at what I was up to. It was easy to chat with them and the whole experience was totally enjoyable. I was amused that they filmed me singing a bastardisation of John Lennon's 'all we are saying, is give peace a chance' which by changing a few notes and words had become 'all I am saying, is vote for yourself,' then sending me a release form for me to sign authorising them to play 'my song' without infringing my copyrights. I nearly passed out laughing.

When it came close to release I found out that the program was to be called 'Britain's weird and wonderful political parties.' I was disappointed as it dawned on me that the reason I had been selected had been purely because of the M.A.D. Party name, and they were hoping for something totally whacky to film

Other parties in the documentary included the 'Common Sense Party' based in Reading who had a yellow submarine on the Thames to promote their cause, and had subsequently constructed a huge yellow submarine that was road worthy to reach more areas. Their policies were salient and clear but that submarine surely couldn't have been doing much for their common sense image.

'The Landless Peasants Party' man had discovered that most of the wealth in Britain is owned by a very small number of people, and we, the vast majority are left with tiny scraps of land to squabble over. His image was pretty good, like a 'man in black' with shades and a black suit. He stood in Gordon Browns Constituency so was always in the background with a black leathered gloved fist raised above his head. His position, too, was utterly salient, a sad truth that is virtually unspoken in the media or by the government.

Then there was Captain Beany. He was from Port Talbot with a thick Welsh accent, and he was just enjoying the ride. He painted himself orange from head to toe and made jokes referring to Big Ben as being Big Bean. Of all those appearing on the documentary he received the most votes, as he works tirelessly for local causes and good works in the community. There were a couple of guys with waxed moustaches who also spoke complete sense about the corruption of the government system, and the squandering of public money, and then there was me.

My position was not about any particular policy, as the whole country clearly needed a good shake up, but about a crowd sourcing of opinion, asking 'if there were a problem in a hospital ward would you rather get the ideas for fixing it from all the nurses who work there or from the single director who doesn't?

This applies all the way through our community. Who knows what you want better than you? How can any representative, even if they really had the will and the power, represent each and every one of their twenty thousand constituents? The answer, is they can't. We have the technology in place for the people to rule themselves with the government being relegated to back office public servants who might advise and legislate the will of the people and that is all their role should be in a democracy.' It went down well and the presenter said that if he lived in my constituency I would have had his vote, and I believed him.

The thought came to me afterwards that actually all the parties on this supposedly 'whacky' documentary had a common theme. We were all disillusioned and we could all see a better and fairer way to do things. We weren't whacky at all, but enlightened and motivated to try and do something about it.

It was my brother, Olly who face-booked me from Chile saying he had done a Google search first putting in Barrack Obama and Democracy and then Andy Kirkwood and Democracy and found that I had two thirds as many hits, which was staggering and comforting.

Next, I created the 'Democracy Wagon', a couple of sheets of eight by four ply with printed laminate attached with the message 'why vote for a faceless stranger when you could vote for yourself?' It was mounted on a small trailer that I pulled and parked in layby's around the constituency, sparking calls from the highways people telling me to move it or they would impound it. It was unfair as you see trailers advertising events at pubs or villages all the time and they don't get moved on. Also there were thousands of placards for the major parties in fields and gardens.

I bought a speaker system and mounted it on the roof of the car which ran a message endlessly blaring out 'Vote Andy Kirkwood, Movement for Active Democracy and decide how your country is run. This is your country, you are an adult, you pay the tax which funds everything so why shouldn't you have your say how your money is spent? Movement for Active Democracy, go MAD and vote for yourself.'

Prior to every election the returning officer calls a meeting for all candidates and their agents to attend. Mine was at the council offices in Weymouth. They lay out the rules regarding the forthcoming night of the count. Each candidate is allowed to allocate a large number of witnesses who can scrutinise any ballot station, the collection of the boxes, the transport of them and the count itself. I wondered as to why they made such a big fuss about this, as I didn't anticipate votes to be stolen or destroyed but realised that the reason attention was diverted to the security of the boxes, was exactly the same reason that a magician makes a huge fuss of how hard and sharp the sword that appears to go through his assistant is. This is of course because of course it has nothing to do with the trick. The deception of 'democracy' had already been put into your head when you were five years old and not even looking for it.

The personal assistant to the returning officer was a smart sassy lady called Sue Gonham-Donett. Sue was pretty, looking like one of those stereotypical supposedly plain ladies in office garb wearing glasses who then whip them off and shake their hair down, thereby suddenly transforming themselves into a saucy stunner. I really liked Sue and I think, at arms-length anyway, she liked me, and we always shared a bit of light hearted banter.

The count goes on all night, and we had had the passes and access explained to us. The meeting was coming to a close and the returning officer asked if there were any questions. I raised my hand. 'Yes, Andy?' 'Is there a bar at the count?' A moments' consideration, 'No, there's no bar but tea and coffee are available. Anything else?' I raise my hand 'Yes Andy?' Are we allowed to go to the pub during the count?' A moment's consideration. 'Yes you can go to the pub. Is there anything else?' I raise my hand. 'Yes Andy?' 'And we can come and go to the pub as often as we like?' A moments consideration and a few giggles, 'yes Andy you can go to the pub as often as you want. Anything else?' Feeling buoyed by the amused reactions I impishly I asked 'yes, just one more thing that's puzzling me. Who exactly is this Count we keep talking about?' To my amazement Sue had been getting wrapped up in the farcical humour and said in a theatrically rasping spooky voice 'I am the Count! I am the Count!' and everyone just fell about, except her boss who glared at her. Sue immediately realised that this wasn't really the time or place for such theatricals and gathered herself back to her professional persona. I liked her very much for that cameo moment.

On the day of the election I went to the polling booth and duly put a cross in my own box, thinking that my decision to have 'Go MAD and vote for yourself' as the party name was a good one. I had had to squabble with the Electoral Commission for weeks to get the logo scanned properly. They refused to do it for a long while until I threatened them with action. The major party logos were perfectly smooth and clear but mine was pixilated so badly you couldn't really make out what it was, and I couldn't help thinking it was to make the upside-down pyramid illegible.

That evening I drove to Weymouth and booked into my guest house. As I was crossing the bridge over the Wey the first person I passed said 'I voted for you.' 'Bloody Hell!' I thought, 'with me that's two out of two! A one hundred per cent success rate! Maybe I've won a landslide!' As soon as I got to the hall and the votes were being sorted it was patently clear that it was to be nothing of the sort. The piles of votes grew into towers of paper with mine forming and embarrassingly meagre spattering next to them.

I spent quite a lot of the evening at the pub and returning to the hall sporadically to be interviewed by local radio and, in my slightly relaxed state, being pretty forthright and direct with my thoughts. 'Have you considered why the elections are still carried out with paper ballots that you have to go to a booth to participate in, and why the count goes on all night with Peter Snow working away at his 'swing-o-meter' and reporting on it like it is a football game? Because that is all part of the trick to make it look like something important is going on. It's an illusion to fool the public into thinking they are participating in a democracy when in fact they are not.' It wasn't what they were expecting but it was live so there wasn't a great deal they could do about it, and anyway, that was, and is, the truth.

I stuck around for the results and I got nearly three hundred votes. As each candidate gets to say a few words I stayed for the laboriously long speeches but by this time I was pretty pissed and last but one on the mic, I just said, 'well, I gave the people the opportunity to choose something different and they have elected not to take it. What I can say with some authority is that unless you shake off the manacles of going between the major parties nothing worthwhile shall change, meaning we are all doomed to die early and horribly and you only have yourselves to blame.' A popular message that would be bound to endear me to the people, I thought.

The next day I awoke with a fearsome hangover and the knowledge that I had lost, again. By miles. I had breakfast and took a tongue in cheek photograph of me standing in the entrance of a guest house called number ten. The results came out and while it could be argued that the three hundred odd votes I got was better than most independents, it was still an embarrassing and ineffectual loss. I was nineteen thousand off the pace and had worked hard on the project. Then I thought that maybe I could build for the next one and election by election my results would improve. Sharpie, a friend from Whiteparish near Salisbury, who I used to go on cricket tour with, produces a spoof tour magazine each year and I was honoured and amused to discover that the back of the mag was devoted to my fantasy election card with the title 'Harry Potter and the lost deposit.' Funny, true, but oh so cutting.

CHAPTER 38

How to rig an election

'Frankly, what we need to be looking at is whether this election was rigged by Donald Trump and his buddy Vladimir Putin'. - Tom Perez

We hear a great deal about election rigging in countries that are well known for high levels of corruption or where a despot is clinging to power. The obvious ways are to hi-jack the ballot boxes, burn the votes, bribe the officials or make the whole result up at gunpoint.

In the U.S. elections, when Al Gore (Democrat) and George Bush (Republican) were in close contest, only the swing states have any relevance, as most states vote the same way election after election. Florida State being one of these, became the crucial battle ground, and had Georges' brother, Jeb, as Senator. Jeb promised the state would vote Georges' way, and orchestrated this by going through the electoral roles prior to the election to determine if anyone had committed any trivial crime, including driving offences, and if they had, removing them. Thousands of people were this way made ineligible to vote. The greater proportion committing minor offences tended to be the poorer section of the community who were traditionally Democrat voters and which Jeb and George didn't want.

Greg Palast in New York on the 31st Oct 2004 wrote for the Guadian saying: *'The claims, made by the BBC's Newsnight, follow alleged attempts by Republicans to illegally suppress the votes in key states. Republican spokesmen deny these allegations.*

One of the more serious claims is that no action has been taken in a complex fraud, where more than 4,000 Florida students were allegedly conned into signing a form which could lead them to be doubly registered and void their votes. The Florida Law Enforcement Department has told the complainants that it is too busy to investigate.

The attempt to purge the list of alleged felons would appear to be a re-run of the attempt by Florida Governor Jeb Bush's secretary of state to remove 93,000 citizens from voter rolls as felon convicts are not allowed to vote.

Investigations appear to have established that only 3 per cent of the largely African-American list were illegal voters.'

Next he had the ballot paper laid out so that George was the first check box, but Al Gore was not the second, but third, as the boxes were meshed with names left and right. Without care it was therefore easy to vote for the second name who happened to be Patrick J. Buchanan, who received an inordinate number of votes, well above his anticipated number, suggesting that many people had inadvertently voted for the wrong person, as Jeb had hoped. The rest, as they say is history, Al Gore marginally lost, and with him went the hopes for a leaning toward a greener planet less dependent on fossil fuels with Texan oil man George winning, taking the U.S. into several oil wars and ignoring all climate change warnings.

Don Van Nattar Jr. and Dana Cannedy wrote on the 9th November 2000. *'Senior Democratic officials seized on disputed votes cast in Palm Beach County to challenge Gov. George W. Bush's slim lead for the state's 25 electoral votes, vowing to fight beyond Thursday's vote recount if the Texas Republican prevails.*

The dispute centers on the peculiar layout of a presidential ballot in Palm Beach County that some Democratic voters say caused them to become confused and mistakenly vote for Patrick J. Buchanan when they had intended to vote for Vice President Al Gore.

After the final tally, with Mr. Gore trailing Mr. Bush by just 1,784 votes in Florida, several senior Democratic officials said if the ballot had not flummoxed their supporters, Mr. Gore would have won enough votes to win Florida and the presidency.

Even though he never made even one campaign stop in Palm Beach County, Mr. Buchanan, the Reform Party candidate, finished with 3,704 votes in the staunchly Democratic county -- nearly 2,700 more than Mr. Buchanan received in any of Florida's other 66 counties. A lawsuit was filed in West Palm Beach challenging the county's election and seeking a repeat of the vote two weeks from now.

"Leading Democrats have become increasingly concerned about the ballot in Palm Beach County," said a senior Democratic Party official. "This issue threatens to become a focal point for us even after the recount."

They play their own tricks in Britain too. There is a big fuss about getting us all to go to the polling station and make our cross. They tell us that people died so that you have the right to vote. They tell you that if you don't vote you don't have a say, which is true, but what they *don't* tell you is that if you *do* vote you *still* don't have a say. They purposefully don't upgrade the system to an easy 'vote from home on line' method for two reasons. The first is that they want us to believe the illusion that we are participating in a traditional and almost sacred activity, that has huge consequences for themselves and their children. Filling out a form months before and having a card come through the post, taking the time to go to the polling station and seeing all the other people queuing there, sitting up all night as the results are counted and broadcast like the results from the World Cup makes it feel like something important is happening. It has to be real doesn't it? All that effort? All that time and expense? Elections must be really important then. Aren't they? No, but it certainly looks that way.

But what influences people which way to vote is their financial position and the way their parents voted, and that is what feeds the nonsense of our first past the post political system.

In the Telegraph.co.uk online on Sunday 12 March 2017 they wrote:

'Does your vote really count? New research shows that more than half of MPs are in safe seats. Find your constituency on this map to discover if you're one of the 25 million people who already know who will be your MP after May 7.

They went on to state that if you have you ever had the feeling that your vote was pointless, you could be right.

Research by the Electoral Reform Society has shown that out of 650 parliamentary constituencies, 364 - or 56 per cent - are all but certain to go to one party.

In these "safe seats", nobody but the incumbent party stands any chance of winning. So, if you live there and you don't like your MP, that's tough luck.

They pointed out that from a population of over 60 million people, 25.7 million of us live in safe seats. Chief executive Katie Ghose claims that the average constituency hasn't changed hands since the 1960s - and that some have been controlled by one party since the reign of Queen Victoria.

They listed the safe seats that included well-heeled Witney (David Cameron) and hard-working Doncaster North (Ed Miliband), and the SNP stronghold of Perth and North Perthshire, and told us that an example of a marginal seat would be South Thanet, where both main parties are ploughing their resources to prevent Nigel Farage from winning it for Ukip.

Of course, the Electoral Reform Society have an agenda (the clue is in the name). They want the UK to move away from its "first past the post" voting system (FPTP), where the winner takes all in each individual seat, to one of proportional representation (PR), where seats are awarded based on the overall share of the vote.

If PR was instituted across the UK, then Ukip would end up with 99 seats rather than none.

Ms Ghose says: *"The fact that we can firmly predict the outcome of over half of the seats being contested this May is a sorry indictment of our outdated voting system...which actively discourages voters and parties from taking part."*

But even if you like the system as it stands, the fact that almost half the country lives in a safe seat should give you pause for thought.'

I call this the 'Dead dog theory' in which, when I lived in East Devon, there wasn't the remotest chance of anyone but a Conservative being returned as M.P. This meant that I could have put a blue rosette on my collie Matilda and she would have won the election. She has sadly passed on, but guess what? With that blue rosette on she would *still* have won the election for that constituency. This is a nonsense at the heart of why more people choose not bother to vote than vote for the winning party.

A feature of living in a seat like that is that there will always be the dominant political parties 'club'. The 'Conservative Club' or

'Labour Club', where local people are invited to enjoy functions and cheap alcohol, in return for a promise to support the party. Think about this for a moment. Cheap booze if you vote for one of the major parties? Is that legal? Yep! Is this a trickle bribe and extortion of the local population? Yep! Imagine if I were to start a Movement for Active Democracy Party bar that sold beer at ten pee a pint if people promised to vote for me. There would be an absolute uproar.

There was even more desperate inequality in the voting process until comparatively recently when successive Reform Acts by 1950 had both extended the opportunity to almost all adult citizens, barring only convicts, lunatics and members of the House of Lords and finally eliminated most of the plural voting for both Westminster and local-government elections, where the privileged could vote more than once.

We have all heard about the women's suffragette movement, when women martyred themselves to obtain the right to vote, men no-one makes a fuss that men had to go through a similar thing only a decade or so before. Previously the qualification was based on land ownership, which was a small minority, and vote-less men were conscripted in their millions. If you were unlucky enough to have been between 18 and 41 in 1914 you were automatically 'deemed to have enlisted', put under military authority and sent to be slaughtered in the French mud of WW1with no rights to make any stand to prevent it without facing a firing squad. It is reasonable to argue that things may have improved since then, but by how much?

The Government also continues with the old paper and ballot box system because if people realised how easy it was to vote securely and instantly from the comfort of their own home they might just start wondering why it is they aren't engaged in voting more often on issues, rather than which stranger to choose as a representative. To allow a sharing of power with the people? Oh no, they wouldn't want that for a moment. Heavens knows what liberties and justices people might clamour for?

'Your vote is a secret between you and the ballot box.' That is also true, but why should any of us care? Does it matter other than to make it seem that this secret you have is so bloomin' important? No, it's just another thing to add to the mystery and make you think you are doing something important, when, given the system we are currently lumbered with, you are not.

Anyway, back to the fixing part. As mentioned, the most obvious corruption of our political system is the set-up of the constituency system and the first past the post way of deciding who wins the seat. All the votes for anyone else who comes anywhere but first are thrown away. There are no silver or bronze medals in this game. The major parties know that they have the very best chance of coming first in each seat thereby winning it, and so they do not want any fair representation in parliament that reflects the overall voting pattern of the country. Some parties can get twenty per cent of the votes but have no seats at all. That is a blatant and purposeful corruption of the will of the people that we only accept as we have been accustomed to this as the only system for as long as anyone can remember.

The winning candidate does not even need to have over fifty per cent of the peoples support, meaning we often see governments in power who have the mandate of only about a third of the people.

The second fix is that the major parties receive massive publicity in a press that other parties do not receive. The press maintains that that every party should have an equal amount of exposure, but that is simply untrue. Front pages of every newspaper for months ahead of the election will have stories of those few parties, ranging from their newly thought up policy that is going to make everything all right (that they didn't get round to doing when they were in power, and will never implement if they get in again) to the colour of the prime ministers wife's shoes and everything in between. It is an avalanche of propaganda that is impossible to avoid.

Third, the party election broadcasts are biased toward the big players and unilaterally scheduled by the BBC. The current government gets three exposures, the next party two and the others, who have enough representatives, one. The other parties get none at all. Broadcasts are beamed out at BBC chosen time-slots, further tilting the exposure as the two main parties being broadcast at peak viewing six to seven slots and others closer to ten-thirty.

Every news broadcast will show the major party candidates going about their electioneering and discussing their policies. There will be radio chat shows talking about them incessantly, Question time with

only the big players, Newsnight the six o'clock and ten o'clock news
and any number of references in the mainstream media twenty four
hours a day.

The party leader debates are televised following the U.S. example.
We are told that these are 'the party leaders' but they are only four or
perhaps five of (the last time I looked) three hundred and eighty one
registered parties that stand in our elections, most of which you will
never have heard of.

Pippa Norris (British Politics Vol 26 No 1, 2006) divides the bias
of media impact into three types:-

'Agenda setting, by choosing which issues to cover and in what way

*- Persuasion, by influencing voters' perceptions of the parties and their
leaders. 1983 is the best example when, partly because of the difference in
the qualities of the parties' management of the media, Margaret Thatcher
was shown in a few appearances in front of cheering crowds and Michael
Foot was shown walking along deserted streets or being heckled from small
groups of voters*

*- Mobilization, by encouraging people to take an interest in the
campaign and its issues and so increasing turnout, or depressing it, if the
media present an election as boring, with little difference between the
parties, or a foregone conclusion.'*

A minor party has so much more to say because their views are
often new to the listener and yet they might end up with a few seconds
if they are lucky, and even that is not assured. How can a minor party
with virtually no exposure hope to compete? The simple answer is,
they can't. It is patently a dishonest and unfair system that, itself, is
also left unreported on unexposed by the press. As an example, in a
recent election where I decided to stand in my birth town of Reading
I went to the street where I had found out BBC Radio Berkshire were
holding a Q and A with candidates and shoppers. I wasn't invited and
had had to make numerous calls to find the location and date. Bear
in mind here that I am a legitimate candidate who has complied with
Electoral Commission regulations and have paid my £500 deposit,
which I am almost certain to lose, especially if I can get no exposure.
When I arrived I was told categorically that I was not allowed to enter
into the debates. I questioned why not, as I had paid my deposit and
this was supposed to be a fair fight. (The major party candidates

deposit is paid by their party who fully expect not to lose it.) Being a party with fresh concepts I told them I had the most to say, and the most to lose. I was not given a reason or an apology.

I was instead given a ten second manifesto. Ten seconds! How can a party that no-one has heard of, and have no clue at to what the policies may be, do that? I started, 'all government decisions are controlled by the banks and corporations, that is why they are getting richer as you and I face austerity and cutbacks. There is a better way, one person one vote on everything, direct democracy, it's our country, we pay the tax and it's only fair we have our say.' When it came out on the radio I was shocked and disappointed to find those lovely people at the BBC had edited the first line about the banks and corporations controlling government decisions out of my 'speech', and so my manifesto was shrunken to a meaningless five seconds.

What are they so afraid of? This is only little me on the radio and they couldn't bring themselves to even let me say my opinion. Why? Because I am right and the government do not want people realising that government follows instructions for a moment. It actually is at the heart of this book as this understanding unravels everything we have been taught about the workings of Westminster. I had clearly touched a nerve, which showed me I was on the right path, but the fact remains. The others got two hours and I got five seconds. I rest my case.

Fourth, and decades before any of this happens, the real trick is carried out. It is done when you aren't looking and are so vulnerable that you have no defence or ability to deflect it. This is the subliminal programming at school with children being told stories about the choices of elections and how it will shape their future. I have a very clear memory of stomping around the playground as part of a small boys army chanting 'conservative, conservative' not knowing what on earth I was backing as I was only six. I only knew the word from the blue posters in peoples' windows. Even then we were willing to take on anyone who had the audacity to support another party. These thoughts are formed at an age where everything we are told by an adult is absorbed as absolute gospel truth and becomes so ingrained it can take ten years of continual agitation and coercion for a grown adult to start opening their mind to other possibilities and wake up the fact they've been duped, and the establishment knows this. This is the reason why the actual polling day process can be so transparent and fair, because you already missed the trick by a decade or two, and the 'voting on the day' part doesn't matter at all.

All major political parties are privately owned businesses which file returns to Companies House, which is extraordinary when you think about it. A registered company that is Hell bent on putting their ideals before those preferred by the people of a country? That is a pretty worrying thought when the glitz of it all is peeled away. All major parties have beneficiaries, supporters who donate large sums of money, amounting to millions of pounds annually. For what exactly? To receive a bogus knighthood, lordship or baronial title, or more sinisterly to receive beneficial and biased support from those who they hope to help to power, for their own financial gain. A profitable contract perhaps? Or maybe a generous grant of a major planning application like Heathrow?

CHAPTER 39

The two-horse race

'Destiny is no matter of chance. It is a matter of choice. It is not a thing to be waited for, it is a thing to be achieved.' - William Jennings Bryan

To ensure that everybody feels enfranchised at some time or other, it is important for their preferred party to be taking a turn. Witnessing the movement of one government to another sure feels like a change is being effected, and that we the people have had our influence and made the difference. Something to celebrate if your party has now taken control, or a reason to steel yourself if your party has just lost. But when did you see any real change in the way things are done or run other than the implementation of policies that offer no more than a little trivial, and almost inconsequential, tickling around the edges.

It is essential that the baton is regularly passed from one party to another thereby perpetuating the illusion that real change is continually happening. If there were no change to the parties 'in power' (as you are fooled into believing, no party is ever in power) there would be no interest in an election. The illusion of change is the only reason why elections are so important to the establishment.

Observations of changes in government bears this theory out. Following are the list of governments that were in place in the post second world war years.

Labour Government, 1945–51
Conservative Government, 1951–64

Labour Government, 1964–70
Conservative Government, 1970–74
Labour Government, 1974–79
Conservative Government, 1979–97
Labour Government, 1997–2010
Conservative Government, 2010–present

Fifth, and the biggest fix of all is the loading of unpopular policies onto any party that is becoming too strong for too long. The longest period for a party to maintain power in all that time was the conservatives eighteen year reign with Margaret Thatcher and then John Major as Prime Ministers, and so it was essential to introduce unpopular policies to 'let the other lot have a go.' Enter stage left coal mine closures, stage right 'the poll tax' and the unemployment of three million, all of which were financially disastrous to the working family. Yep, that should swing it labours way, and sure enough in 1997 it did with the most humiliating defeat (165 vs 418) that the conservatives have seen in modern times. John Major was in fact meant to lose the election before as the conservative reign was going on too long, but he scraped his way through with the smallest majority against all the odds.

Elections are designed to continually produce an apparent transfer of power from one party to another to ensure that the majority of people get to see their chosen (big) party 'in control', giving those who do not understand the illusion, something to celebrate. If you are looking for further evidence of this deliberate ping-ponging of power a reasonable place to start might be with 'Short Money'.

Short Money was introduced by the Harold Wilson Government of 1974–76 following a commitment in the Queen's Speech (which is written by the government so it's not actually the Queens speech at all, just a speech she is reading out) of 12 March 1974: *"My Ministers will consider the provision of financial assistance to enable Opposition parties more effectively to fulfil their Parliamentary functions"*. I wish I could write a few of her speeches for her *'my husband and I think that Andy Kirkwood is knob-tastic and should get lots of short money – somewhere between two and four million a year to put him in line with the rest of the spongers. . . .'* for example.

Edward Short fleshed out the proposal in a statement on Members' allowances in July 1974:

'A more immediate need is to provide additional support for the Opposition parties in Parliament — support which they certainly require if they are to play their full part here. The then Opposition and, I believe, the whole House benefited greatly from the Rowntree scheme (the provision of a funded 'chocolate soldier' or secretary to the opposition front bench), but more permanent arrangements are now necessary. (Why??) *Following our commitment in the Queen's Speech, I have had very helpful discussions with the parties opposite. I now plan to bring firm proposals before the House in the autumn.'*

The current scheme is administered under a Resolution of the House of Commons of 26 May 1999. Short Money is made available to all opposition parties in the House of Commons that secured either at least two seats or one seat and more than 150,000 votes at the previous general election but is not available to parties whose Members have not sworn the Oath of Allegiance to the Queen her family and descendants, such as Sinn Féin. (which raises another question about the level of the Royal Family's true roll in modern politics that we shall look into later.)

The scheme has three components. Funding to assist an opposition party in carrying out its Parliamentary business, for the opposition parties' travel and associated expenses and for the running costs of the Leader of the Opposition's office.

Now this all may sound like harmless stuff and common sense on the face of it however the sums that are paid, your taxes by the way, are simply staggering.

BBC news reported on 13th May 2015 that *'the amount payable to qualifying parties is £16,956.86 for every seat won at the most recent election plus £33.86 for every 200 votes gained by the party. There is also a travel fund of £183,336 which is shared between the parties in line with the same formula. In addition, the Leader of the Opposition's office is entitled to about £777,500 to help with running costs. The parties receive a monthly payment.*

They calculated that as a result Labour was in line to get at least £6.2m each year - about the same as it received in the last Parliament. The SNP would get something in the region of £1.2m - a big increase on the £187,000 it received in the last Parliament, in recognition of the massive increase in votes and seats it saw at the general election.

The Lib Dems, who did not receive Short money in the last Parliament because they were part of the government are likely to get about £540,000 a year this time.

The BBC told us that UKIP and the Greens were in the unusual position of having gained millions of votes between them but ending up with just one MP each. Meaning Green MP Caroline Lucas and UKIP's Douglas Carswell would be the most well-funded MPs in British history. UKIP, which was not entitled to Short money in the last Parliament, will be entitled to about £650,000. The Green Party was in line to get about £212,000 and Plaid Cymru would receive £81,000, and Northern Ireland's DUP £166,000' (and let's not forget the £1,500,000,000 bribe of our taxpayers money as a gift from the rest of Britain to Northern Ireland made by the Conservatives Party to persuade The DUP to vote with the conservative agenda, thereby keeping the blues in control.)

Remember that all of these figures are for money handed over *every year* and are paid from YOUR taxes. And here's the crunch. According to a paper by the Commons library *"Very little information is published about the qualifying parties' use of their Short money allocation in carrying out their parliamentary business. There has been some concern over the years about whether Short Money is being used appropriately."*

And the really scary bit. If the party in opposition cannot band with other parties to outvote the government, they will have absolutely no power whatsoever in 'opposing' other than to make glib comments and sly remarks. They are all utterly powerless. Their influence is zippo, zilch, nada, bugger all. But hey, I can't really think of anything I'd rather waste over ten million pounds a year on, can you?

Another thing that should be noted is that minor parties, that do not have any representation, and so are in need of the greatest funding, get nothing at all, as the rules say you must have at least one serving MP to qualify. I get no help at all with any of my election expenses or campaigning.

The most important thing for the establishment is for them to keep the people engaged in the political process, but only just enough.

Too much and we start trying to interfere with protests and strikes, but with disengagement they have no mandate whatsoever. The race has to be exciting enough for people to argue about who is their favourite 'horse' in the pub, so it requires a close finish with regularly changing winners.

The money the opposition parties receive encourages the 'two or three horse race' as the losing horses get loads of free money to work up their profiles by raising advertising campaigns and press exposure that the party in power does not. It also widens the void between them and the 'also rans' as it is virtually impossible for a minor party to compete with the limelight these vast sums of money generate. If a diversity of opinion was really wanted then it would be reasonable for every minor party to receive some form of financial assistance to enable them to further their message.

As I have mentioned, the party in power, if they get too far ahead, shall be given unpopular policies, thereby lessening their support base, because each unwelcome policy shall shake off a number of their supporters.

For example, Theresa May called an election shortly after the Brexit vote for no reason, except the establishment wanted Labour to win and put an end to all this Brexit 'nonsense.' Whatever your position on that, the ruling elite know that a unified Europe run by a single unelected civil servant is an easier entity to control than a large number of independent countries. The Conservatives had a majority in parliament and the time to put everything in place for a finalised Brexit, so why then call an election? Anyone in business will tell you, a majority share of 51% is enough to have your sway, and likewise an overall majority in parliament is all you need to steam roller through any legislation. May had that in place.

In the month leading up to the election Theresa May announced that the Conservatives were planning to call another vote on fox hunting, a highly emotive issue that is not supported by the majority of people, thus she shall have shed some support. Next, she introduced zero tolerance on speeding, so 31mph became an offence, goodbye more votes. Scrapping the winter fuel allowance for the elderly was always going to be a vote loser, and the introduction of the 'dementure tax', meaning that sick elderly people risked losing their homes, should have been enough to do the trick. Why would any sane person trying to win an election talk about all those things in the very month before? Because she was following orders to lose her majority.

The result of a hung parliament wasn't quite what the elite wanted, but a hung parliament introduced the DUP problem leading to all the border questions that are causing all manner of doubts and problems about UK/EU borders, and have muddied the process, just as the elite had hoped.

At the same time Jeremy Corbyn was lambasted in the press to such an extent that it started upsetting our great British sense of fair play, and he began to attract the sympathy vote, thus boosting Labours challenge.

A first past the post system that bins millions of votes, massive press propaganda, skewed representation of election broadcasts, lying to infants by telling then that choosing a different party shall change their lot, and that their vote means they are in control, massive investment of public money into the big players and the introduction of unpopular policies at a critical time are exactly how elections are rigged in Britain.

But let's keep a close eye on those ballot boxes to make sure there's no foul play!

Oh, incidentally, the cost of running the 2010 general election (not including any party funding) according to the Independent, 17th April 2015, was £113,255,271 of public money to administer – an increase of nearly 60 per cent on 2005 and more than twice as much as in 2001. Just over a quarter – £28,655,271 – was spent on distributing candidates' mailings, and Returning Officers' expenses came to £71,613,784 (£110,000 each! How?) For an exercise that is an illusion of choice to pacify the workers into thinking they are enfranchised, when they are not. This is a pretty big show they are putting on at our expense. That is how important it is to them to maintain the deception that something important is going on.

CHAPTER 40

Broken election promises

'No wonder Americans hate politics when, year in and year out, they hear politicians make promises that won't come true because they don't even mean them - campaign fantasies that win elections but don't get nations moving again.' - Bill Clinton

Every five years, give or take, we are allowed to hear a load of stuff from the major political parties that tell us of all the wonderful things they are going to do for us if we give them our vote. These things have almost nothing with our past experiences and, more often than not, are pledges that shall be broken without any repercussions for the party or the candidate. If you want examples I could fill a whole other book, but here are only a chapter of lies to make the point:-

The BBC reported on Friday, 3 May, 2002, that Labour stated in their 1997 Labour party manifesto: *'We have made it our guiding rule not to promise what we cannot deliver"*

But critics are likely to point out that in several crucial areas - such as waiting times for cancer treatment, crime and electoral reform - Labour has failed to deliver. Conservative leader Iain Duncan Smith used Labour's fifth anniversary to launch an attack on Mr Blair's record on crime and transport.

Mr Duncan Smith mocked Deputy Prime Minister John Prescott's 1997 promise that there would be "far fewer" cars on the road within five years.

"In this government no one takes responsibility, no one apologises and no one resigns," Mr Duncan Smith told MPs during prime minister's questions on Wednesday.'

Patrick Hennessy, Political editor in the Telegraph wrote on the 25ᵗʰ April 2010 about Labours miserable empty and broken promises record -

'THE ECONOMY

Mr Brown sees his stewardship of Britain through the worst recession in living memory as one his greatest electoral strengths. In its 2010 manifesto, Labour sets out its plan to halve the deficit by 2014, introduce a new global levy on banks and create more than one million high-skilled jobs.

Patrick said that five years ago, at the height of the boom, there was of course no mention of the impending global storm – let alone any plans to nationalise British banks, but a declaration that Britain would march "forward to increased prosperity, not back to boom and bust". The reality is that the UK now produces less per head of population than it did five years ago.

He told us that under Tony Blair in 2005 Labour promised to maintain Mr Brown's prized fiscal rules – borrowing only to invest and keeping net debt stable. Three years later, as Alistair Darling, the Chancellor, battled the forces of financial hell, he was forced to admit he would have to abandon the fiscal rules.

Meanwhile, net debt is soared, hitting £1.4 trillion according to the government's own figures.

In 2005 Labour stated that it would "maintain [the] inflation target at two per cent. Last month it was 3.9 per cent.

The party also pledged to eliminate youth unemployment – it is currently running at more than 920,000 among 16-24 year olds

TAX

In the run up to the 1997 election, Mr Brown famously pledged not to increase the base rate or the top rate of income tax for the lifetime of the forthcoming parliament. He did so again in 2001 In 2005 the party made the same pledge on income tax, however, in 2008 Mr Darling announced a new 45p top rate of tax for those on £150,000, putting this up to 50p in 2009. The new tax rate came into force this month.

We were told that Labour's plans for a National Insurance rise from next year is a "tax on jobs" and a world away from Labour's 2005 declaration. Council tax, which Labour said it was "committed to reform", and pledged to keep "under control" in 2005, has gone on rising with plans for a property revaluation in England kicked into touch.

TRANSPORT

In June 1997, at the start of New Labour's years in power, John Prescott, the former deputy prime minister, rashly declared: "I will have failed if in five years time there are not ... far fewer journeys by car." By June 2002, car traffic was up by seven per cent.

EDUCATION

Mr Blair began his final term of office with a renewed zeal for major reform of the public services – with education top of his list.

However, literacy and numeracy targets for 11-year-olds, which the 2005 manifesto promised would be met, have not been hit. Nor do all children receive two hours of PE or sport per week, which the document pledged they would do by this year.

In 2005 Labour promised a "nationwide week-long summer residential programme for school students". Nothing like this has been introduced.

The party also promised a "bigger, better" higher education system with increased public spending. However, about half of Britain's universities will have their budgets cut this year as the sector becomes one of the first big victims of government savings.

In 2005 Labour's "aim" was for 50 per cent of young people to go on to higher education by this year – by 2008 the figure was only 39.8 per cent – a rise of 0.6 percentage points since 2000.

HEALTH

The 2010 manifesto promises patients a maximum 18 weeks' wait for treatment. Laudable – until you remember that the same promise was made in the party's 2005 manifesto and that for one in 10 patients this target has not been met.

Patrick tells us that another great Blair idea – patient choice – saw a pledge that by 2009 all women would be able to choose where

ANDY KIRKWOOD

they had their baby as well as what sort of pain relief. However, the National Childbirth Trust suggests this is not true for 95 per cent of women.

Labour has not been able to do much to meet its plan to reduce health inequalities between rich and poor. 2010 targets in this area for both life expectancy and infant mortality are set to be missed.

Labour's plan for "comprehensive" out-of-hours service by GPs sounded good – until 90 per cent took up a contract to opt out of such provision.

Even a relatively minor, achievable-sounding pledge, such as the 2005 promise to make fruit and vegetables part of every school meal, has not been met.

CRIME

More officers on the beat – tough action on problem families – a crackdown on anti-social behaviour. The pledges in Labour's 2010 manifesto would surely be backed by any political party in any democracy.

So would their predecessors from 2005, however, which included a pledge for "historically high numbers of police officers". Unfortunately, according to MPs, only four out of 43 police forces in England and Wales plan to maintain current staffing levels.

By 2007, Labour said, every offender would be "supervised after release." Currently those who spend less than a year in jail are not supervised.

FOREIGN AND DEFENCE

In one of the most blatant examples of broken promises, Labour pledged in 2005 to put the European Union Constitution to a referendum in Britain. However, two years later the government forced through the Lisbon Treaty – substantially the same as the Constitution – without a public vote

Jon Ashworth of the Mirror on the 6th December 2015 compiled a list of the top ten promises that David Cameron used to win votes that subsequently were broken. Now while we all know the Mirror are notoriously anti-Tory the list of broken promises (which can also be described as lies) is truly shocking.

Jon wrote *'David Cameron has been Tory Leader for 10 years [and] in the decade since he became leader of the Conservative Party a lot has changed in our country, and in politics. Along the way he has tried to redefine himself, but the consistent theme of his leadership has been one of broken promises and letting down working people.*

Broken promise #1 – balancing the books by 2015. His Government has completely failed to deliver. As the independent Office for Budget Responsibility showed last month the deficit is set to be more than £73 billion this year.

Broken promise #2 – David Cameron repeatedly promised that there would be no top down reorganisations of the NHS. But, despite opposition from health professionals, patients and the public, the Tory-led Government did impose the biggest top-down reorganisation in NHS history.

Broken promise #3 – David Cameron said he had "no plans" to increase VAT. But he broke this promise almost immediately in government, hiking VAT to 20 per cent in a move that costs a family with children £450 a year.

Broken promise #4 – David Cameron has twice broken his promise not to cut tax credits.

Broken promise #5 - In his acceptance speech David Cameron spoke about wanting to "give this country a modern compassionate Conservativism that is right for our times and right for our country". Instead of compassion, five years' of a Tory government has delivered the cruel and unfair Bedroom Tax and a growing reliance on food banks while at the same time cutting taxes for millionaires.

Broken promise #6 –David Cameron said: "I want this message to go out loud and clear: the Conservative Party recognises, will measure and will act on relative poverty." But following the 2015 General Election his Government has scrapped Labour's target for tackling relative child poverty.

Broken promise #7 – most family friendly government ever: – but his policies and decisions have hit families hard

Broken promise #8 – greenest government ever: - but has completely failed to deliver. Since 2010 David Cameron's Government has cut support for solar panels on homes, scrapped the Green Deal to help people insulate old homes, scrapped green building standards for new homes and cut support for industrial solar projects.

Broken promise #9 – well paid jobs and good careers for our young people: David Cameron said he wanted them to have "well-paid jobs and good careers". But 10 years on, those about to head to university face being saddled with decades of debt as a result of the Tories' decision to treble tuition fees. And one of the first acts of the Tory majority government was to pave the way for even higher tuition fees in some universities. Those going straight into work are facing increasingly insecurity, entrenched low pay and a rise in zero-hours contracts.

Broken promise #10 – David Cameron pledged that for people over the age of 65 "their safety, their dignity in old age will be our priority". But cuts to social care are hitting the elderly hard while his Government's plans to introduce a cap on social care costs have been delayed until 2020.'

David Cameron said he wanted to lead the "greenest government ever", and even cycled to work for a few months (jumping a few red lights that just happened to be photographed thereby getting front page coverage to ensure we all got to hear about it) to get the green lobby behind him but has completely failed to deliver.

Rowena Mason, political correspondent of the Guardian wrote on Thu 21 Nov 2013 *'David Cameron was at the centre of a storm over whether he ordered aides to "get rid of all the green crap" from energy bills in a drive to bring down costs.*

The language, attributed to Cameron in the Sun newspaper by a senior Tory source, sparked a furious reaction from campaigners accusing the prime minister of abandoning his promise to run the greenest government ever.' And his slogan to help the conservatives win seats? "Vote blue go green". The cynicism is frankly insulting.

But David Cameron and the Conservative party are far from alone in the complete lack of regard for pledges made to a sleepwalking, conditioned public. Nick Clegg of the Liberal Democrats was no better. Patrick Wintour, political editor, and Hélène Mulholland of the Guardian wrote on Thu 20 Sep 2012 *'A contrite Nick Clegg drew both scorn and applause on Wednesday when he apologised for promising at the last election to oppose any increase in tuition fees, saying: "We made a pledge, we did not stick to it, and for that I am sorry."*

The admission of error, rare in a modern politics, came before next week's Liberal Democrat party conference in Brighton at which his ability to take the party into the next election will be under scrutiny. In a released broadcast he conceded: "There is no easy way to say this."

It was stressed that Clegg was apologising for making the pledge to the National Union of Students before the election not to raise tuition fees, but not for the eventual decision by the coalition to lift the cap on fees to £9,000.

Some of his advisers urged him against the apology, saying it would be taken as a sign of weakness, or merely disinterring an issue best left buried

What can we glean from this? An admission of 'errors' is rare, and Nick's advisors told him not to do it as he may be seen as weak, and that it should all just be buried and left unmentioned. Well I don't find any of that overly comforting, do you?

At the last election where I stood in South Dorset, one of the independent candidates had this joke on his website. 'A guy dies and because his behaviour on earth is in balance he gets to choose whether to go to Heaven or Hell. So, he goes up to Heaven to have a look. It's very pleasant and calm but appears a little boring, so he decides to have a look at Hell. When he arrives he is warmly welcomed by the Devil, who slaps him on the back, stuffs a Havana cigar into his mouth and shoves a large single malt whiskey into his hand. The Devil turns out to be charming and funny and the guy has a great afternoon. Next day, the guy goes to St Peter and says 'right, I've chosen, and it's Hell for me!' 'You sure?' replies a slightly stunned St Peter. 'Yep!' Replies the guy with a big smile on his face, and with a flash he appears in Hell, but this time everyone is running around screaming and gnashing their teeth and there is an unbearable inferno raging. The guy sees the Devil and screams 'what the fuck happened? It was so nice here yesterday!' and the Devil gives him a wink and says 'ah yes, but yesterday we were electioneering!'

So there you have it. The political parties can tell you anything they like to entice you to give them your vote and afterwards they can decide whether or not to be held by their own promises. The very worst that can happen to them is they may have to make a public apology in an attempt to save what little face they have left, as was the case with Nik Clegg, but, as we read, that is 'rare' and 'unadvised'.

But if elections are so important (which I obviously question) then promises and pledges should be legally binding and punishable by law.

Your candidates make promises of what they shall do for you, and in return ask you to give them your tiny bit of power in the form of your five yearly vote. They have made a pledge, a promise and a commitment to you. If anyone were to make an agreement with you to give you a quarter of a million pounds for your flat, and after you had handed over your keys and deeds they decided that they were no longer going to hand over the money there would be law suits, demands for the payment, a court would rule in your favour and the perpetrator would be punished. Of course.

CHAPTER 41

The inability to solve problems

'When solving problems, dig at the roots instead of just hacking at the leaves.' - Anthony J. D'Angelo

Many issues have been raging my entire life, that in a few hours could be easily and inexpensively fixed. The question, therefore, is why aren't they? If you could find a government that tackled these thorny problems efficiently, surely they would get more votes than they know what to do with, right?

Consider this. If the government were to say we were to have, for example, fewer cars on the roads they would have the car and petrochemical industries rioting for their jobs. If they tried to make farming environmentally friendly there would be tractors spraying shit all over Westminster Abbey. How about just trying to utilise prisoners in social projects then? Well there would be a huge hoo-haa about the unemployment figures. But all of those things are actually sensible initiatives that would serve the wider community.

This is why, when it comes to election time, all that the parties will normally want to talk about is improving education, increasing prosperity, cutting NHS waiting times and cutting crime. This is because everyone in their right mind wants those things (well, with the exception of burglars who might want more crime.) You don't lose a vote from any sector of society by not fixing the issues, but you also don't make any inroads into solving them and, if left unresolved those issues are likely to escalate.

A better approach is to apply vision and balance. For example, if you really wanted to take cars off the road a reduction in manufacturing would be essential, but then there is a need for a marked increase in the mass production of renewable energy units, whether it be wind or deep-sea turbines, heat-pumps or solar panels. It would be relatively simple to make the transition from cars or bombers to renewable energy generators. These manufacturers already have premises, purchasing, fabrication, warehouse space, design teams, electrical and mechanical engineering skills, and a qualified workforce in place. It would be a comparatively simple transition for them to start fabricating something that humanity desperately needs, rather than, for example, Trident which is estimated at over £100 billion, and if ever used would make the northern hemisphere virtually uninhabitable.

In every need for the change in the way we have traditionally done things there is bound to be a trade-off. Yes, it may cause some upheaval, yes, there would be growing pains but remember always that to do nothing is to stick your head in the sand and await the four horsemen of the Apocalypse.

CHAPTER 42

The collapsing economy

'The government's view of the economy could be summed up in a few short phrases: If it moves, tax it. If it keeps moving, regulate it. And if it stops moving, subsidize it.' - Ronald Reagan

Have you noticed how many times you hear about 'improving the economy' or 'boosting the economy', or 'helping the economy', or 'stabilising the economy', or 'propping up the economy?' It's the same rhetoric day in day out. We hear it on almost every news programme and buried in every speech made by any party leader. The other considerations, the amount of work you have to do, the tax you have to pay or the adverse effects on an environment in which your kids are growing up, hardly counts a jot, and yet, despite all of this apparent effort the economy sucks. How is that possible? I mean, if we are sacrificing everything else to support this single ambition of bolstering the economy thereby competing against our neighbours, and yet we are still losing ground, then something is out of whack.

A pretty good measure of how well the economy is doing can be estimated by examining the exchange rates that you receive from other countries. For example, when the UK joined the E.U. in 1973 (or actually the Common Market was what we joined but let's not go there right now), according to fxtop.com's historical exchange rates, you would have received 2.2864 Euros for your pound. The rate almost immediately slumped and has continued its zig-zag downward path hitting an all-time low of 1.0219 in 2010 (way before, and nothing to do with, Brexit.)

From that we know that half of the value of everything you ever owned whether it be land, houses, jewellery, cars or money in the bank went down to less than half of the value it was when we joined the E.U. All the time this decay on your net worth was going on, every news item and political speech was talking about improving the economy. So how is that possible? Well, since you ask, I shall tell you.

It is because the government, while pretending to you that they were doing everything in their power to make you wealthier were scheming to purposely collapse the pound. Can they really do that I hear you cry? Yes, and this is how it was done.

The first thing you have to do is get rid of your gold reserve, as that props up your currency when things aren't looking so very rosy. Bullion Vault, a website specialising in the trade of precious metals, on Wednesday, 5/07/2014 wrote – *'Fifteen years ago today, the UK government announced it would sell 415 of the country's 715 tonnes in gold reserve.*

Although everyone else in Europe was at it, that decision still looked crazy enough at the time. Gold prices were at a 20-year low. No one had prepared the ground for Britain to join Switzerland, the Netherlands and the rest. The market was sure to take fright. But run by New Labour, the UK government went further, giving the market two months' notice before the sales started.

That told the market to expect lower prices still, forcing prices lower straight away. By the time the UK's three-year sales programme began in July 1999, prices had dropped a further 10%.

But that still wasn't enough for Gordon Brown's ham-fisted strategy, however. The then chancellor, the man who would be prime minister during the UK banking crash of 2007-2010...reaping the whirlwind...in fact sold gold which the Bank of England already had out on loan.

That enabled speculators wanting to bet on lower prices...caused by the UK's sudden, clunking sales announcement...to borrow gold, sell it, and then buy it back lower down, before returning metal to the Bank of England and banking a profit.'

The price Gordon Brown sold off one of our countries greatest assets was $275 an ounce. If he had waited until the market was at a high he could have expected to net $1,905 an ounce just ten years on – and as there are 32,150 oz in a ton, and he sold off 395 tonnes, he thereby made a staggering loss of over 20 billion U.S. dollars. Thanks for that Gordon. Our gold standard halved and 20 billion pounds lost. Good job.

Thomas Pascoe of the Telegraph on 5th July 2012 ran story that suggests there were even more sinister intentions afoot. He tells us *First, he [Gordon Brown] broke with convention and announced the sale well in advance, giving the market notice that it was shortly to be flooded and forcing down the spot price. This was apparently done in the interests of "open government", but had the effect of sending the spot price of gold to a 20-year low, as implied by basic supply and demand theory.*

Thomas then told us that second, the Treasury elected to sell its gold via auction. Again, this broke with the standard model. The price of gold was usually determined at a morning and afternoon "fix" between representatives of big banks whose network of smaller bank clients and private orders allowed them to determine the exact price at which demand met with supply.

He stated that the auction system again frequently achieved a lower price than the equivalent fix price. The first auction saw an auction price of $10c less per ounce than was achieved at the morning fix. It also acted to depress the price of the afternoon fix which fell by nearly $4.

Thomas added that the Treasury was trying to achieve the lowest price possible for the public's gold, because, faced with the prospect of a global collapse in the banking system, the Chancellor took the decision to bail out the banks by dumping Britain's gold, forcing the price down and allowing the banks to buy back gold at a profit, thus meeting their borrowing obligations.

Goldman Sachs, which is not understood to have been significantly short on gold itself, is rumoured to have approached the Treasury to explain the situation through its then head of commodities Gavyn Davies, later Chairman of the BBC and married to Sue Nye who ran Gordon Brown's private office.'

Our gold, our inheritance, our wealth, purposefully flogged off at the lowest price possible to help Goldman Sachs and J.P. Morgan banks, and no jail sentence at the end of it for Gordon. Well that's British democracy for you.

OK, so that done the second thing you have to do is get rid of the 'slush fund.' Any spare cash lying around has to be squandered so there is no chance of the country easily paying its way out of a financial problem. The market crash of 2007 gave the government the perfect opportunity. The FTSE 100 index reached a peak of 6703 on 18th June 2007 but by 9th March 2009 the value of all shares had crashed to nearly half their value, with the FTSE top 100 plummeting to 3542. During this panic the UK government told us they wanted 'to recapitalise the banks', thereby, they said, attempting the slide from worsening.

Nick Mathiason of the Guardian wrote on Sun 28 Dec 2o08 *'By Wednesday, Brown and Alistair Darling were ready to announce their £50bn bank bail-out. The day began with a 5am crisis meeting at Number 11 Downing Street to put the final touches to the 'recapitalisation' that Brown would then urge the rest of the world to emulate. At 19 minutes to 12, as Brown prepared for his first prime minister's questions since parliament's summer recess, his phone rang: it was Mervyn King, informing the prime minister that interest rates would be cut by half a percentage point, at noon, in a move co-ordinated with central banks around the world.*

Like Brown, King had at times seemed caught on the back foot by the mounting financial and economic crisis of the summer and early autumn; but the Bank, too, was now ready to gallop into action. For Britain's borrowers, it marked the beginning of an unprecedented period of reductions, bringing rates down to 2 per cent, with another cutting spree expected. The scale of October's internationally co-ordinated cut was unprecedented; but still the markets plunged'

Bang! £50 million of our money gone in a flash, trying to prop up a market that was collapsing because of the foolishness and greed of the banks. The injection caused a upward spike in the markets, the money men celebrated, cashed in the stock as they knew the fix was temporary, and then the markets slid back down again, so all the government did was throw away fifty billion pounds of our hard earnt cash thereby saving the greed merchants who control them, at our expense, and nothing had changed.

The third trick to collapse a currency is drop interest rates, as mentioned in Nick Mathaisons' previous article. If you want to be sure that no-one invests in your bank simply offer a lousy return. If you want to be sure that no-one invests their cash in your country you only have to (deep breath) offer a lousy interest return. Simply, if you want the value of the pound to slide the last thing you need is someone shovelling money into the country.

To give us some idea of the changes to base bank rates, they were at 17% in 1980 but are currently at their lowest ever at a measly 0.25% today. Who in their right mind would invest in a country that is only offering 0.25% in interest? And who is it who makes the decision on what the interest rates should be? Graeme Wearden of the Guardian explains that *'Since 1997 rates have been decided by the nine members of the Bank's [of England's] monetary policy committee, which is chaired by the Bank's governor. It meets each month to vote on whether to raise or lower rates, or leave them unchanged.'*

In other words, when you hear on the news 'the bank of England have decided to keep interest rates at X per cent', what they really mean is the Governor and an inner circle of eight other people unilaterally decide what is going to happen next.

This leads us to an important and little understood side issue, that, while you and I are gambling on what interest rates are going to do next (whether you should you take a fixed or floating interest rate deal on your mortgage for example) these people know *exactly* what is going to happen. While we are staring at the roulette table willing the ball to land on 'red', they are placing the ball where they choose and will have all of their affairs (and presumably those of everyone involved in the scam with them) arranged perfectly to make sure they can never get it wrong and that they financially benefit from every rate revision decision.

Fourth you devalue the currency, through a measure called 'quantitative easing.' Katie Allen and Larry Elliott of the Guardian wrote on the 4th of August 2016 *'Reacting to early economic indicators suggesting demand and output had slowed across all parts of the economy since the June referendum, the Bank announced a cut in official interest rates to 0.25%, the first such move since March 2009, plans to pump an additional £60bn in electronic cash into the economy to buy government bonds, extending the existing quantitative easing (QE) programme to £435bn in total, and another £10bn in electronic cash to buy corporate bonds from firms "making a material contribution to the UK economy";*

As much as £100bn of new funding shall be given to banks to help them pass on the base rate cut. Under this new "term funding scheme" (TFS) the Bank will create new money to provide loans to banks at interest rates close to the base rate of 0.25%. The scheme will charge a penalty rate if banks do not lend.'

Ok so let's think about those figures for a moment. £435 billion of electronic money equates to over £6,500 for every man woman and child (or if you prefer £40,000 for every retired person) in the country. This is a vast amount of cash to suddenly magic up and it waters down the existing money, causing the value of it to slide on the international currency exchanges. And who is it who gets this unsupported imaginary cash? The banks! Who were you expecting? You? Me? Are you not paying attention here? You didn't get a fat brown paper package with over six grand through the post did you? You should have, because that is how much you lost by the Government taking this measure.

Katie Allen and Julia Kollewe of the Guardian on 4th of August 2016 wrote: *'In a QE programme, a central bank [Bank of England] creates new money electronically to buy financial assets such as government bonds or corporate bonds from banks or other financial institutions. The hope is that they will use the extra funds to boost lending to households and businesses. Over the following three years it expanded QE five times, to £375bn in July 2012 when the UK faced a prolonged double-dip recession*

However, the Bank [of England] later admitted that the richest 10% of households in Britain had benefited the most from QE. (What a surprise!) *The strategy has been criticised by groups representing savers and pensioners because savings rates, annuity rates and gilt yields have all fallen.'*

Fifth you have to ensure that money generated in Britain somehow ends up in the coffers of another country. Impossible? Well Jim Armitage of the Independent on 20 November 2014 wrote: *'Foreign governments are making hundreds of millions of pounds a year running British public services, according to an Independent investigation highlighting how privatisation is benefiting overseas – rather than UK – taxpayers.*

Swathes of Britain's energy, transport and utility networks are run by companies owned by other European governments – meaning foreign exchequers reap the dividends while UK customers struggle with increasing fares and bills.

Jim told us that in the past two years from 2014, overseas taxpayers have taken dividends totalling nearly £1bn from companies which make their profits from UK households and passengers.

An analysis of companies' financial filings for the last financial year shows that currently 20 national train lines are run or owned by foreign state-owned or controlled companies.

Only last month, the ScotRail franchise was offloaded to the Netherlands' state-owned Abellio.

Christian Wolmar, a rail industry analyst, said: "It is a completely daft situation where state-run companies in foreign countries can bid for our rail services but UK ones can't. It is specifically banned by law for the likes of Transport for London, or Directly Operated Railways to bid for UK rail contracts."'

And sixth on the list, you need to rack up debt. Lots of it. And guess what? Our national debt, money that the government have borrowed over the years now stands in 2018 at a slither under £2 trillion. This is a vast amount, two thousand billions or, if you prefer, two million millions. This amount equates to about £31,000 for each of us or £54,000 per tax payer. And who pays the interest payments on this bonkers loan? You do!

The Daily Mail had this to say on Jan 16th 2018: *'Britain pays £8m an HOUR to service the national debt: Figures show Government borrowed £8bn in October as it continues to spend more than it receives in tax.*

Government borrowed £8bn in October, £500m more than same month last year Debt interest payments jumped by 25 per cent to £6billion last month alone National debt now stands at £1.79trillion and has tripled since turn of the century. Britain plunged deeper into the red last month as the country was forced to pay £8million an hour servicing the mammoth national debt.

The national debt currently stands at about 85% of GDP, which means that if every erg of effort that you and I and everyone else in Britain makes were put into reducing it to zero it would take 10 months, or three years if you add and take into account the annual tax burden on each of us. And each year the burden increases by another 9.9% of GDP.

Personal debt is a further problem, likely to burden by the less well off in our community who continually have to 'rob Peter to pay Paul.'

Phillip Inman and Jill Treanor of the Guardian had this to say about it on Mon 18 Sep 2017 *'The government needs to step in to help tackle the mountain of debt being racked up by the most vulnerable consumers in Britain, the chief financial regulator has warned, as new data shows that personal debt burdens are continuing to rise.*

New figures seen by the Guardian showed the worsening consequences of Britain's borrowing binge. According to the Money Advice Service, there are now 8.3 million people in the UK with problem debts.

The debt charity StepChange, which has also released fresh data, said the percentage of its clients falling behind on payments went over 40% in the first half of 2017, while the average debt of the people it helps has also risen, from £14,251 in 2016 to £14,367 in the first half of the year.'

And that, my friend, is how you collapse an economy and successfully drive down the value of the pound on international markets (while gassing on about improving the economy at every opportunity – of course.) And you are still voting these lying, cheating bastards in?

Oh, and in case you didn't join the dots - who makes money when the gold reserves are sold off on the cheap? The banks. Who makes money on national debt? The banks. Who makes money on personal debt? The banks. Who receives the money in quantitive easing measures? The banks. Who makes money when the stock exchange is propped up by the government? The banks. Who knows interest rate fluctuations before anyone else, because they are the ones who make them up? The banks. In which sector of business are all companies permanently underwritten by the government? The banks.

So, who is it who actually runs our country? All together now. . . . .!

CHAPTER 43

The Great British discount store

'We reward people for making money off money, and moving money around and dividing up mortgages a thousand times over, selling it to China... and it becomes this shell game.' - Michael Moore

Now, the next logical question has to be why? Why would the government be doing all of these despicable things that are undermining our country and our efforts? After all they represent the people don't they? They want what is best for Britain surely? I mean, they are always talking about the economy right?

Er, actually, and surprisingly for those who have never dug this deep, the answer is no. They actually are, as is being demonstrated in a common theme running through this book, the puppets of the banks and corporations, taking their instructions from those greed merchants, the 1% elite who care nothing for quality of life for the common man, only in control, personal profits and in increasing their share.

So how do the corporations benefit from all this jiggery-pokery? They buy up our utilities, our family jewels, at a bargain price. Because the pound has been collapsed, if you happen to have spare euros, roubles, or dollars you can do a little shopping in the UK and pick yourself up a right bargain. A water company perhaps or maybe a nice little energy monopoly, at half the price it should have been if our government weren't screwing us all over, because the exchange rate is so favourable for those outside the pound.

Jim Armitage of the Independent on 20 November 2014 goes on:- *'While privatisation was meant to bring the business acumen of the corporate sector into public utilities, increasingly it has allowed foreign governments and their state-owned operators to make vast profits out of the UK. Meanwhile, British firms have almost no presence in overseas utilities markets and, since the takeover of Arriva by Germany's state-owned Deutsche Bahn, only a small share of global public transport.*

As a result, vast amounts of British citizens' bills and fares leave the country in the form of dividends to taxpayers in continental Europe, funding their schools and hospitals.

Foreign taxpayer-owned transport companies received £102m in dividends from UK train fares during the past two years, The Independent has calculated. That figure is dwarfed by the £900m sent back to foreign governments from British household energy bills. These came from dividends taken out of the UK by EDF, majority-owned by the French state, and the industrial energy supplier GDF Suez, part-owned by France.

Other foreign energy players are also taking huge dividends from UK electricity bills but are remitting them to private investors. For instance, Scottish Power's Spanish owners Iberdrola took a £600m payment. With consumers paying an average of £410 more a year for energy compared with a decade ago, The Independent's findings shine new light on the motivations of foreign energy suppliers.'

The lovemoney website tells us of our energy companies only British Gas is UK based and owned. They *continue: 'EDF Energy is a subsidiary of the French Government-owned energy company EDF (Électricité de France) Group. Over the years it has bought UK energy companies London Electricity, SWEB, Seeboard and British Energy.*

E.ON is a German-owned group formed from the merger of German companies VEBA and VIAG. The group bought UK energy company Powergen back in 2002 but it wasn't until 2007 that its UK energy operations were renamed E.ON.

Npower is a subsidiary of German energy company RWE Group. It was bought in 2002, having evolved out of National Power, later renamed npower, which had bought the likes of Calortex, Independent Energy and Midlands Electricity following privatisation.

ScottishPower is a subsidiary of Spanish company Iberdrola, who bought it in 2006. The company was formed in 1990 from the South of Scotland Electricity Board. It later bought Manweb, the energy company supplying Merseyside and North Wales.'

Water is big on the list of utilities that foreign investors want to get their mitts on, partly because Offwat, in their five year review system, guarantees a profit for the company, no matter how bad things get. Who wouldn't want a slice of that pie? So where are they owned? Thames Water, has been controlled by the Macquarie Group of Australia, since 2006. Northumbrian Water Group, was bought by Chung Kong Infrastructure in 2011, others include Kemble Water (Australia), South East Water (Australia), Wales and West Utilities (China).

Sir Alan Rudge, Chairman of the ERA Foundation (a non-profit organisation which supports engineering skills development and aims to bridge the gap between engineering research and its commercialisation.) writes *"But foreign ownership of UK firms is increasing. From 2000 to 2007, in the manufacturing sector and measured in terms of output, foreign ownership rose from 25 to 40 per cent. Among larger companies, it is now between 70 and 80 per cent: 2,000 firms taken into foreign ownership in one decade. I see no sign it has slowed. In mining and quarrying in 2007, 70 per cent were foreign owned; in utilities, it was 50 per cent and is now much higher. Our next generation of nuclear power stations will also be decided overseas. Only one national newspaper is wholly UK owned, while legislation to free up television station ownership is on the cards."*

Under EU law corporation tax is levied in the designated country of the Head Office of a multinational so losing UK Companies means an immediate loss to the UK tax payer. The losses in corporation tax are in the region of £20 billion a year or more to the Exchequer.

Of the railways Gwyn Topham of the Observer on Sat 2 Dec 2017 wrote *'At Romford station, in the Essex centre of "taking back control", there's a choice of trains into London: those run by the Dutch, or those run by the Chinese. Anyone heading for nearby Basildon has to change at*

Upminster and pay a fare to the Italian firm that has been operating C2C since January.

He told us that Welsh railways fell to German-owned Arriva long ago, while ScotRail is also in the hands of the Netherlands' Abellio. The French, as part of Govia, own much of Britain's biggest commuter franchises, including Southern Rail. Still, the news last week that South West Trains – serving destinations such as Weymouth and Windsor from Waterloo – would from August be operated by First MTR, partly owned by the Hong Kong government, marked a tipping point in Britain's rail franchising.

Gwyn adds that with the transfer of this network, which has been operated since 1995 by Britain's Stagecoach, one in two of the 1.7bn passenger journeys made in the UK each year will be on trains operated by foreign firms. And all of those firms are ultimately owned by foreign states – which outrages unions and others who call rail privatisation into question.

Mick Whelan, general secretary of train drivers' union Aslef, said: "It is savagely ironic that the Tories say they don't believe in state control, yet are perfectly happy to allow Britain's train companies to be run by state-owned railways – as long as it's another state!" It's because they are lying to you mate! Work it out!

And it isn't just the utility companies. Famous brands that we naturally assume are British through and through have been snapped up. HP is the famous brown sauce of the Houses of Parliament (hence the name). Nevertheless, it is owned by Americans: Heinz purchased it in 2005. House of Fraser is owned by the Sanpower Group, a Chinese corporation that bought it in 2017 for £450 million, and before that it was owned by the Icelandic group Baugur. What could be more British than Sarson's vinegar on a plate of fish and chips? A Japanese vinegar manufacturer, Mizkan, bought Sarson's in 2012 for £41 million. Branston Pickle was also acquired by Mizkan in 2016 for £92.5 million. Walkers Crisps produce 56% of all crisps and popcorn sold in Britain. The brand was bought by PepsiCo back in 1989. (In America, Walkers are called Lays.) Weetabix, the famous breakfast cereal, has been in Chinese hands for years. Shanghai-based consortium Bright Food bought it in May 2012. Hartley's Jam was bought by American corporation Hain Celestial in 2012, for £200 million. The car manufacturer Jaguar was bought by India's Tata in 2008. Before that it was owned by Ford, based in Detroit, Michigan. Manchester United and Queen's Park Rangers both play in the English Premier League. United is owned by the Glazer family of the US; QPR by Malaysian tycoon Tony Fernandes. Fernandes also owned of another glory of British sport: the Caterham Racing Team in Formula One. He sold it to an undisclosed consortium of Swiss and Middle Eastern investors in July 2017. A third of the milk drunk in Britain is owned by foreign companies: Wiseman Milk is now part of the German group Müller, which bought it in 2012. Cadbury has a similarly dominant position in the British chocolate market. It was bought by Kraft in 2010 and is now incorporated into Mondelēz International, a US company. British law states that everyone must eat a Terry's Chocolate Orange at Christmas, but Terry's is also owned by Mondelēz, and the orange factory is in Poland. Tetley has traded on its English heritage for decades, however, it is owned by India's Tata Global Beverages. Another Indian group owns Typhoo Tea: Apeejay Surrendra bought it in 2005 for £80 million. Newcastle Brown Ale was purchased by Heineken of the Netherlands in 2008. The beer is produced in Yorkshire in the same factory as John Smith's, also owned by the Dutch. Bass was one of the first 30 companies to be listed on the London Stock Exchange. It was bought by Interbrew in 2000, and it is now part of America's AB-InBev. For many people, Beefeater Gin means London and the Tower, but the French group Pernod Ricard has controlled it since 1987. The same company owns Chivas Regal, which claims to be crafted by the oldest distillery in Scotland. Glenlivet, an icon of Scotch single malts, is the best-selling whisky in the US (and owned by Pernod Ricard since 2000). Mobile networks are not exempt: O2 was bought by Telefònica, a Spanish group, in 2005. EE is the largest mobile network in Britain. It is a joint venture between Deutsche Telekom and Orange SA. (Orange used to be a British company, before it was bought by France Telecom in 2000.) Even Heathrow Airport is owned by foreigners: a consortium of international investors, led by the Spanish Grupo Ferrovial, has controlled it since 2006. TfL (Transport for London) is controlled by the Greater London Authority, but its famous red double-deckers operate through international partners. The biggest, Arriva, is a subsidiary of Deutsche Bahn, the German national railway, since 2010. It is hard to forget that Britain's 'paper of record', The Times, is owned by the Australian-American Rupert Murdoch. Hamley's was owned by Baugur, before being sold to the French Ludendo Groupe for £60 million. ASDA is actually a Wal-Mart subsidiary since 1999. The American giant bought it for £6.7 billion. Umbro has passed from one foreign corporation to another: The US's Iconix Brand Group took it from Nike in 2012 for £141 million. Boots UK is the latest British brand to defect: Walgreens, the biggest pharmacy company in the world, bought it this August for £5.65 billion. It was previously owned by Stefano Pessina, an Italian entrepreneur.

This list, while exhausting, is not exhaustive, and is seemingly never ending. MG-Rover is Chinese, Rowntrees is Swiss, P&O Ports are owned in Dubai, Corus is Indian, Camelot is Canadian, ICI is Dutch, Selfridges, Fortnum & Masons and the Savoy are all Canadian.

Aside from the companies that have been selling out to foreign investors the UK housing market has also attracted a great deal of outside investment, some from individuals of course but a truly worryingly amount is coming from gigantic offshore corporations who are looking for investments only, and never use the buildings, that should be homes for British people, for that use. This is causing immense hardship to the people of Britain and the government has stood idly by. Well almost idly by, they have been counting the money while watching the agony and refusing to intervene. So at least they are doing *something*!

To expand, the Business Insider website had this to say about it:- *'The average house in London now costs about 12 times the average income, according to data from HMRC crunched by The Guardian. Londoners are not bidding against each other for houses. They are bidding against all of the world's rich people and the shell corporations they control. British people just don't own that much property in central London anymore. In the ultra-rich Mayfair neighbourhood — yes, the one that's most expensive square on the Monopoly board— building after building is owned by foreign investment companies.*

A typical example is Flat 21 in Avenfield House on Park Lane (the other Monopoly board trophy). It was bought for £6.2 million by "Hung

Yip Developments" of the British Virgin Islands. We tried to contact Hung Yip Developments for comment but were unable to reach them.'

According to the BBC, foreigners own £122 billion in property in the UK, via offshore holding companies. More than 100,000 UK property titles are registered to overseas companies, with more than 36,000 properties in London owned by offshore firms.

That value is the equivalent of the entire GDP of Kuwait or Vietnam. Here's the Guardian, to put that into real-money terms:

In 1995, the median income in London was £19,000 and the median house price was £83,000, meaning that people were spending 4.4 times their income on buying a property. But by 2012-13, the median income in London had increased to £24,600 and the median house price in the capital had increased to £300,000, meaning people were forced to spend 12.2 times their income on a house.'

Here is a scary thought. Normally when you sell off an asset, your home, your car, your diamond ring, you benefit by the increased prosperity the money that it brings. You actually get to enjoy the money. Now with so much of the U.K. being sold to overseas investors you would be right in thinking that we should have seen a turnaround in our financial circumstances. A period of milk and honey, at least for a little while.

However, at the same time as selling off our assets hand over fist, injecting our money like there is no tomorrow and screwing us by every available means, our country has still driven up debt we have faced austerity measures, like the closing of libraries and the thinning down of public services like the police or ambulance services. The corruption of the system controlling our own government is shocking.

Now here is the million pound question. What is it that all those overseas companies that have bought into the UK have in common? All together now, they all got their deals at half price because the government purposefully drove down the pound. Q.E.D.

CHAPTER 44

Whipping

'Our diversity is our strength. What a dull and pointless life it would be if everyone was the same.' - Angelina Jolie

So far, we have only been dealing with the façade. Only the stage show that is going on in front of our eyes, to bamboozle us all into thinking something important is going on. It certainly does look that way.

But what if all that hype really is there just to fool us all into thinking we are participating in a great choice that will shape the lives of our children, when in fact it is just a sham that we keenly watch with the same facial expressions as a dog being shown a card trick.

Let us assume for a moment that you have voted and that your choice of candidate wins and is duly appointed as a member of parliament. If that candidate happens to represent any party other than the one that wins an outright majority in the house, then that is the end of your M.P.'s role in the running of the country for the next five years. They can comment and make statements to the press, they can disagree with the incumbent party's policies and they can vote against them in an attempt to show them to be unpopular, but they have no real power to effect change.

But here is the real trick, even if your choice of MP *is* part of the majority party they *still* don't have any power to effect change. Why? Because of 'whipping.'

The party whip is the name given to an official of a political party whose task is to ensure party discipline in a legislature. Whips are the party's 'enforcers', they invite their MPs to attend votings and to vote according to the official party policy. The term is taken from the 'whipper-in' during a hunt, who tries to prevent the hounds from wandering away from the pack. In the UK and Ireland, a party's endorsement of a member of parliament to 'withdraw the whip' is to expel an MP from his or her parliamentary party.

In British politics, the chief whip of the governing party in the House of Commons is customarily appointed as Parliamentary Secretary to the Treasury so that the incumbent, who represents the whips in general, has a seat and a voice in the Cabinet. By virtue of holding the office of Parliamentary Secretary to the Treasury, the government chief whip has an official residence at 12 Downing Street, although the chief whip's office is currently located at 9 Downing Street. Whips report to the prime minister on any possible backbench revolts and the general opinion of MPs within the party, and upon the exercise of the patronage, which is used to motivate and reward loyalty.

In the United Kingdom, there are three categories of whip that are issued on particular issues. An express instruction on how to vote could constitute a breach of parliamentary privilege, so the party's wishes are expressed unequivocally but indirectly. These whips are issued to M.P.s in the form of a letter outlining the parliamentary schedule, with a sentence such as 'Your attendance is absolutely essential' next to each debate in which there will be a vote, underlined one, two or three times according to the severity of the whip:

A single-line whip is a guide to what the party's policy would indicate, and notification of when the vote is expected to take place; this is non-binding for attendance or voting.

A two-line whip, sometimes known as a double-line whip, is an instruction to attend and vote; partially binding for voting, attendance required unless prior permission is given by the whip. A three-line whip is a strict instruction to attend and vote, breach of which would normally have serious consequences. Permission not to attend may be given by the whip, but a serious reason is needed. Breach of a three-line whip can lead to expulsion from the parliamentary political group in extreme circumstances and may lead to expulsion from the party.

The nature of three-line whips and the potential punishments for revolt vary dramatically among parties and legislatures. Disobeying a three-line whip is a newsworthy event, indicating as it does a potential mutiny; an example was the decision on 10 July 2012 by 91 Conservative MPs to vote against Prime Minister David Cameron on the issue of reform of the House of Lords.

And your MP had better not think they can vote with their conscience and buck the system. Taken from an article in the Guardian on 13ᵗʰ July 2014 was the following paragraphs. *"For young and idealistic backbenchers, the whips' tactics were a brutal introduction to Westminster. One MP from the 1992 intake recalled last week how they rang members of his family at all hours. "They even kept phoning my wife and saying 'you should tell him to vote with the government'. It was quite extraordinary," he said. "They would try everything – threats and inducements – saying they knew things that they didn't want to have to make public, implying they would if they had to. With some it was affairs, or things like visits to gay nightclubs. It didn't matter if it wasn't true, or was gossip, they still tried it on."*

A member of the whips' office during that period recalls how, every day, he and all the other Tory whips would be expected to write notes into a "black book", and that these entries would be discussed each morning at a team meeting in the chief whip's office. "It was mostly fairly mild stuff, about who said what at some meeting of the 1922 Committee, or that kind of thing. But it might be rumors of one sort or another about private things."

Political leaders also have at their disposal a great deal of patronage, in the sense that they make decisions on the appointment of officials inside and outside government, for example on quangos, that according to BBC News 14ᵗʰ October 2010 cost the British taxpayer 'between £34bn and about £60bn'. Annually.

At the heart of the government is the 'Cabinet of the United Kingdom' which is the collective decision-making body of Her Majesty's Government of the United Kingdom, composed of the Prime Minister and some 21 cabinet ministers, the most senior of the government ministers.

Ministers of the Crown, and especially Cabinet ministers, are selected primarily from the elected members of the House of

Commons, and also from the House of Lords. And who do we think it is who decides on who those people are going to be? The Prime Minister. If your M.P. wants to have any kind of authority there they had better shut up and put their hand up when they are told to, like a good boy/girl/person/whatever. Cabinet ministers are heads of government departments, mostly with the office of 'Secretary of State for (for example) Defence or Heath.' The collective coordinating function of the Cabinet is reinforced by the statutory position that all the Secretaries of State jointly hold the same office, and can exercise the same powers. So should your M.P. decide to vote on merit or conscience they are unlikely to hold any position of consequence and shall be sent to the back benches where they shall take no further active part in the process other than to occasionally raise a hand and will never get their face on the television again.

So where have we got to? Ah yes, you think your vote is important so you bothered to do your homework. You listened to a load of stuff from various strangers that may or may not be true, and if it is untrue there is no repercussions for those that told the 'un-truths'. You walked to the polling booth and put your cross down for your chosen candidate who may either lose or be in a minority, so shall have no power. Possibly your choice of candidate might win *and* be part of the majority, so that's ok then? Staggeringly they will *still* have no power as they have to go along with what they are told by the whip. Is this sounding like a democracy to you? Are you glad you bothered to take the time to place your cross on that bit of paper?

But now is here is the really horrible part. Even all of this is a charade. Even at the level of Cabinet there is nothing of any importance is really going on, and the reason is? Permanent Secretaries.

CHAPTER 45

Permanent secretaries

'Assuming either the Left Wing or the Right Wing gained control of the country, it would probably fly around in circles.' - Pat Paulsen

Now we are starting to get a little closer to the core of the problem. In most departments the official title is the Permanent Under-secretary of State or PUS, and this is the most senior civil servant of a British Government ministry, charged with running the department on a day-to-day basis.

Permanent Secretaries are the non-political civil service heads or chief executives of government departments, who generally hold their position for a number of years (thus 'permanent') at a ministry as distinct from the changing political Secretaries of State (who are promoted elected M.P.s) to whom they report and provide advice. To put this into Google translate for a moment, this means that while the Secretary of State chops and changes, as they are just the MPs who put their hands up at the right time and so made it into the cabinet, they can be removed or reshuffled at a whim, whereas the Permanent Secretary is not, exactly as the title suggests.

On 17th July 2016 the Mirror described newly elected as PM (by her own party not the people of Britain) Theresa May's reshuffle as *"These are the Tories who will join Theresa May around the Cabinet table for the first meeting chaired by a woman PM at No.10 Downing Street in 26 years.*

The mirror reported that she had stamped her power from the start as she ditched George Osborne as Chancellor, leaving him to slip out Number 10's back gate with his reputation in tatters. Tory big guns Michael Gove, Nicky Morgan and John Whittingdale were also sacked in quick succession in a brutal piece of justice for the backstabbing Justice Secretary.

They added that Jeremy Hunt, whose catastrophic handling of the junior doctors' strike enraged tens of thousands of NHS staff, grinned, waved and trolled critics on Twitter as he kept his job as Health Secretary, and Boris Johnson had popped eyes out of their sockets across Westminster by being made Foreign Secretary. He once called black people "piccaninnies".

They told us that leadership rival Andrea Leadsom was rewarded with a new job as Environment Secretary despite wanting to bring back fox hunting, and that Priti Patel became head of the Department for International Development, which controls foreign aid, despite suggesting three years ago it should be scrapped.

So, what we can say for sure is that none of these people have any clue how to do their job. One day you are the minister for health, the next, defence. So, what do you know about defence exactly? Er, is that nothing? 'Well I know you need an army and stuff and lots of money to build weapons that you can never use but other than that. . .' So where does all the information that is fed into the decision process come from? The Permanent Secretaries of course.

The Permanent secretary is probably male (there are three women holding posts in a total of nineteen), mature, white, Eton or Harrow and Oxbridge educated and is definitely unelected and virtually anonymous, rarely making appearances in the press or on television news. For example, who is your Permanent Secretary for defence? Give up? I'll tell you. It's Stephen Lovegrove! Of course! When he was recently appointed he said "I am thrilled to be joining the Ministry of Defence: keeping Britain safe (from who?) and employing over 250,000 people all over the world in a hugely (expensive!) diverse variety of roles."

Health? No idea? Chris Wormald, although Dame Una O'Brien had been doing it for the last twenty-five years. When he was appointed the Cabinet Secretary, Sir Jeremy Heywood, said: "Chris has done a superb job leading the Department for Education." Secretary of State for Health, Rt Hon Jeremy Hunt MP, said "I'm delighted, Chris has done excellent work across the public sector." Secretary of State for Education, Rt Hon Nicky Morgan MP, said "Chris Wormald has done a superb job in leading the Department for Education". Not too much back slapping going on there then!

But now it's time to get serious because here is a little-known fact, taken from Wikipedia. 'Her Majesty's Home Civil Service forms an inseparable part of the British government. The executive decisions of government ministers are implemented by HM Civil Service. ***Civil servants are employees of the Crown and not of the British parliament.***' Huh? When I was a kid I was taught that the monarchy didn't have anything to do with the running of the country, and that the Queen was simply a figure head. That is clearly untrue if the Crown are paying the wages for the top civil servants who advise the cabinet, who form the inner circle of government.

CHAPTER 46

The Crown

'If you ever start feeling like you have the goofiest, craziest, most dysfunctional family in the world, all you have to do is go to a state fair. Because five minutes at the fair, you'll be going, 'you know, we're alright. We are dang near royalty." - Jeff Foxworthy

So, what role does the Queen and her family really have? In the Telegraph on march 14th 2017 Alice Feinstein, editor of Woman's Hour (who was not part of the judging panel to assess who was the most powerful woman in the world), says she wasn't surprised by the Queen's position *"I can see why she is at the top of the list of the world's most powerful women. She's the head of state and Commonwealth. The Queen has a lot of potential power she could exercise, but doesn't [so we are told]. I know that the panel considered her weekly meeting with the Prime Minister to be a key indicator of her power. She has been doing the job a long time – and is a major repository of knowledge. The Queen is highly respected because of her experience and access."*

The Guardian on the 14th January 2013 printed this shocking exposé bombshell, *"The extent of the Queen and Prince Charles's secretive power of veto over new laws has been exposed after Downing Street lost its battle to keep information about its application secret.*

Whitehall papers prepared by Cabinet Office lawyers show that overall at least 39 bills have been subject to the most senior royals' little-known power to consent to or block new laws. They also reveal the power has been

used to torpedo proposed legislation relating to decisions about the country going to war.

The Guardian told us that the internal Whitehall pamphlet was only released following a court order and shows ministers and civil servants are obliged to consult the Queen and Prince Charles in greater detail and over more areas of legislation than was previously understood.

They said the new laws that were required to receive the seal of approval from the Queen or Prince Charles cover issues from higher education and paternity pay to identity cards and child maintenance, and went on the say that In one instance the Queen completely vetoed the Military Actions Against Iraq Bill in 1999, a private member's bill that sought to transfer the power to authorise military strikes against Iraq from the monarch to parliament.

They told us that in the pamphlet, the Parliamentary Counsel warns civil servants that if consent is not forthcoming there is a risk "a major plank of the bill must be removed".

"This is opening the eyes of those who believe the Queen only has a ceremonial role," said Andrew George, Liberal Democrat MP for St Ives, which includes land owned by the Duchy of Cornwall, the Prince of Wales' hereditary estate.

Andrew went on to say that *'it shows the royals are playing an active role in the democratic process and we need greater transparency in parliament so we can be fully appraised of whether these powers of influence and veto are really appropriate. At any stage this issue could come up and surprise us and we could find parliament is less powerful than we thought it was'.*

The Guardian found out that Charles has been asked to consent to 20 pieces of legislation and this power of veto has been described by constitutional lawyers as a royal "nuclear deterrent" that may help explain why ministers appear to pay close attention to the views of senior royals.

Apparently the guidance also warns civil servants that obtaining consent can cause delays to legislation and reveals that even amendments may need to be run past the royals for further consent.

"There has been an implication that these prerogative powers are quaint and sweet but actually there is real influence and real power, albeit

unaccountable," said John Kirkhope, the legal scholar who fought the freedom of information case to access the papers.

The release of the papers comes amid growing concern in parliament at a lack of transparency over the royals' role in lawmaking. George has set down a series of questions to ministers asking for a full list of bills that have been consented to by the Queen and Prince Charles and have been vetoed or amended.

The guidance states that the Queen's consent is likely to be needed for laws affecting hereditary revenues, personal property or personal interests of the Crown, the Duchy of Lancaster or the Duchy of Cornwall.

Consent is also needed if it affects the Duchy of Cornwall. These guidelines effectively mean the Queen and Charles both have power over laws affecting their sources of private income.

The Guardian told us that Queen uses revenues from the Duchy of Lancaster's 19,000 hectares of land and 10 castles to pay for the upkeep of her private homes at Sandringham and Balmoral, while the prince earns £18m-a-year from the Duchy of Cornwall.

A Buckingham Palace spokeswoman said: "It is a long established convention that the Queen is asked by parliament to provide consent to those bills which parliament has decided would affect crown interests. The sovereign has not refused to consent to any bill affecting crown interests unless advised to do so by ministers."

Graham Smith, director of Republic, the campaign for an elected head of state, has also called for full disclosure of the details of the occasions when royal consent has been refused.

"The suggestion in these documents that the Queen withheld consent for a private member's bill on such an important issue as going to war beggars belief," he said. "We need to know whether laws have been changed as the result of a private threat to withhold that consent."

The Cabinet Office fought against the publication of the 30-page internal guidance in a 15-month freedom of information dispute. It refused a request to release the papers from Kirkhope, a notary public who wanted to use them in his graduate studies at Plymouth University. It was ordered to do so by the Information Commissioner. The Cabinet Office then appealed that decision in the Information Tribunal but lost."

What? A legal and valid request for the information was made and the Cabinet Office refused to supply anything and then, even when told to release them, went to a tribunal to try and keep this a secret from the public? Hardly fills one with confidence does it? So, lets continuing the Guardian story here is a list of government bills that have required the consent of the Queen or the Prince of Wales. It is not exhaustive and in only one case does it show whether any changes were made. It is drawn from data gleaned from two Freedom of Information requests.

The Queen
Agriculture (miscellaneous provisions) bill 1962
Housing Act 1996
Rating (Valuation Act) 1999
Military actions against Iraq (parliamentary approval bill) 1999 – consent not signified
Pollution prevention and control bill (1999)
High hedges bills 2000/01 and 2002/03
European Union bill 2004
Civil Partnership Act 2004
Higher Education Act 2004
National Insurance Contributions and Statutory Payments Act 2004
Identity cards bill 2004-06
Work and families bill 2005-06
Commons bill 2006
Animal Welfare Act 2006
Charities Act 2006
Child maintenance and other payments bill (2006/07)
Rating (Empty Properties) Act 2007
Courts, Tribunals and Enforcement Act 2007
Corporate Manslaughter and Corporate Homicide Act 2007
Fixed term parliaments bill (2010-12 session)
Prince Charles
Conveyancing and Feudal Reform (Scotland) Act 1970
Land Registration (Scotland Act) 1979
Pilotage bill 1987
Merchant Shipping and Maritime Security Act 1997
House of Lords Act 1999
Gambling bill 2004-05
Road Safety bill 2004-05

Natural environment and rural communities bill 2005-06
London Olympics bill 2005-06
Commons bill 2006
Charities Act 2006
Housing and regeneration bill 2007-08
Energy bill 2007-08
Planning bill 2007-08
Co-operative and community benefit societies and credit unions bill 2008-09
Local Democracy, Economic Development and Construction (Lords) 2008-09
Marine and Coastal Access (Lords) 2008-09
Coroners and justice bill 2008-09
Marine navigation aids bill 2009-2010
Wreck Removal Convention Act 2010-12"

Now some of these may look harmless enough but energy? Planning? ID cards? Housing? Higher education? Scotland? Europe? Agriculture? Rates? Commons? House of Lords? Local democracy? Environment? War? These look like pretty big issues to me for a family to be having influence over, that are lying to us by pretending they are simply a figure head and don't get involved.

CHAPTER 47

Lobbying

'After all, Wall Street is clearly the most powerful lobbying force on Capitol Hill. From 1998 through 2008, the financial sector spent over $5 billion in lobbying and campaign contributions to deregulate Wall Street.' - Bernie Sanders

Lobbying (also known widely as 'Persuasion') is the act of attempting to influence the actions, policies, or decisions of officials in their daily life, most often involving legislators or members of regulatory agencies. Lobbying is done by many types of people, associations and organized groups, including individuals in the private sector, corporations, fellow legislators or government officials, or advocacy groups (interest groups). Lobbyists may be among a legislator's constituencies, meaning a voter or bloc of voters within their electoral district, or not; they may engage in lobbying as a business, or not.

Professional lobbyists are people whose business is trying to influence legislation, regulation, or other government decisions, actions, or policies on behalf of a group or individual who hires them. Individuals and nonprofit organizations can also lobby as an act of volunteering or as a small part of their normal job (for instance, a CEO meeting with a representative about a project important to their company, or an activist meeting with their legislator in an unpaid capacity). Governments often define and regulate organized group lobbying that has become influential.

The ethics and morality of lobbying are dual-edged. Lobbying is often spoken of with contempt. The implication is that people with inordinate socioeconomic power are corrupting the law (twisting it away from fairness) in order to serve their own interests. When people who have a duty to act on behalf of others, such as elected officials with a duty to serve their constituents' interests or more broadly the public good, can benefit by shaping the law to serve the interests of some private parties, a conflict of interest exists. Many critiques of lobbying point to the potential for conflicts of interest to lead to agent misdirection or the intentional failure of an agent with a duty to serve an employer, client, or constituent to perform those duties. The failure of government officials to serve the public interest as a consequence of lobbying by special interests who provide benefits to the official is an example of agent misdirection.

The major parties in the UK spend heavily in the run up to a general election. The amount according to the Independent 17th April 2015 was *"a total of £45.5m spent by individual candidates and national parties. Of this, the parties spent about £31.5m and the candidates about £14m. A further £3m was spent by registered third parties.*

Of the £31.5m spent by parties, £16.7m was spent by the Conservatives, £8 m by Labour, and £4.8m by the Liberal Democrats. Just under a third – £9,095,766 – was spent on advertising, while £821,054 was spent on press conferences." So this begs the question, where does this money come from?

The Financial Times reports that between May 2010 and December 2014 the lobbying in the form of party donations from private individuals, companies and organisations was vast. £109.9 million to Labour, £90.1 million to the Conservatives and £23.5 million to the Lib Dems. Even the BNP received donations of just over £900 thousand.

But who are the big financial investors in political parties? Well, in that four years Labour received £34 million in 'public funds'(your taxes), £29 million of it from our old friend 'Short Money.'

Another £341 thousand a year came from the Electoral Commission (who at time of writing have fined me £200 for putting in a late declaration of having spent just £25 in a year, and a further £600 for telling them a day late that I did not receive any loans during an election by the way) in the form of something called the 'Public funds Policy Development Grant.' From the E.C.'s website they say *'Policy development grants are prescribed under the Political Parties, Elections and Referendums Act 2000 (PPERA). They are awarded to help parties in developing policies to include in manifestos for elections.*

The total grant is £2 million per year and distributed via a formula based on representation and performance at national and devolved legislature elections. To be eligible for the grant, a party must have at least two sitting Members of the House of Commons and have taken the oath of allegiance provided by the Parliamentary Oaths Act 1866.

There are currently eight political parties eligible for the grant:

- *Conservative Party*
- *Democratic Unionist Party – D.U.P.*
- *Labour Party*
- *Liberal Democrats*
- *Plaid Cymru – The Party of Wales*
- *Scottish National Party (SNP)*
- *SDLP (Social Democratic & Labour Party)*
- *Ulster Unionist Party*

The grant is distributed based on a formula drawn up by the Electoral Commission and approved by Parliament. The first £1 million is distributed equally amongst the eligible parties. The second £1 million is divided based on the proportion of the registered electorate where the party contest elections (England, Wales, Scotland and Northern Ireland), and weighted share of the vote received by each party in each part of the UK.

Policy development grants paid to political parties published. Published: 10 Oct 2013Policy development grants paid for financial year 2012-13:

Party	Total grant paid
Conservative and Unionist Party	*£397,097*
Democratic Unionist Party – D.U.P	*£136,816*
Labour Party	*£455,193*
Liberal Democrats	*£455,193*

Woah! Hold on a minute – these figures are from the Electoral Commission supposedly published on 10th October 2013. So how is it that the D.U.P., who are now in bed with the Conservatives since 2017, have shot their position up the league table to second, on something published four years previously? And way more worrying is the Conservatives are referred to as the Conservative and Unionist Party. Was that their title in 2013? Surely not. And the Electoral Commission are the ones who are supposedly in place to ensure fair play in party registration, party housekeeping, transparency and legal accountability in all elections. Hmmmmmmmm,

But I'm getting a little sidetracked. Outside of the gifts of public tax money the biggest individual donators are:- £48.5 million which comes to Labour from the Trade Unions, and £11.8 million from individuals with John Mills topping the list at £1.7 million, and Lord David Sainsbury, now Baron Sainsbury of Turville don't you know, coming in second with £1.2 mill. For the conservatives the biggest donations come from individuals with Michael Farmer (who?) coming top with a staggering personal donation in the four years of £4,232,042. So, who is he exactly? Metals tycoon, and treasurer for, wait for it, the Conservative party, where he (of course quite randomly and luckily) has been, in August 2014, nominated to become a working peer in the House of Lords and on 5 September 2014 was created a life peer as Baron Farmer, of Bishopsgate in the City of London. How nice for him. (Incidentally Baron Farmer of Bishopsgate has spoken extensively on social mobility and social issues. In November 2015, he contributed to a House of Lords debate on the impact of pornography by noting that "greater numbers of...teenage girls...in a leafy suburb of Surrey...were suffering from after effects of frequent anal sex, like incontinence" – but I digress.)

Another big donor to the Tories is James Lupton who has given over £2.5 million to them. He was created a life peer taking the title Baron Lupton, of Lovington in the County of Hampshire on 6 October 2015, and was appointed Commander of the Order of the British Empire (CBE) in the 2012 New Year Honours. Oh, I wonder how our great democracy, where we get one measly vote twice a decade, really works?

More worrying are the companies that make donations. Their ambition it is to make money it is disturbing that they can make huge donations to a political party on the assumption that they shall be thought kindly of an should that party get into power, and so benefit financially.

Now it gets way worse, because the really telling piece of information is not about who *is* donating, but who *isn't* donating. So, who do you think was the largest company to donate to the Conservatives between 2010 and 2014? A bank perhaps? Or maybe an oil industry giant? Or maybe a pharmaceutical company? Ok then, how about a property company? Insurance? Some organisation in the City? Perhaps a car manufacturer or road builder? Nope. None of those. Coming in at £2.3million was, drum roll please, JCB. JCB?! Ok – I know it's a pretty sizeable firm, but really? And who was second biggest donor? At a measly £827k it was Lycamobile. What? What is going on here? Lyca-bloomin'mobile? Second biggest company to donate to any political party?

If we think carefully about this revelation for just a moment and the realisation becomes clear that the really big players aren't making any donations at all - because they don't *need* to. The don't make donations to any political party because . . . .*they already control government policy.* Why would any money crazed corporation throw good money at any party when they already dictate policy? Route one to goal means there need not be any route two. Why try to influence from those below you when you already control the top?

This ten begs the question, where do the policies that our government generates actually come from? We know that your bog-standard MP doesn't have the influence, and the cabinet is shuffled around so often those guys could never have a proper grip on things, and I struggle to believe that it all comes to the Prime Minister in a dream in the middle of the night. The only place left for policy to come from is the Permanent Secretaries.

They are the ones who normally hold a role for long periods, they are not voted in, have comparative anonymity and so have the flexibility of proffering policies that are unpopular with the people. But where do *they* get the policies from? Well I'll tell you. 'Think tanks.'

CHAPTER 48

Chatham House

'The governance of Chatham House is overseen by its Council as laid out in its Charter and Bylaws. Council members are drawn from and elected by the Institute's membership. Governance responsibilities for the operation and management of the institute reside fully with the Council, led by its Chairman and Executive Committee, along with its Finance Committee.' – from the Chatham House website

In their website, Chatham House tells us *'Chatham House, the Royal Institute of International Affairs, is an independent policy institute based in London. Our mission is to help build a sustainably secure, prosperous and just world.'* Ahhh, they are so lovely, aren't they? Just like those nice people at Coca-Cola teaching the world to sing.

First clue. Chatham House is the *'Royal* Institute of National Affairs'. Royal means in this context to be under the patronage of a sovereign. Don't tell me the Queen has nothing to do with this.

From the Chatham House website:- *'Founded in 1920, Chatham House engages governments, the private sector, civil society and its members in open debate and confidential discussion on the most significant developments in international affairs. Each year, the institute runs more than 300 private and public events – conferences, workshops and roundtables – in London and internationally with partners. Our convening power attracts world leaders and the best analysts in their respective fields from across the globe.'* The key words in that paragraph are of course 'confidential discussion' and '300 private (and public) events'.

From the Milner-Fabian Conspiracy page we can read, *'Chatham House a.k.a. Royal Institute of International Affairs (RIIA) is the British sister organization of America's Council on Foreign Relations – the CFR. Like the CFR, Chatham House was created by the Milner Group in collaboration with the Fabian Society and associated interests.*

From inception, Chatham House was financed by banking and industrial interests including J. P. Morgan, Rockefeller and Rothschild. One of Chatham House's main objectives – which reflected those of the interests behind it – was to deconstruct the British Empire and incorporate it into a world organization aiming to establish world government.'

Although the majority of its activities are publicly accessible, it is, perhaps tellingly, for its policy on keeping certain meetings private that the organization is best known. The policy is called The Chatham House Rule and states:

"When a meeting, or part thereof, is held under the Chatham House Rule, participants are free to use the information received, but neither the identity nor the affiliation of the speaker(s), nor that of any other participant, may be revealed."

In the end, what is perhaps most intriguing to those who are interested in examining how power functions in society is not necessarily the secretive origins of a group like the Royal Institute of International Affairs, or even the way that it has covertly manipulated, shaped and controlled British foreign policy for decades, or how it has managed to wield such considerable influence over world affairs through its various branch organizations. Instead, what is most fascinating about Chatham House is that it is so very much open.

Many of its meetings and proceedings are publicly available. Its partners and corporate members are published on its website. Its journal is accessible to all. Its history, once shrouded in mystery, has been laid bare for over half a century thanks to the work of scholars like Quigley. And yet still, for all that, the RIIA is rarely discussed as an important power centre in 21st century society.

In some ways, perhaps this is its greatest accomplishment: to hide its enormous influence and its ongoing role in steering global geopolitics, not by hiding under a blanket of secrecy like Freemasonry, the Bilderberg

Group, Skull and Bones, or other secret societies, but by putting itself so much in the public spotlight that it seems mundane. It should be noted, after all, that this is precisely the way that Rhodes envisioned such an organization to function, and the continued existence and influence of that idea, manifested most openly in Chatham House, the CFR, and their brethren think tanks around the world, might serve as the perfect example of how some of the world's biggest secrets are hidden in plain sight.

To put that through Google translate, Chatham House is a club bristling with ex-ministers and the occasional Prime Minister (John Major used to be a member for example.) The Queen is invited along together with a plethora of influential member of banks and multinationals. They hold meetings, the key ones in secret, and decide what is best for the UK in policy. Of course, if you happen to be the CEO of an oil company you are likely to say that sticking with oil and gas is best and that a bit of fracking is a good thing for everyone. If you happen to be the CEO of a car manufacturer then obviously road building and low investment in public transport systems is best for everyone, or a top dog for a pharmaceutical company probably thinks that alternative medicines should be banned unless they have gone through a prohibitively expensive testing process (that the little companies cannot afford to do).

There are several levels of membership at Chatham House, but if you want to be in the top echelon that is going to set you back a cool '£50 thousand plus' a year. It is called the President's Circle. Now you might like to ask yourself why anyone would want to spend that kind of money? The answer is of course is that *this* is where much of the policy for the UK government is truly made. If you want the UK government to be discussing building new nuclear power stations or reintroducing neonicotinoid pesticides that are tearing our wildlife to shreds then this is the place to be, to get that message to across.

And where can we find the influence that Chatham House has with government – well on their own website of course. It's so up-front and in your face it's hard to imagine there is anything sinister going on at all. They say:-

'Government Relations. Chatham House delivers independent, policy-relevant analysis and new ideas to decision-makers around the world, much of it achieved through government briefings, high-level roundtables

and conferences, testimony to parliamentary committees and dissemination of the institute's research.'

Evidence to Parliament. Chatham House experts regularly provide evidence to parliamentary committees in the UK and elsewhere on a range of international issues'. Parliamentary Briefings. The institute's Parliamentary Briefings provide a forum for open and informed discussion between parliamentarians and Chatham House experts.'

They discuss and involve themselves in a huge number of issues, and the 'confidential discussion' and 'private events' ensure that we are not privy to all of them. I did find this about climate change, which is public but staggering in its content if you take a moment to think about it.

'Climate. Chatham House research on climate focuses around two broad areas: climate change and low-carbon development. Work on this topic includes research on global climate action and climate policy; the impact of livestock, animal agriculture and western diets on climate change; EU climate and energy policy; and managing the political economy of low-carbon development.' Huh? 'Impact of livestock, animal agriculture and western diets?' Is that the most pressing contributors to climate change? What about the flippin' cars man?! The oil? The proliferation of drilling in the last vestiges of wilderness we have on this planet? The fracking? The dash for gas? You don't suppose there would be a lot of oil and high rolling money people sitting in those expensive dialogue clubs do you? Well let's have a look shall we?

At the top of the pile we have the President's Circle. It costs £50,000+ (that's a minimum of £50,000) a year to be a member and the current members are:-

Ayman Asfari, Group Chief Executive, Petrofac, a Syrian-born English businessman, and the chief executive of Petrofac, a 'tax efficient' Jersey-registered multinational oilfield services company serving the oil, gas and energy production and processing industries His net worth is US$ 1.2 billion with an annual salary is $2,603,000. Holly Watt and David Pegg of the Guardian had this to say on 12th of May 2017: 'The Serious Fraud Office has launched an investigation into a company run by a major Conservative donor who is one of the prime minister's business ambassadors.

Petrofac, which provides services to the oil and gas industry, is being investigated by the SFO over suspected bribery, corruption and money laundering.

Its chief executive, Ayman Asfari, and his wife have given the Tories more than £700,000 since 2009, with the party receiving £40,000 last December. The Syrian-born businessman has been questioned under caution by the SFO, along with another member of Petrofac's senior management team.'

A billionaire, tax dodging oil man who donating like a mad-man to the Tories and is being investigated by the Serious Fraud Office, how nice!

Edward Atkin CBE, The Atkin Foundation - net worth of $300 million. Israel aligned, Atkin has made significant donations to the Conservative Party, as well as the climate sceptic think tank Global Warming Policy Foundation of which he is a board member. Hilary Aked of The Electronic Intifada on 14th March 2016 wrote 'New documents seen by The Electronic Intifada, obtained under freedom of information laws, show that the British Council has been quietly working to thwart the boycott, divestment and sanctions (BDS) movement in support of Palestinian rights. The Atkin Foundation, whose founders Celia and Edward Atkin have also supported BICOM, gave an undisclosed amount to BIRAX. The revelations about the government-funded program come as the UK attempts to ban local government from boycotting companies complicit in Israeli human rights abuses.'

So, a multi-millionaire trying to stop Palestinians getting aid, like medicines for their kids, and on a panel that attempts to disprove and block measures to combat climate change. What a charming man.

Celia Atkin, The Atkin Foundation, wife of Edward, fourth on the Telegraphs list of 'Wonder women' with a net worth of £80million, Celia made her fortune from redesigning babies feeding bottles.

Garvin Brown IV, Chairman of the Board, Brown-Forman Corporation, one of the largest American-owned companies in the spirits and wine business with annual revenues of $3.08 billion, he is Canadian and his family was worth $12.3billion in 2016.

A billionaire Canadian who flogs booze. Great.

The late Dr Carlos Bulgheroni, President, Bridas Corporation. Bridas

Corporation with a net worth ⌐US$ 4.8 billion (September 2016) is an independent oil and gas holding company based in Argentina. Since March 2010 it is 50% owned by China National Offshore Oil Corporation, 'Bridas began expanding into the Central Asian energy sector in 1987, and secured its first large-scale contract (gas exploration rights in Turkmenistan), in 1992. The BBC on 4th December 1997 told us *'CEO Carlos Bulgheroni was personally involved in negotiations between Bridas and the governments of Pakistan and Turkmenistan, as well as the ruling Taliban faction in Afghanistan, to build the Trans-Afghanistan Gas Pipeline'*

A billionaire Argentinian oil man who is dealing with the Taliban. Lovely!

Tim Bunting, an ex-partner at Goldman Sachs Bank Tim moved to Balderton Capital in 2005 which is a London, UK-based venture capital firm that invests early-stage, primarily in Europe-based technology and Internet start-up companies. It only has 25 employees but has a net worth of $2.2 billion.

A billionaire venture capital ex-banker.

Louis G. Elson, ex-investment banker with Goldman Sachs and Co he became Co-Founder, Palamon Capital Partners, a private equity and venture capital firm specializing in investments in medium-sized lower middle market companies and growth capital investments. With a net equity of 1.3 billion euros. In January 2017, Palamon acquired a majority share in the Swedish retailer Happy Socks, valuing the company at US$85.4 million.

A billionaire venture capital ex-banker. Are we starting to see a pattern forming here?

Richard Hayden, Non-Executive Chairman, Towerbrook Capital Partners (UK) LLP which is an investment firm specializing in direct funds investments, with funds raised from investors of $9.4 billion. He was also a non-Executive Director of Deutsche Börse, Non-Executive Director of Abbey National Bank, LLC, and Vice Chairman of GSC Group where he had responsibility for the European Mezzanine Funds and the Global CLO business. Prior to that, he was Deputy Chairman of Goldman Sachs International, where he was head of investment banking for EMEA and Chairman of the Global Credit Committee.

A billionaire investment specialist and ex-banking executive.

André Hoffmann, Vice-Chairman, Board of Roche Holding is the holding company for F. Hoffmann-La Roche AG is a Swiss multinational healthcare company that operates worldwide under two divisions which are Pharmaceuticals and Diagnostics. It's annual profits were CHF 9.576 billion (Swiss francs) in 2016, and their net worth is CHF 35.5 billion.

A billionaire pharmaceutical executive officer.

Hon. Marc E. Leland, President, Marc E Leland and Associates, USA, an investment advisory firm. He is Attorney and Co-Chairman of German Marshall Fund of the United States, an honorary member of the Panel of Senior Advisers at Chatham House, national advisor at the Centre for the Study of the Presidency and Congress, director of Noble Corporation, an offshore drilling contractor based in London, United Kingdom, with revenues of $2.302 billion in 2016. He is also former assistant secretary of the Treasury for International Affairs, senior advisor to the Mutual Balanced Force Reduction Negotiations, General Counsel of the Peace Corps, managing director of the J. Paul Getty and Gordon P. Getty Trusts, member of the Board of the U.S. Institute of Peace, member of Council on Foreign Relations and International Institute for Strategic Studies.

An American billionaire oil man. And blimey! What doesn't this guy try to get involved in? I'll bet he's on the school board as well.

Robert Ng, Chairman, Sino Land Company Ltd is a major developer and property companies in Hong Kong, a member of Sino Group owned by Singaporean Ng Teng Fong family. His net worth was $9.7 billion in June 2017, jointly owned with his brother Philip Ng. The brothers are the wealthiest Singaporean billionaires by net worth (world rank: 150).

Billionaire Singaporean property developer.

Sir Simon Robertson, Founder, Simon Robertson Associates LLP. He worked for Kleinwort Benson (a private investment bank) for 34 years, where he eventually served as Chairman of the Board. He then worked as President of Goldman Sachs Europe. In 2004, and he became Chairman of Board of Directors of Rolls-Royce in January 2005. He has a net worth of £95million.

A billionaire banker.

Next down we come to the Director's Circle which only requires a measly £25,000 a year to sit on. Its current members are (briefly as this gets tedious)

Baha Bassatne, Executive Chairman, BB Energy Holdings NV. (Oil infrastructure and funding)

David Blood, Private Investor (Goldman Sachs Bank)

Gavin Boyle, Private Investor Derby Hospital Chief on £190,000 a year (Daily Telegraph)

Sir Trevor Chinn CVO, Senior Adviser, CVC Capital Partners CVC Capital Partners is a private equity firm with approximately US$80 billion in secured commitments across European and Asian private equity, credit and growth funds. In total, the CVC Group manages over US$52 billion of assets.

Victor Chu, Chairman, First Eastern Investment Group. Investment, of course.

Robert Conway, Partner, Goldman Sachs – Banking.

Sir Mick Davis, The Davis Foundation - Charity with varied aims including the environment and education. Hurrah!

Helen L. Freeman - Real estate.

Ronald M. Freeman, Corporate Board Director - Real estate.

Michael Hoffman, Co-Founder, Palamon Capital Partners, UK - (again! Private equity)

Timothy Jones, Private Investor - Barrister in major planning debacles

Karim Khairallah, Managing Director, Oaktree Capital - Management Investment and corporate advice.

Sara Burch Khairallah – wife of said Karim (why exactly would you need both you and your wife on the committee? To double your voting power?)

Chris Rokos, Private Investor hedge funds worth more than $1 billion.

Ron Sandler CBE, Chairman, Centaur Media – marketing and financial services with a turnover of £71million in 2015.

Richard Sharp, Private Investor. This article in the press says it all for me. *'Richard Sharp: Bank of England denies rule breach.*

Fresh concerns may be raised about a multi-millionaire former Goldman Sachs banker, who was controversially appointed to sit on the

Bank of England's most senior regulatory committee by George Osborne last year.

It went on to say that documents obtained by the Bureau reveal that Richard Sharp, who was appointed an external member of the Bank's Financial Policy Committee, FPC, attended the Conservative fundraising party last summer just weeks after giving assurances to parliament that he would not let his past political connections compromise his independence.

They added that the bureau can further reveal that the banker, who has donated more than £402,420 to the Tories, has since become a partner in Roundshield, a firm that lends to distressed businesses and buys assets from them, including residential property, care-related real estate and agricultural machinery.

Sharp's position as one of four partners in this commercial venture may raise fresh questions about his access to privileged and confidential Bank papers on UK financial stability and mortgage lending.

Edward Siskind, Founder & CEO, Cale Street Partners - ex-Goldman Sachs – fund management.

Lance West, ex-Partner and Managing Director of Goldman Sachs - Senior Managing Director, Centerbridge Partners Centerbridge Partners - a multi-strategy private investment firm focused on leveraged buyouts and distressed securities. The firm manages over $25 billion of assets and is based in New York City.

The Lionel Curtis Group is next down at only £10,000 a year to join and has 30 members

and at the bottom of the pile we have the William Pitt Group at a paltry £5,000 a year and which has 45 members.

And what do all these good people have in common? They all make more money than is good for them, and they are all striving for more.

The results of these discussions, *'by the corporations for the corporations'*, are then fed to the relevant permanent secretaries and they, in turn, feed the policies to their relevant departmental minister. Easy! And the government, who you made all that effort to vote for, doesn't play any role other than telling us all the bad news. They have no more power than the sergeant major telling us the officer's decisions that have as much thought and compassion for the common man as wanting us all to go over the top of the trench into a hail of machine gun fire. Again.

These powerful individuals may be making huge donations to political parties because they want to be on the honours list, but not one of these big corporations makes a single significant donation to any party. They don't need to. They already have whatever party comes into power in their pocket because that is how the system works. A puppet government.

Now, at this point I fully expect some of you to put this book down, thinking I am some kind of radical loony. I can sympathise with that sentiment, for when I was first told that the prime minister wasn't at the top, I thought the person who told me was crazy. I had had that programming put into me so deeply when I was five, and it had been reinforced on pretty much every six o'clock news since then. It took an effort, in my case about two years of researching and considering, to change all that. But once I had re-evaluated and established the truth, all the pieces started to fall into place. It took a while - but man, it was worth it!

CHAPTER 49

The shadow government

'Men fear thought as they fear nothing else on earth -- more than ruin – more even than death.... Thought is subversive and revolutionary, destructive and terrible, thought is merciless to privilege, established institutions, and comfortable habit. Thought looks into the pit of hell and is not afraid. Thought is great and swift and free, the light of the world, and the chief glory of man.' - Bertrand Russell

It's a rather simple and clever trick that dupes us. To choose a subject dear to my heart, if BP came straight to us and said 'OK, we want to frack the hell out of the UK including under your house. Yeah, we know it all went horribly wrong in Pennsylvania USA, and Queensland Australia, where there is loads of space and low populations but still thousands of people got sick and the very nature around communities started dying off because of poisoned water, air and rain, but this is a really good thing for Britain', we would stick two fingers up to them and tell them to go 'frack' themselves.

If British Aerospace and Rockwell came to us and said 'listen, we've got a shed load of bombs that are going to go to waste unless we use them so we are going to invade some tin-pot country because we think their democracy stinks' we'd give them the finger.

But because these horrible corporate crimes don't come from BP or British Aerospace (or Roche, or Smith-Kline-Beecham, or HSBC, or Pepsi-Cola, or Toyota or ICI or blah blah) directly, but appears to come from our government who we voted in, and who most people, despite their own common sense and observations, believe have our best interests at heart, we accept the crimes of these money generating corporations.

Using fracking as the example, the vile process is backed by a tidal wave of propaganda in the press about how we shall all making a fortune, and anyone who is against is just some sort of hippy loony, we just go along with it. After all we have busy lives and it's the job of the government to take care of these things for us anyway – right?

You shall read in the press that 'We need to be self-sufficient in energy and don't want to be dependent on Russia.' That seems like a perfectly reasonable sentiment, it's just a pity it isn't true. We do get gas from Russia, but not so much that we couldn't shop around for other sources. 'We cannot obtain the energy we need from green renewable sources.' The truth is we could easily get all our energy form renewables but the problem is the way the government have been dragging their heels. They pretend to be doing everything in their power to introduce renewable energy schemes, while doing virtually the opposite, ignoring real opportunities like deep sea tidal turbines and algae cultures. Why? Because the corporations want to crack on with oil as there is pots of money in it for them still, and don't need the competition, and they control Chatham House, that controls the Permanent Secretaries, who control cabinet, who control M.P.'s who control you. Are you getting this yet?

To give you some evidence of the kind of oil relationships that go on the Guardian 20th May 2015 printed *"Revealed: BP's close ties with the UK government"* which said:

"At that meeting, BP was assured by the Department of Energy and Climate Change (Decc) that it would do what it could, with lawyers from the Treasury, the Foreign Office and the business department, to find "an operational solution" to allow BP to reopen the major North Sea gas field it owned jointly with Iran despite the EU's sanction regime against that country. The solution, a couple of years later, would be for Iran's share of the profits to be held by the British government in a frozen account.

The Guardian went on to say that these extraordinary insights into the extreme closeness between the British government and one of its biggest companies came to light after a Freedom of Information (FoI) request, and that nobody, perhaps, should be much surprised by it. After all, they have shared mutual interests since the first British involvement in commercial oil exploration in the Gulf over 100 years ago.. . . .

They told us of the 'revolving door between BP and government.' It earned the company the moniker Blair Petroleum under Labour the governments. It continues to revolve today, with former BP chief executive Lord Browne brought in to the Cabinet Office by the Conservatives in 2010 to help appoint business leaders to new boards of each government department, and former BP executive John Manzoni now chief executive of the Civil Service.

They went on saying that BP had appointed the recently-retired head of the UK's secret intelligence services to its board. The former MI6 spy chief, Sir John Sawers, *would bring invaluable geopolitical experience*, said BP's chairman.

The significance of all this for climate change is profound. Being embedded in Whitehall, it appears, has given the oil and gas multinationals confidence that the government will not act on emissions in a way that will restrict their growth.

BP experimented with moving towards renewables, only to retreat after a shareholders' savaging, says the oil companies know climate change represents "an existential threat" to their business.

"They've worked it out. The only people who have done as much thinking as them on this are the military. BP is certain that government won't act on their obligation to keep the rise in global temperatures below 2C and in fact will be allies to keep the revenues flowing."

BP's hold on the government is so tight they don't even need to use the Chatham House to Permanent Secretary route although there is bound to be assistance from the oil riddled committee.

This jiggery-pokery is often summed up in the term 'shadow government' where it is understood that the government you see is simply a piece of theatre, that even many of the players (M.P.s) have no concept of. A puppet show aimed at bamboozling the people into believing they are living in a true democracy when the decisions are in fact being made by a very small number of extremely wealthy individuals, who unilaterally decide policy that benefits themselves.

From Wikipedia: *The shadow government (cryptocracy, secret government, or invisible government) . . .theories based on the notion that real and actual political power resides not with publicly elected representatives (for example, the United States Congress) but with private individuals who are exercising power behind the scenes, beyond the scrutiny of democratic institutions. According to this belief, the official elected government is in reality subservient to the shadow government who are the true executive power.*

Shadow government theories often propose that the government is secretly controlled by foreign elements (such as aliens the Vatican and Jesuits), internal minorities (such as the Jews, moneyed interests and central banks, or Freemasons), or globalist elites and supranational organizations, who seek to manipulate policy.

Well, I'm not exactly saying it is the aliens (although both the Russian and American governments have departments dealing with extra-terrestrial activities, and maybe being run by aliens would be better than what we currently have?) but the other sources of control look highly likely. The Vatican? Well, the Pope did once split the world in two and gave half to Spain and the other half to Portugal (who then fought over a disagreement of where the line was!) The Jesuits? Well, they are pretty influential in the Catholic Church. The Jews? Well, Hitler obviously thought they were a pretty big problem in Germany in the 1930's. The Central banks? That is where my money is! The Freemasons? Well they have got their logo on the U.S. dollar and MI5 badge so they must be up to something.

Or how about the Bilderberg Group? Joe Sommerlad of the Independent on Friday 1 June 2018 had this to say:-

"The secretive Bilderberg Group gathers for its annual meeting next week, which this year takes place in Turin, Italy.

Joe explained that the members consist of a collective of elite North American and European politicians, business leaders, financiers and academics and that the group has attracted a good deal of suspicion over the last half-century, with conspiracy theorists confidently asserting that its members are plotting the New World Order and are hell-bent on global domination.

Joe continues, 'protesters who believe the Bilderbergers represent a "shadow world government" regularly picket their yearly meet-ups, creating a need for high security at all times, but attendees insist the group is simply a debating society taking place outside the glare of the political spotlight'.

He tells us that the group publishes its guest list the day before its annual get together - between 120 and 150 are invited by its steering committee - along with a list of the subjects they intend to discuss as a gesture towards transparency. This typically consists of broad issues like macroeconomic concerns, the threat of terrorism and cyber-security.

'No minutes are taken, however, and the outcome of their discussions are not made public, hence the assumption that they are a sinister cabal of the rich and powerful with something to hide.

The group hoped to revive a spirit of transatlantic brotherhood based on political, economic and military cooperation, necessary during the Cold War as the USSR tightened its iron grip on its eastern satellites."

One of the most concise academic papers critical of Bilderberg's 'Deep State' role in influencing geopolitical events out of the public spotlight was written in 1996 by Prof. Mike Peters of Leeds Metropolitan University and published in Lobster. Entitled "The Bilderberg Group and the Project for European Unification", Peters expresses incredulity that so few academics have examined the Bilderberg Group's international financial and political lobbying clout but closely examines links between the post-war effort for a united Europe and specific individuals connected with the Bilderberg Group.

In 2005, former chairman Etienne Davignon discussed accusations of the group striving for a one-world government with the BBC: *"It is unavoidable and it doesn't matter. There will always be people who believe in conspiracies but things happen in a much more incoherent fashion. ... When people say this is a secret government of the world I say that if we were a secret government of the world we should be bloody ashamed of ourselves.'*

And then we have the Skull and Bones group, featured in theories claiming the society plays a role in a conspiracy for world control. Theorist, Alexandra Robbins suggests that Skull and Bones is a branch of the Illuminati, founded by German university alumni following the Order's suppression in their native land by Karl Theodor, Elector of Bavaria, with the support of Frederick the Great of Prussia. It has been strongly suggested that Skull and Bones controls the Central

Intelligence Agency, and has had many recent Presidents of the U.S.A. as its members, including President Bush (senior) and Alphonso Taft, the latter Secretary of War under Ulysses S Grant and the father of 27th president William Howard Taft, George W Bush, the 43rd president; John Kerry, Democratic presidential candidate and Secretary of State.

Others known to have been members include actor Paul Giamatti; William F Buckley, Republican commentator and editor of The National Review; McGeorge Bundy, advisor to John F Kennedy; Morrison Waite and Potter Stewart, both Supreme Court Justices; Frederick Wallace Smith, founder of FedEx; Lyman Spitzer, theoretical physicist and space telescope pioneer; and William Camp, godfather of American football.

And how about Freemasonry? After all their logo is found on the U.S. one-dollar bill (the pyramid) and also forms the MI5 logo of a pyramid with the all seeing eye at the top. Research involving Freemasonry reveals that hundreds of conspiracy theories have been described since the late 18th century. Generally, these theories fall into three distinct categories: political (usually involving allegations of control of government, particularly in the United States and the United Kingdom), religious (usually involving allegations of anti-Christian or Satanic beliefs or practices), and cultural (usually involving popular entertainment.) Many conspiracy theory writers have connected Freemasons and the Knights Templar, with worship of the Devil, based on accurate interpretations of the doctrines of those organizations.

Of the claims that Freemasonry exerts control over politics, perhaps the best-known example is the New World Order theory, but there are others. These mainly involve aspects and agencies of the United States government, but actual events outside the US such as (from Wikipedia) the Propaganda Due scandal in Italy. Also named P2, it was a Masonic lodge under the Grand Orient of Italy, founded in 1877. However its Masonic charter was withdrawn in 1976, and it transformed into a clandestine, pseudo-Masonic, ultra-right organization operating in contravention of Article 18 of the Constitution of Italy that banned secret associations. In its latter period, during which the lodge was headed by Licio Gelli, P2 was implicated in numerous Italian crimes and mysteries, including the collapse of the Vatican-affiliated Banco Ambrosiano, the murders of journalist Mino Pecorelli and banker Roberto Calvi, and corruption cases within the nationwide bribe scandal Tangentopoli. P2 came to light through the investigations into the collapse of Michele Sindona's financial empire.

P2 was sometimes referred to as a "state within a state" or a "shadow government". The lodge had among its members prominent journalists, members of parliament, industrialists, and military leaders—including Silvio Berlusconi, who later became Prime Minister of Italy, the Savoy pretender to the Italian throne Victor Emmanuel and the heads of all three Italian intelligence services are often used to lend credence to claims.

The Observer Business. Nick Mathiason on Sun 7 Dec 2003 01.29 GMT wrote

'Who killed Calvi? Reopening the inquiry into the 'suicide' of 'God's banker' has exposed links with the mafia, masons and Vatican fraud.'

In 1833, John Quincy Adams wrote to Edward Livingston, explaining his anti-Masonic stance in the wake of the Morgan Affair said *"I do conscientiously and sincerely believe that the Order of Freemasonry, if not the greatest, is one of the greatest moral and political evils under which the Union is now laboring.'*

Not convinced? Well these influential people of substance and governmental knowledge had this to say about it all:

"The real menace of our Republic is the invisible government, which like a giant octopus sprawls its slimy legs over our cities, states and nation."—John Hylan, Mayor of New York City, 1922

In their book 'Prolonging the agony' (where a meticulously cross-referenced and strongly evidenced case is made of how a select band of just five powerful men in Britain pushed Germany into the first world war with a view to crushing the greatest competitor to the British Empire. They then ensured the war went on long enough to annihilate Germany by, amongst other things, supplying them with coal, food and ore from the Empire at hugely inflated and profitable (to them) prices, so that Germany could maintain the struggle until completely destroyed (accidentally leaving a vacuum for Hitler to fill.) All of this was done with complete disregard for the lives of valiant soldiers who continued to be slaughtered in the trenches as a result) Jim MacGregor and Gerry Docherty write *'The Anglo-American Establishment, the expanding Secret Elite so effectively identified by Professor Carrol Quigley, placed power and influence into the hands chosen by friendship and loyalty to their cause, rather than merit, and have controlled politics, banking, the press and much else in Britain and the United States for the past century. Sometimes referred to obliquely as the 'Deep State', the 'money people', the 'money-power', the 'hidden power' or the 'men behind the curtain' these utterly ruthless individuals amassed vast profits for their companies, banks, and industries through the war against Germany. Their complicity in the sinking of the Lusitania and its cover-up demonstrated just how far their influence extended inside both Whitehall and the White House.'*

From the Platform of President, Theodore Roosevelt's Progressive ("Bull Moose") Party stated that: *"Behind the ostensible government sits enthroned an invisible government owing no allegiance and acknowledging no responsibility to the people."*

Ron Paul, former U.S. Representative, November 2016 (following Donald Trump presidential election win) said *"But quite frankly there is an outside source which we refer to as the 'deep state' or the 'shadow government'. There is a lot of influence by people which are actually more powerful than our government itself, our president."*

Edward Bernays, the "father of public relations," writing in his influential 1928 book, Propaganda, said, *"The conscious and intelligent manipulation of the organized habits and opinions of the masses is an important element in democratic society. Those who manipulate this unseen mechanism of society constitute an invisible government which is the true ruling power of our country. We are governed, our minds are molded, our tastes formed, our ideas suggested, largely by men we have never heard of."*

To provide a stark recent example of how the banks and corporations exert their power on government we need look no further than the heartbreaking story that unraveled in Greece in 2015. The Syriza party had only first stood in elections in 2004 and their power had swiftly grown, based on the platform of fighting bank-imposed austerity measures and the strangle hold of debt over the county, rising to become the leading party in the 2014 elections.

Faced with the choices of greater debt and austerity or opting out of Europe altogether Syriza's parliamentary leader Alexis Tsipras put a referendum to the people. Mark Lowen of BBC News, Athens, takes up the story on 11th July 2015.

"Just over a week ago, Alexis Tsipras stepped on to a podium in Syntagma Square in Athens. In his trademark open-necked white shirt, his sleeves rolled up, he punched the air.

"I call on you to say a big 'no' to ultimatums, 'no' to blackmail," he cried. "Turn your back on those who would terrorise you."

His thousands of fans roared in approval. The Greek public followed his lead and 61% voted "oxi" ("No").

Mark then tells us that if we roll forward just seven days, Greece's prime minister signed the very measures he had fought against. Corporate tax and VAT to rise, privatisations to be pursued, public sector pay to be lowered and early retirement phased out. Mark says that in a late-night speech to parliament, a chastened Alexis Tsipras compared negotiations to a war, in which battles are fought and lost.

"It is our national duty to keep our people alive and in the eurozone", he said. *There was not a fist-punch in sight.*

Mark told us that the old adage of a week being a long time in politics could not be more relevant. *'But even for us Greece-watchers, the past few days have left us scratching our heads.'*

"When we started five months ago, it was very difficult to realise how this thing that we call the European Union was going to behave," says Dimitris Tsoukalas, general secretary at the interior ministry.

"We, the government, thought we could convince them that a country in this mess could take a completely different path. But it wasn't possible."

He sighs, flicking through the recently signed document of reform measures. ***"We couldn't overcome the bankers and northern European elite who have absolute power in this continent."***

What a nightmare – a government that cannot overcome the 'absolute power of the bankers and Northern European elite.' One has to question Mr. Tsipras' quick turnaround from winning the result he wanted so badly and worked so hard for, to fully capitulating, (even giving away more than he was asked for) within three days. What happened? There is clearly a part of this story that we don't know. Was he threatened? His family's health and well-being put at stake perhaps? Blackmailed? Shown the JFK film but taken from 'the grassy knowle?'

Well, something drastic certainly happened. Some powerful wealthy people stood to lose lot of money, so it's not difficult to imagine.

And there we have it. The government is a charade, a show to encourage you to believe you are exercising an important democratic right when you vote . I have seen a fridge magnet that succinctly stated, 'British Democracy - the illusion of choice in return for the loss of freedom.' The bit you missed, that would help you better understand what you are really watching, is before ministers are seen jabbering away on the TV a bell should ring with a voice on a loud speaker announcing, 'ladies and gentlemen, please take your seats, the performance will start in two minutes.' Then two big red velvet curtains should open from the middle to reveal a surreally lit stage.

CHAPTER 50

The role of the banks

'I believe that banking institutions are more dangerous to our liberties than standing armies.' - Thomas Jefferson

We all know about banks right? We've seen all the adverts on the box, black horses running through people's lives creating opportunity and stability, growing trees, happy smiling cartoon children, that whacky black guy riding around on a swan, bankers taking the role of 'the wizard of Oz' and in every other way possible suggesting caring prosperity, and a rosy future for you and your family.

When I took out my first mortgage, I was thrilled to think that I had been entrusted with a loan that, without it, would have made the buying of my first house an impossibility. It was suggested to me that I should take out an endowment mortgage as this was likely to accumulate and pay off the loan early, perhaps as soon as twelve years away. It didn't actually work out that well, but I was one of the lucky ones. I got in early enough while the return rates were fairly good, and despite coasting for the last few years I scraped over the bar on my mortgages twenty fifth birthday.

But then I got to thinking, why was the loan over such a huge period? I mean twenty-five years is a huge chunk of your life to be paying interest on a loan. I looked into it and it transpired that if I had increased by endowment by a meagre twenty pounds a month the loan would have been paid off after fifteen years. And the reason that option was never discussed with me? Because the upper echelons of the western world thrive on debt. The longer they can keep you in that position the more they can siphon off the cream of all your efforts and striving to make a reasonable life for yourself. Like a tapeworm in your gut they take what they want while leaving just enough for you to survive, thereby also ensuring their own survival.

Not many people realise that by the time they have paid off their mortgage they have, while buying one house for themselves, actually paid enough to also buy two for the bank, for doing no more than a bit of paperwork. Now here is the really scary bit. The money that the bank 'lends' you never actually existed. The bank is allowed to loan ten times what they have, which by definition means that 90% of the money is made up from nothing. Now if you happen to default on your loan, the bank doesn't only want the 10% they actually had, but the whole 100% including the 90% they never had.

It is rarely understood that the American great depression of 1929 was purposefully orchestrated by the banks. In the 1920's the Federal Reserve Bank, which is not a government agency but a private bank, printed a massive increase to the money supply of 60%, allowing people to get into debt. This was combined with the creation of 'margin loans.' These loans enabled anyone to purchase stock market shares with just ten percent of the market value paid, with the broker holding the other ninety percent on account.

The purchaser would receive the whole of the profits from 100% of the shares which obviously made them very popular as, with a thousand dollars someone could own ten thousand dollars' worth of shares. However, there was a nasty and orchestrated catch. If the stock dipped in value the balance could be called in with only twenty four hours' notice. This is known as a 'margin call.' The banking cartel, which included J.P. Morgan and the Rothschild family, quietly offloaded their own shares from these stocks and then on October 24th 1929 they started calling in the 'margin loans.' The result was that everyone who held this stock was forced to sell within 24 hours, and as they were all selling on the same day the market crashed. Sixteen thousand independent banks went bust, losing all of the peoples' money that they held.

The Federal Reserve Bank then reduced the money supply so no-one could borrow their way out of trouble and people were forced to sell everything they owned to cover their debts. The banking cartel moved in and bought up property, farms and businesses at a few cents in the dollar, creating the vast wealth for themselves that they still hold on to today, at the cost of everyone else.

Louis McFadden who spoke out against President Herbert Hoover and the banking cartel was murdered by poisoning for his troubles. What nice people they are!

And guess what? Those same wealthy banking families now make up the International Monetary Fund, whom our government regularly borrows from and is in debt to the tune of two trillion pounds. Think about this for a moment. A country borrowing money from a ruthless family cartel, who have purposefully made the lives of millions of people so utterly miserable that many committed suicide? That can't be good can it?

Now that we have the insight that the corporations run the government policy making machine, let's have a quick peek at the list of 'easily solvable problems' that I wrote about all those years ago and see if we can now spot why the fixes are not forthcoming.

If you want to refresh yourself read Chapter 19 - Financial Meltdown.

Nick Mathiason in The Guardian on Sunday 28 December 2008 told us

"It was the year the neo-liberal economic orthodoxy that ran the world for 30 years suffered a heart attack of epic proportions. Not since 1929 has the financial community witnessed 12 months like it. Lehman Brothers went bankrupt. Merrill Lynch, AIG, Freddie Mac, Fannie Mae, HBOS, Royal Bank of Scotland, Bradford & Bingley, Fortis, Hypo and Alliance & Leicester all came within a whisker of doing so and had to be rescued. Western leaders, who for years boasted about the self-evident benefits of light-touch regulation, had to sink trillions of dollars to prevent the world bank system collapsing."

Of all the people who shouldn't need the assistance of public money supplied by a complicit government it has to be the banks. The fact that these banks received vast sums of our money without any obstacle tells you all you need to know about the hold they have over government.

CHAPTER 51

So why have elections?

'If the United States of America or Britain is having elections, they don't ask for observers from Africa or from Asia. But when we have elections, they want observers.' - Nelson Mandela

An obvious question must surely be, having put all this effort into proving there is if there is no point in voting why have *I* been participating in the elections? Well, firstly, I am not beholden to any major party and can say what I like.

Second, elections provide something a platform for me to put the case in this book to people who are engaged in the process, in an attempt to open their eyes.

Third. the ultimate goal is to start an avalanche of support by the people to, rightly, start demanding true, direct and crowd sourced democracy. Should this happen in great enough numbers, the existing corrupt power base would become eroded and ultimately destroyed. The result would wrench power from the hands of the big parties, and their corporate overlords, who have had it all their way for far too long.

Once exposed, the complacency and willingness to deceive the people should make further support for these self-serving organisations untenable. I believe the old system is at a critical tipping point as people awaken and question, but it had better happen soon as we are running short on time.

Elections are the key as collectively we do hold the power for radical change if we would just stop swallowing the lie and act in unison. People should have the opportunity to choose genuinely independent candidates pledged to assist them along the first faltering steps of introducing a true direct democracy.

It is admirable to be putting out the fires that the corporations, approved by their puppet government arrangement, are starting. But it is an impossible task to attend to them all. Problems can be started behind closed doors in a few hours, that then require thousands of people to sacrifice years of their lives by protesting, writing letters, marching and hindering in an attempt to put things right. Meantime another, and yet another greed driven problem can be started, over-stretching resources of those wanting to stop the lunacy and fighting for common sense to prevail.

The solution is not to fight the fires, but get to the heart of the system and confiscate the matches. Make the all-important changes from within by creating a system that truly represents, and is run by, the people. The way this can be easily achieved, but what is surprisingly difficult is the reprogramming of people to believe just how simple it really is.

The hardest prison to escape from is one where you cannot see the bars.

CHAPTER 52

Closer to true democracy

'We have a Scottish Parliament and National Assembly for Wales, both elected by fairer votes - involving proportional representation.' - Charles Kennedy

For people to feel truly enfranchised in the running of the country changes must be made. There are many small steps that can be made toward what must surely be the ultimate goal. The people being in control of their own affairs.

A first step for many is proportional representation, where the number of seats won by a party directly correlates to the number of votes cast for it. At least then the smaller parties would have some sort of a voice reflected by some amount of column inches in the press and the start to obtain a power base from which to grow from.

A better step would be to do away with political parties completely. At least people would then vote for the person who they thought had the greatest integrity and drive to get the job done, and each candidate would politically live or die by the peoples' assessment of their own actions and energy they put into the job. Debates in the house would become genuine discussions between representatives who were truly doing their best for their supporters on an honest, open, free and fair basis.

But this still wouldn't make the change necessary if the permanent secretaries are still feeding an agenda to a select body such as the government cabinet is today. This also still means that you and I would be relying on a representative to make decisions for us. What do you want for dinner tonight? You probably know that don't you? Does your M.P. know better? I don't think so. Surely, you'd rather pick your menu yourself? And that is my point.

To gain a better understanding what a people want, ask them. An obstacle is the establishment deciding how much authority should be given to the people. Switzerland has the best democratic model in the world. If 100,000 people do not like a decision made by the government, they can force a referendum for everyone to become involved, and the result is binding on the government. If someone wants to start an initiative and can collect the support of 100,000 people, they can force the government to undertake a referendum.

These figures are so large that, pre-internet days, it was very difficult for anyone to gather that level of support. Since the advent of the internet this threshold has become increasingly easy, but still quite difficult. As a result, there is talk in Switzerland of raising the bar, which tells you all you need to know about the grip on power that the minority wishes to preserve, even in Switzerland.

In the U.K., by raising 200,000 signatures, people do have the opportunity to force the government to debate something once in the house, but then the subject can be dropped like a hot brick or, if merited, voted on but only by the representatives in Westminster, again.

To properly engage people, the involvement needs to be way higher, with the implementation of a direct democracy that demotes the Government to the 'back office', carrying out the will of the people, to whom any country really belongs.

Benefit 1 – Decisions faithfully reflect the will of the majority.

Enabling the people to take an active role in the making of decisions for their country would remove the power from the hands of the few and place it in the hands of the many. As most people want the same things (peace, fairness, equality, opportunity, freedom, a future for their children etc.) by giving everyone the opportunity to participate, these wants would most likely come to the fore, resulting in policy that positively affects all of us and the world around us.

Benefit 2 – Corruption by big business would be removed.

This system would not be corruptible, as 45 million adults would be participating, and it would be impossible to influence that number other than by bogus and contentious reporting in the press. That is why fair and unbiased reporting and a free source of all information pertinent to any decision being made is a requirement of any true democracy. A system that involves the population at large wouldn't suffer so severely from corporate outside influences or vested interests that currently and sinisterly lurk above the governmental veneer.

Benefit 3 – True participation would create feelings of enfranchisement.

By letting the people take control of their country, a spark of national pride and interest that is sadly lacking in Britain today would be lit. Being a voting and participating shareholder in 'Great Britain plc' would encourage people to take an active interest in the day to day running and decisions affecting their country and their future. Conversations with your family and friends about any issue would no longer just be a conversation, collectively you would be your own parliament assessing and deciding the future for yourselves and your country.

Benefit 4 – A huge participation means an accurate result.

Allowing a small handful of individuals to make decisions cannot, and will never be as accurate as taking the opinions of the whole voting population, even if there were no corruption or hidden agendas. Further, by making the answers from the people incremental, rather than binary and by applying simple mathematics, such as the drawing of a probability curve and finding the mean, the general will of the people can be ascertained and the direction the majority wish things to go can easily be established. Statistically speaking, the larger the sample the more accurate is likely to be the result. Currently the number of people involved in making any particular decision on which we must all abide can be as few as 5, or one nine millionth of the voting population, or, graphically, the same proportion as one second is in 1000 days.

Benefit 5 – No pledges or manifesto.

The removal of 'party politics' ensures that there would no longer be any need for large manifestos full of policies and election promises as there would be no governmental party in power.

Benefit 6 – Power to the people.

The power of government would be curtailed in that each member of parliament (should the people decide they still want those), while welcome to enter into the discussions, and having some influence as being an elected voice, would only have the power of a single vote in a voting population of around 45 million, ensuring that debate is encouraged but the people would ultimately make the decisions. After all you are an adult, it is your country, you pay the tax that funds everything, so it is only fair that you have your share of the power to decide how your money is spent.

Benefit 6 – Uncorruptable.

Because the whole voting population would be involved, mathematics takes over. Any attempt to distort the outcome through extreme influences would be ironed out, and entirely random entries, because they would swing both ways, would tend to cancel each other out and have little, if any, influence at all.

CHAPTER 53

The Mechanism

'While the State exists, there can be no freedom. When there is freedom there will be no State.' - Lenin

A paradigm involving the people could be implemented by updating the constitution. As Britain's constitution was written in 1214, Magna Carta it isn't unreasonable to assume that an update is overdue.

It is essential that the majority of the power is held by the people, so there would be no way for any party or body to hi-jack it, and restore the injustices that we suffer today. If we are to learn anything from the recent histories of Iceland and Greece, who attempted to buck the grip of the banks off their backs, we must assume the establishment shall continue to fight doggedly to overthrow any attempts at bringing about freedom and free choice. In those cases the people were pulled back under their boot through threats and tax bribes.

There is no reason why there should not be some comparatively powerless elected body of representatives who are given the authority of handling mundane day-to-day dealings in a transparent manner on the behalf of, and scrutinised by, the people.

In a true direct democracy, while government might still discuss issues as it does today, it would not hold the power to decide, meaning no parties grouping thoughts or agendas being driven by an individual or small influential lobby. All representatives would be openly elected based on their merit and ability.

Any policy would be open to the 'the House of the People', where all voters could put forward concerns should they choose to in a simple on-line process. If, say, 5,000 (an arbitrary number I have plucked from thin air) people choose to raise a 'significant concern' an on-line referendum on that policy would take place, the result of which would be binding.

Similarly anyone would have the right to put forward a policy that, if supported by, say, 5,000 people, would be placed onto a 'ladder of suggestions.' Anyone would then have the opportunity to promote or demote each suggestion once. As in a squash ladder the best concepts, that received the most support, would then percolate to the top. The top idea would monthly (again just a suggestion) become a 'peoples initiative' and go to referendum and, if passed by a majority of the people, would be passed to the government, as back office workers, to implement into law.

Voting would be done via internet, mobile apps, touch tone phone or, if none of those were available to an individual, by utilising slips at the post office for the non-computer minded. Voters would input their national insurance number to prove they are a resident, a six digit pin to verify it is indeed them that is voting, an issue reference number related for the item on which they are voting, and their preferences, which would be incremental rather than binary.

It is essential that issues should not normally be decided on a binary 'yes' or 'no' basis, but analogue, with a scale of one to ten, to provide a more accurate picture of just how important an issue is to anyone. For example, plastics are very useful in our daily lives – how important is it to you for there to be a policy that ensures complete recycling? 1 – not really important – 10 imperative. Which services are more important to you for increased investment? How would you like to see the fiscal budget split (having been given the whole budget and normal running costings information in a simple diagramtic form.)

Integrity of the system is everything, so the votes could be registered in multiple locations and results compared to eliminate tampering. Bitcoin is a peer to peer system that avoids a central authority and has integrity software that allows people to interact with the service via the internet instantly and with total security. This software is available right now.

Even though the whole process of voting in a referendum would be brief and from the comfort of your own home it would be optional with no pressure on any individual to participate should they choose not to. Typically voting would be open for a month and the result binding. If a referendum fails then the issue should not be placed onto the register for voting on again within three years. Ideally there would be 12 such monthly referendums in a year, which more or less reflects the number of significant policy votes currently taken in parliament annually.

So, the Government would be an elected assembly of independents and the House of Lords would have their powers reduced with their mandate to provide checks and balances to ensure concepts meet with basic test criteria, such as non-violation of human rights, fiscal viability, querying 'a nonsense', and so forth. Any new policy chosen by the people would need to be formed into a workable and legally supportable document acceptable to the people, and assisting this might also be their role.

Mistakes are bound to happen, like a child finding its first faltering steps, but as the population becomes enfranchised and starts to enjoy and experience the benefits of living in a free and fair system of true democracy the joint decisions made by the people shall become better focused and the path to fairness, fulfilment and peace clearer and clearer.

CHAPTER 54

Representative democracy vs. true democracy.

'Liberty means responsibility. That is why most men dread it.' -
George Bernard Shaw

The word 'democracy' stems from the Greek 'demos' - the people
and 'cratia' rule. Created in Athens, democracy was an attempt to
provide a fair government system with the power fairly shared amongst
the eligible people.

Greek 'Athenian' democracy developed around the fifth century
BC in the city-state of Athens and the surrounding territory of Attica.
It is the first known democracy in the world. Other Greek cities set up
their own democracies, most following the Athenian model.

It was a system of direct democracy, in which participating citizens
voted directly on legislation and executive bills. Participation was only
open to adult, male citizens who had completed their military training.
Women, slaves and foreigners were excluded.

In any event, while the system they had may not have been perfect
it did mean that the government couldn't do anything until the
people had approved it. This foresight and comparative fairness should
be applauded, as it was the best attempt that could have been made
without the common place technology that we possess today.

The birth and rise of the internet has opened up all sorts of
opportunities and one significant possibility is for it to be the tool
that shall enable a true direct democracy that enfranchises the whole
population (even including the ladies! Joke.) to come about.

In order to underline the differences between what is being proposed here and the position we find ourselves in today here are some of the myths, or perhaps lies is a better label, that we have been fed our entire lives.

We are constantly told that we are living in a democracy. You hear it every day, but this is untrue. We live in a representative democracy, and the difference that adjective makes is staggering. It is like saying you are on a diet, but leaving out the adjective 'chocolate cake'. Anyone can see the difference that makes.

In a representative democracy you only get to choose, as the name suggests, a representative. You have no further input for the term of the government. In a direct democracy you would hold your power and engage on issues directly and frequently.

In a representative democracy your representative can be manipulated, cajoled, bribed, leant on and may have no power at all. In a direct democracy you would exercise your opinion directly and that is the end of it. There would be around 40 million voting adults and so the mean of the sample would be the collective will of the people and is uncorruptible by a group or with money.

In a representative democracy issues are decided upon behind closed doors (cabinet meetings) and the true agenda is hidden from the people. In a direct democracy is would be up to you to decide if you wanted to keep your preferences secret or discuss them in an attempt to influence your friends.

As most people want the same things, opportunity, peace, fairness, freedom, love, hope, health, education, fulfilment, leisure time, family and a healthy world for us to live in, the outcome of voting directly would lean those ways.

CHAPTER 55

The press

'For most folks, no news is good news; for the press, good news is not news.' - Gloria Borger

Let me start by saying there are a handful of good old-fashioned reporters working in the industry, properly researching and writing honest and articulate reports that can be critical and damning of the establishment and their activities. Sadly, that is becoming increasingly rare. You will have noted that I have taken quotes from the press all the way through this book to support my statements. What is printed on the press or broadcast on the television is supposed to meet regulating standards of accuracy, but a problem arises as many press companies have an agenda or political bias and so the story can be skewed to support that bias. People tend to believe what they read in the press vebatim.

The Leveson Inquiry revealed a pervasive culture of mutual interest between the press and politicians. It exposed how politicians attempt to gain favour with press proprietors, just as newspaper owners expect access and influence to senior political players. Unchecked media concentration over several decades has allowed some media groups to accumulate vast amounts of revenue and influence. One consequence of this has been the development of intimate relationships between political and media elites which, according to Lord Justice Leveson, *'has not been in the public interest'*, and which presents adverse consequences for ethical journalism and democracy.

This 'culture of mutual interest between the press and politicians' distorts democracy in two ways: first by restricting public debate to those agendas favoured by press elites; and second by failing to insulate government policy making from the private interests of media proprietors.

Over the last thirty five years the political parties of UK national government and of UK official opposition, have developed too close a relationship with the press in a way which has not been in the public interest. In part, this has simply been a matter of spending a disproportionate amount of time, attention and resource on this relationship and a matter of going too far in trying to control the supply of news and information to the public in return for the hope of favourable treatment by sections of the press.

Evidence provided to the inquiry regarding the relationship between David Cameron, both in government and opposition, and the press, documented *'1,404 meetings with media figures as leader of the opposition'*. According to Robert Jay, counsel for the Leveson Inquiry, this, *'equates to around 26 meetings or interviews per month, which is more than one every weekday.*

As Rupert Murdoch noted, *'the motivation for politicians to maintain relations with the press in the hope that their views will be 'put across', so that they might influence public opinion via a favourable press. The counterpart to politicians' influence over public opinion is the attempt by press proprietors to affect government policy'*. As Lord Justice Leveson outlined in his findings from the Inquiry, *'there have been those in positions of leadership of the press who have shown themselves to be exceptionally dedicated, powerful and effective political lobbyists in the cause of their own (predominantly commercial, but also wider) interests. That lobbying has been conducted in part overtly and editorially, and in part covertly and through the medium of personal relationships with politicians'*.

An in depth report published by the Media Reform Coalition, April 2014 www.mediareform.org.uk, had this to say:-

'Media ownership has long been the 'elephant in the room' when it comes to analysis of the state of our media: obvious to all but rarely discussed. We view it as crucial to the health of the press, and therefore of a functioning democracy, that the news and views consumed by the public

are spread across a sufficient range of independent providers. But we have a serious problem with plurality in the UK.

Just three companies (News UK, DMGT and Trinity Mirror) control nearly 70% of national newspaper circulation. Just five companies control some 70% of regional daily newspaper circulation. Out of 406 Local Government Areas, 100 (25%) have no daily local newspaper at all while in 143 LGAs (35% of the total) a single title has a 100% monopoly.

Online news sources are overwhelmingly accounted for by traditional news providers while online news consumption is also dominated either by established news providers or digital intermediaries who rely predominantly on traditional news providers for their content.

A single news provider, Sky, provides news bulletins for virtually all of national and regional commercial radio. While the BBC accounts for a majority of television news consumption, a single company, ITV, accounts for a majority of non-BBC TV news consumption. Concentration within some news and information markets has reached endemic levels and is undermining the quality and diversity of output on which citizens rely'.

'What does it mean to have a 'free' media when the nation's TV channels, news outlets, radio stations, search engines and social media platforms are owned by a handful of giant corporations? What does it mean to have 'independent media' when many of our most influential media organisations are controlled by individuals and Boards that are so closely connected with vested interests?

This report shows that just three companies dominate 71% of the national newspaper market – a market that may be shrinking but is still crucial when it comes to setting the agenda for the rest of the news media. When online readers are included, just five companies dominate some 80% of market share. In the area of local news, six giant conglomerates account for 80% of all titles while the 50-plus publishers have less than 20% of the remaining titles.

We are facing an increasing number of news deserts given the fact that 36 million UK citizens – some 57% of the total population - do not have a local daily paper that is able to dedicate itself to matters of concern to their community. And where there is still a local press presence, some 85% of local government areas are faced with a monopoly or duopoly supply of local outlets.

Sky, effectively controlled by Rupert Murdoch's 21ˢᵗ Century Fox empire, is by far the UK's biggest broadcaster and continues to dominate the pay TV landscape.

ITV is making huge profits on the back of its format sales and faces fewer and fewer obligations to serve domestic audiences. Meanwhile, Channel 5 is already owned by a US giant, Viacom International, and there are constant rumours that the government is keen to sell off Channel 4 to the highest bidder. Two companies have nearly 40% of all commercial local analogue radio licences and control two thirds of all commercial digital stations. Only 14% of non-BBC stations are now independently owned while radio news is provided either by the BBC or by Sky.

Is the internet any different to this? UK search is overwhelmingly dominated by Google while the most popular apps like Instagram and WhatsApp are owned by Facebook, itself by far the most popular social media site.

The BBC remains a powerful presence in broadcasting and online but its budget has been severely cut by the last two licence fee deals, its independence has been undermined, and it is increasingly being told by government to be mindful of its impact on the wider commercial market.

We believe that concentration within news and information markets in particular has reached endemic levels in the UK and that we urgently need effective remedies. This kind of concentration creates conditions in which wealthy individuals and organisations can amass huge political and economic power and distort the media landscape to suit their interests and personal views.

Urgent reform is needed in order both to address high levels of concentration in particular media markets and to protect against further concentration in others.'

So how does a story get from the event to our papers and screens exactly?

In the U.S. for example, there are the six media companies that exist today, once there were eighty-eight. These six all get their news from just two sources. Reuters or the Associated Press.

The six companies holding the press includes General Electric Television Holdings which includes13 stations of NBC entering 28% of US households. Their shows include NBC Network News, the Today Show, Nightly News with Tom Brokaw, Meet the Press,

Dateline NBC, NBC News at Sunrise, CNBC business television; MSNBC 24-hour cable and Internet news service (co-owned by NBC and Microsoft). The chances are that if you tune into the news in the U.S. you are highly likely to get a story that has been put through G.E.'s propaganda filter.

The problem here is that General Electric also owns GE Power Systems, producing turbines for nuclear reactors and power plants, and GE Plastics, producing military hardware and nuclear power equipment, so their stories are hardly likely to contain any emphasis on, or even mention of, the dangers of toxic waste created that will last a billion years, or of children dying of leukaemia because they live downwind of a plant, but will be gushing about just how great nuclear fuel is (or how necessary a war is).

Another is Westinghouse / CBS Inc. Their television holdings includes 14 CBS stations and over 200 affiliates in the US including CBS Network News, 60 minutes, 48 hours, CBS Evening News with Dan Rather, CBS Morning News and Up to the Minute.

Westinghouse Electric Company however is part of the Nuclear Utilities Business Group of British Nuclear Fuels (BNFL). Westinghouse Electric Company provides services to the nuclear power industry through Westinghouse Government Environmental Services Company who disposes of nuclear and hazardous wastes (if only they could.) They also operate 4 government-owned nuclear power plants in the US. Energy Systems provides nuclear power plant design and maintenance. I think we can see a pattern developing here.

Even those nice people at Disney who love to entertain our kids so much, are at it. Disney / ABC / CAP provides 10 stations transmitting into 24% of all US households, including ABC Network News, Prime Time Live, Nightline, 20/20, Good Morning America, ESPN, and Lifetime Television. The problem here is that they also have major share-holdings in Sid R. Bass crude oil and gas, so bang goes your chances of proper climate change reporting on any of those news channels.

The holocaust encyclopaedia tells us that *During the first weeks of 1933, the Nazi regime deployed the radio, press, and newsreels to stoke fears of a pending "Communist uprising," then channelled popular anxieties into political measures that eradicated civil liberties and democracy.'* Whatever your opinion of Hitler may be, we know that he was no fool and he clearly saw a controlled press as being a most important tool in getting his party off the ground. In Mien Kampfe he recognised and noted the presses ability to utterly destroy and discredit someone's reputation that had been built up over decades, or to make a complete unknown appear to be a superstar within a week, and was deeply concerned about how much of the press was controlled by the Jews, that he considered to be to the detriment of the German people.

Well that's the nasty Nazi's for you. Of course, here in the UK you wouldn't expect David Cameron to –er – have lots of meetings with high profile press figures would you? I mean, we would never have to suffer that kind of nonsense would we? No-one here would continually talk about terror then propose all sorts of measures aimed at controlling our liberty, like the introduction of I.D. cards, surveillance or random searches would they? We would never have our sporting icons lambasted or praised continually would we? Gazza - baddy, Lineker – goody, Botham – baddy, Gower – goody, Sue Barker – goody. Nigel Farage even – baddy, and so it goes on.

In the U.S., the 'war on terror' has been constructed to go on indefinitely, and is hammered home by press propaganda aimed at spreading fear, thereby gaining public support for the removal of civil liberties, and not a Hitler in sight. Sound familiar? 9/11 led to the introduction of the Patriot Act which, apart from having a 'world turned on its head' title, and which, among other things, authorises the FBI to listen at all your telephone calls, read your mails, examine your bank accounts, credit history and web browsing, all without the authorisation of a court (as incidentally can MI5 in the UK now.) Further they can enter anyone's property, search it, remove your personal possessions and not even tell you that they have been there. Nice! Oh, and by the way, the number of terror threats diverted by the use of the patriot act, which was used 192,000 times between 2003 and 2006? None.

Ah well - that's the Americans for you, but here in the UK. . . . it's just as bad. The Investigatory Powers Act, passed in November 2016, legalises a whole range of tools for snooping and hacking by the security services unmatched by any other country in western Europe or even the US. All phone and internet companies must keep your conversations, mails and browsing for a minimum of one year and relinquish them to the authorities if requested to do so. Jim Killock, the executive director of Open Rights Group, said: *"The UK now has a surveillance law that is more suited to a dictatorship than a democracy. The state has unprecedented powers to monitor and analyse UK citizens' communications regardless of whether we are suspected of any criminal activity."* Renate Samson, the chief executive of Big Brother Watch, said: *"The passing of the investigatory powers bill has fundamentally changed the face of surveillance in this country. None of us online are now guaranteed the right to communicate privately and, most importantly, securely."*

I can recall the overthrowing of President Ceausescu in Romania and the shocking news broken to us by the BBC that many ordinary people in Romania had exhaustive files on their private lives, and even had their holiday postcards copied and filed. Well that is how it is here with us right now in the UK, and it's just as shocking. Thinking of posting a holiday picture on facebook? Better make sure you keep the receipts because the Inland Revenue have a magic password to enter everyone's account and if they see you on the beach will want to know where the money for the flight came from.

So, who are the two companies that all our media information comes through? Well they are called Reuters and the Press Association. The Press Association website tells us it provides *'News from the national news agency'.*

Our agenda-setting news coverage is used by every major national and regional media organisation. PA Media has journalists across the country filing the best in local and national news, as well as specialists in topics such as Finance, Business, Health, Education, the Royal Family and Transport, plus staff at Westminster and the Law Courts

Providing a million words, 2000 images, 400 videos and 100 graphics every week.

I have to say that seems to cover it. Have you ever wondered why you see the same picture on the front page of three or four unrelated newspapers at the garage? It is because the editors of those different papers didn't send a photographer to cover the story, they just paid a monthly fee and have the right to copy them from the Press

Association or Reuters site, and happened to have chosen the same one as their competitors.

With the advent of social media there has been an explosion of worthy news items and personally filmed footage or photographs taken with mobile phones that often exposes the shortcomings of the purposeful misrepresentations of the mainstream media. I'm not saying everything you see is true, we all have to use our common sense to filter what we are shown however my personal experience is a far more accurate picture is presented in this way.

I have watched footage of police telling everyone to get under tables in a bar saying there was a terror attack happening when you could see by their body language and lack of urgency that this was untrue. I have seen a photograph of the guy who was supposedly a terrorist shot dead in combat trousers that was on the front of every UK paper, changing into those clothes in front of a group of police. I have seen video footage of the puffs of smoke emerging from the twin towers on 9/11 as the charges on every floor were detonated, and I have seen accounts disparaging the Corona Virus plandemic by qualified medical personal that you would never see on the main stream news.

A sinister turn of events is the rise in the use of the 'fake news' label, to forcibly remove perfectly credible footage and comment on social media, not because it is incorrect, but because it clashes with the government agenda.

For a final thought about the news and how it is delivered, consider the newsreader on the television. Now, whether we tend to use the skill or not, we are all capable of telling who is lying and who isn't by their body language. The newsreader is only reading from the auto-cue, and so is not considering the implication or content of the text. We, on the other hand, are paying attention to the content while subconsciously watching his or her body language. As the newsreader is only reading, their body language is completely neutral, which auto-suggests to us subliminally that whatever they are saying must be the truth, otherwise our perceptions of body language instinct that we are born with would have alerted us. Very clever.

In a fridge magnet nutshell, 'the most dangerous weapon is not a gun, but government controlled media.'

CHAPTER 56

The picture revisited

'Don't fear failure so much that you refuse to try new things. The saddest summary of a life contains three descriptions: could have, might have, and should have.' - Louis E. Boone

So where have we got to? It's a huge mess isn't it? OK, so let's assume there is an election coming up.

The major parties get vast funding of tax payers money to canvass and promote their pretend ambitions.

They also receive vast funds from individuals and companies looking for favour in the way of business contracts or honours.

They all will have up to thirty meetings weekly with the heads of media meaning the papers will be swamped with stories about them. Because the heads of media have agendas of their own these stories are likely to be gushingly positive.

The manifesto that they present (and are given half a million a year of public money to prepare) is not binding and so can contain anything that the party might think will win them votes.

Because of disillusionment one third of voters will not bother to vote at all.

Because of 'first past the post' two thirds of all votes cast shall be disregarded and thrown in the bin.

The new government will win without anything like a majority mandate from the people

When your M.P. gets in they will be told how to vote on each issue through whipping.

If they say yes enough, they may make it to the cabinet. If they go against the advice they and their families shall be threatened and blackmailed by the party whip, they will be relegated to the back benches, and eventually they can be de-selected by the party for the next election.

If they are good they can get into cabinet where they shall be told what to do by a permanent secretary (who is unelected and was in place before the election regardless of which party was in meaning it is academic which party 'wins') who in turn will receive their instructions from Chatham House, a select club of CEO's of multinationals and banks dressed up and passed off to the people as a 'think tank.'.

All this time the media will try to tell you the terrible decisions you are witnessing are in your best interest, as will your M.P.

If your M.P. is really good at saying yes but loses an election, they shall get a free ticket into the House of Lords. If not they will spend their days sitting on executive boards of corporations earning high end six figure salaries and doing after dinner talks at £20k a pop.

And people STILL think that Britain has one of the finest democracies in the world!

Right. Are you as tired as I am from reading all this doom and gloom? So now here's the fun uplifting bit of the book.

CHAPTER 57

The one pill fix

'When I'm working on a problem, I never think about beauty. I think only how to solve the problem. But when I have finished, if the solution is not beautiful, I know it is wrong.' - R. Buckminster Fuller

The situation we are living in today is clearly untenable, unsustainable and unacceptable. This has to change or the very likely outcome is that mankind shall destroy itself, the planet that gives every organism life, or both. Without a complete revamp of how the power is distributed, the mechanisms in place shall ensure that the pursuit of greed by the few shall continue to rape and dismantle the nature that supports us all. Collectively we have to ask if that is what we want of our future, and that of our children. I struggle to believe it is.

And so how do we, the people wrest the power form the tiny minority that are causing havoc in our society and across our planet? Surely the solution to such an enormous and diverse set of problems must be equally as exhausting? But no. The answer is so simple that many people simply dismiss it out of hand and refuse to believe it possible. Most people want to see a massively complex plan that involves cunning and subversive action, but the truth is all we need, collectively, is belief in ourselves that, by applying ourselves and pulling in the same direction as the majority we can be the change we wish to see. *All we, the people, have to do is win an election on the platform of 'true direct crowd sourced democracy.' One person, one vote, on everything.*

Each of us is given a tiny little piece of power to exercise once every five years or so. We are allowed this one choice, and those in power, backed by a controlling media, would have us believe that our choice must be between the major parties. This is a fallacy. If we were to simply, and collectively, take our power and band it together in a completely different direction, by voting for representatives whose sole ambition it was to degrade the power of all representatives, including their own, everything changes. By breaking the strangle-hold of the major parties from within the citadel of Westminster, and introducing a crowd sourced direct democracy, the people would give themselves the authority to take care of their own lives and futures. Surely that would be something worth voting for?

As it stands, there is nothing anyone can do to forbid us from exercising that power. Pretty much anyone can stand as a candidate, and there is no reason why a candidate shouldn't be standing on a platform of creating a free and fair democracy run by the people. That is why the only policy the Movement for Active Democracy ever had was exactly that. All subsequent choices would then become the responsibility of the people. That is true direct democracy.

The problem here is that people are so childhood-programmed they are unable to believe that this is a viable option, when it is so obviously possible. When I first started the party, I assumed it would be simplicity itself to awaken people from their sleepwalking and that candidates would flock to the banner. That hasn't been the case. Yet. That said, there are movements all over the globe with similar ambitions and with the aid of the miracle called the internet all things are now possible.

The steps to creating a direct democracy are:

1) Wake up a population that is sleepwalking into the abyss. Ironically our current leaders are doing a pretty good job of that. The ceaseless wars and tightening controls over the freedoms are causing people who have traditionally been content to ignore the world and watch football, to sit up and wonder what on earth is going on. Donald Trump is doing a particularly good job as his attitudes and

methods are extreme enough that people are starting to pay attention to his rhetoric.

2) Band together. The small parties cannot hope to make a dent against the big boys if they remain separated and pulling in different directions. The case of the Democratic Alliance (D.A.) in South Africa is a fine example of this. South Africa is governed by deceased Nelson Mandela's African National Congress A.N.C. Because of the countries divided and checkered history the black Africans traditionally vote for that party. As they make up about 80% of the total population, it was always going to be a tall order for any other party to achieve a presence. There were several parties standing against this overwhelming situation and getting nowhere when there was a complex spate of amalgamations and joinings of the opposition parties and the D.A was born, promptly winning the Western Cape election where Cape Town is situated. Since then they have made inroads into the rest of South Africa as they have shown what wise and good governance can achieve, while the A.N.C. remains riddled with corruption and embezzlement. It doesn't matter what skin colour you may have, nobody wants their kids to be sitting in a bookless classroom that looks like a bombed-out shelter while the chairman of the council and his secretary are driving around in a fleet new Mercs (as is what happened in Port Elizbeth, where 95% of the school budget was stolen and when the D.A. won the next election half of the A.N.C council members were sentenced to jail.) So, to attract all of the current parties, the platform must be, and only be, to install a fair and free crowd sourced democracy empowering the people having their input on all major decisions. The concern is that if any other specific policy is introduced, divisions of opinion between existing party candidates may be created, causing a resistance to promoting this single initiative.

3) Find additional candidates. It is necessary to expand the candidature so that there is at the least one candidate for every sixth constituency. By achieving this a free party election broadcast on terrestrial television would become available. While this would only consist of five minutes of airing, it could be enough to raise the profile of the party which, as it has a different approach to the system of

government to which any of us have ever known, surely generating interest, resulting in the all important increased media coverage.

4) Pray. If the people grasp the concept and see the opportunity of dismantling the patently unfair, outdated, cumbersome and corrupted system of government that we have been burdened with, then there is the real potential for the snowball to start an avalanche of support. This would elevate hopeful candidates to elected representatives and that is when the beginnings of this bloodless coup would start to come together.

5) Use the media attention to promote the concept of self-rule and encourage people to join the groundswell. Funding and good candidates are also essential ingredients to winning. I can only feel that this is a rocket waiting to go off, requiring only a spark to get it started. The advent of the internet allowing news to flow without the controls of the traditional participants of T.V. news coverages and the press, and will play an important part in this process.

6) Win a majority in the House of Commons. From here that looks like a tall order but it has to be possible. Once this is achieved the majority of M.P.s shall have the power to put though legislation for the introduction of a 'Direct Crowd Sourced Democracy', passing on the power of self-rule to the people, enabling the desire for the common good to form policy.

7) Spread the philosophy around the planet. In most of my writings I have been referring to the UK, simply because that happens to be my home country, but why should direct democracy end there? Every country has similar problems, and some much worse. Once one working example of direct democracy is in place and shown to work, it would only be a matter of time before peoples all around the planet started clamoring for that change.

When the people start to see the blossoming of the benefits of having an uncorrupted and fair, true and direct democracy, that actually cares about the common man in place, the system shall rapidly become loved and cherished, and the way things are today shall appear so unjust and chaotic they shall come to be thought of as the dark days of man, and there will be no way back. And then, my friend, we shall have peace and equality on earth. Imagine.

And so, realistically, can an election be won in the U.K. on the platform of direct democracy? For encouragement we can take succour from the brief history of 'None of the Above' who's only mandate was 'if you don't think any of the candidates on the ballot deserve your vote, then just vote for 'none of the above.' And do you know what happened next? Within a month, parliament proposed, voted on and passed a law forbidding any party being called 'none of the above.'

So why would they bother to do that? And with such urgency? Certainly the name is not any wackier than some of the choices currently registered with the Electoral Commission, so could it be that those in power really thought that 'none of the above' could catch on and become so popular amongst those who are rightly disillusioned with the system, as the religious preference of 'Jedi' remarkably did on the census form That they could see a hole appearing in their power base? A chink in their armour? That is the only possible reason, and must give us all a great deal of hope.

The system is tied up as tightly as they can make it, its Achilles heel is that one of the big parties still has to get voted in every five years for this unjust system that serves the wealthy elite to proliferate, and we collectively have to put them there. While no longer a party 'none of the above' still campaigns to have a NOT box as a default on every ballot sheet, which would give the people the opportunity to show their dissatisfaction with all the choices available.

The Houses of Parliament at Westminster, sit grandly by the Thames under the shadow of Big Ben but what have we really got here? A building, with six hundred odd people in it, who happen to have worn the right coloured rosette? Some person sitting on a wool sack? Is that it? It's a farce, and together we can put a stop to it all, just like that.

One thing history tells us is that those in power do not go away quietly. They will use their enormous financial backing to undermine and cheat their way back into power if we are not vigilant. And they will stop at nothing. Do you think the Kennedy assassination was carried out by Lee Harvey Oswald? Or do you think arms inspector, Dr. Kelly, who found no evidence of any weapons of mass destruction, and was on the verge of stopping the whole Iraq war after millions were invested in its build up, when the allies were already divvying up the oil supplies, was simply depressed when they found him dead (with slashed wrists but no blood on the ground) while walking his dog?

CHAPTER 58

Who is trying to make a difference?

'The revelation is that when you lift the curtain, history is decided by a very small group of people, and their own interests guide their actions, not necessarily the laws or principles we think our country rides on.' - Mira Sorvino

An important thing to remember is that today there are already a plethora of pressure groups and campaigning organisations that work tirelessly trying to persuade the government to do the 'right thing'. Environmentally speaking there are quite a few groups doing what they can to protect our planet and the creatures that we share it with. As examples, every county in Britain has a 'Wildlife Trust', and then there are privately run organisations like 'People for the ethical Treatment of Animals', 'Save our Seas', 'Campaign for Better Transport', 'Campaign for the Protection of Rural Wales and England', 'Climate Camp', 'Greenpeace', 'Forum for the Future', 'Friends of the Earth', 'Plane Stupid', 'Population Matters', 'Sandbag', 'The Soil Association', 'Surfers Against Sewage', 'Rights Of Way Alliance', 'Rowers Against Thames Sewage', 'Royal Society for the Protection of Birds (RSPB)', 'Waste Watch', 'Women's Environmental Network', 'World Wildlife Fund for Nature (WWF)', 'British Union for the Abolition of Vivisection', 'Hunt Saboteurs Association', 'League Against Cruel Sports', 'OneKind', 'Royal Society for the Prevention of Cruelty to Animals' and 'Vegetarians' International' 'Voice for Animals', all of which are operational in the UK (as well as worldwide), and this selection is by no means all of them. And that is just in the animal and environmental field. Clearly a lot of people care.

Many large pressure groups exist with hundreds of thousands of members. Avaarz is one of the biggest with a worldwide membership of a staggering 46 million members based in 194 countries. In the UK alone it has a formidable 1.8 million members. The group campaigns tirelessly about a wide range of issues, many of them environmental. Looking at their website on February 2018 their top campaigns were:

'Demanding the release of all Palestinian children wrongly held in military prisons.' 'Saving bees from insecticide poisoning - we're in the middle of an environmental holocaust that threatens all of us, because without pollination by bees, our whole food chain is under threat.'

'Help end unbearable cruelty of meat - 56 billion animals are crammed into filthy, windowless cages and slaughtered every year to feed our meat addiction.'

'End the plastic plague - it's a planetary crisis and, unless we act now, there'll be more plastic than fish in the sea by 2050.'

'End tax havens today - the level of global inequality is appalling - 8 people own as much wealth as half the planet.'

'The miracle recovery plan for our planet - the facts are terrifying: species are going extinct at 1000 times the natural rate. 90% of the Great Barrier Reef is dead or dying. Oceans are so choked with plastic that fish are addicted to eating it. But scientists have discovered something else -- a kind of miracle that could save us. If we can protect 50% of our planet from human exploitation, our ecosystem will be able to stabilise and regenerate. Life on earth will recover.'

'Hong Kong: End ivory, not elephants! - Hong Kong is like ivory island -- home to a booming trade in their butchered body parts. As long as it's legal, more and more beautiful elephants will be slaughtered. At this rate, they could literally be wiped out in our lifetime.'

Now who wouldn't support each and every one of those campaigns – unless of course you are yourself profiteering from the misery that is being caused?

The fight to ban the ivory trade in Hong Kong was finally won on the 6th February 2018, but why should it have taken the efforts of 1.166 million people writing to the Hong Kong Legislative Council to make that happen?

A UK member of Avaaz writes:- *'So what am I doing on Avaaz? Here we only make a small effort, as simple as following an e-mail and adding our name, to a good cause. It's not much, but when thousands of us do the same thing it becomes worth a great deal.*

"Nobody made a greater mistake than he who did nothing because he could do only a little." (Edmund Burke)'

What all of these groups have in common is they generate funds through donations and do what they can to raise awareness within the public domain hoping to get enough exposure that the government finally feels compelled to do something about it. The question is of course, why does the government need such persuasions when something like the ill treatment of animals or sewage being pumped into the Thames, or the decimation of our countryside, or the proliferation of plastics is so transparently wrong and unacceptable. Of course, it's our old enemy, corporate greed and control by corporations over the government (are you getting tired of hearing that yet?)

Another UK based pressure group is 38 Degrees, so named as this is the critical angle at which melting snow will avalanche. This is a great image they have created that if a snowball can start an avalanche, one person can create a change. If these campaigns were open for the public to vote on and you could score 1 (being don't care or against) to 10 (very important to me or strongly agree) how would you vote? A sample of their campaigns are listed and for fun I have put my own vote score against each:-

Stopping use of plastics in tea bags. (10)

Forcing the Government to obey the law and stop spying on the people. (10)

Stopping the government from signing up to the Trans Pacific partnership (TPP) that empowers the big corporations allowing them to, among other things, prevent us obtaining widely used alternative medicines. (10)

Pressuring the government to stop big corporations tax-dodging. (10)

Stop the Government prohibiting input on the vetting of trade deals. (7)

Supporting a crack-down on gambling machines in the high streets. (5)

Stopping the government giving private security companies the same powers of arrest as the police. (10)

Pushing the government to introduce deposits on plastics that are choking our seas. (10)

Giving people the right to paid leave to attend a funeral of a close relative. (7)

Forcing the government to put a cap on the profits of the big energy suppliers. (7)

Forcing the government to publish the report about the impact of fracking on the UK climate. (10)

Forcing the government to save our parks. (10)

Force the government to keep the ban on bee-killing pesticides. (10)

So, if you had the power, how would you vote on each of these? It would be fun wouldn't it? Knowing you could make that difference, and knowing that you were engaged and driving the future of your country and the planet? It is how it is meant to be, if only you will just see the lie you are being told, and believe in yourself. As it stands it takes about a million people exercising good common sense to unravel the corrupted and moneyed opinions of just one or two people in government, and that can't be right.

CHAPTER 59

Who is fighting for direct democracy?

'Eventually I foresee voting on the Internet, which will lead to much more direct democracy.' - Dick Gephardt

The concept of introducing an engaged people driven form of government is a seed that is germinating all over the planet. There are dozens, if not hundreds, of groups and small parties actively engaged in creating a fairer form of democracy. A few examples are listed below.

The Net Party (*Partido de la Red*) is a political party headquartered in Argentina, with a global projection based on the Internet, that proposes an online form of liquid democracy that it calls "net democracy", with the goal of electing representatives who will reliably vote according to what the citizenry decide online.

The party was founded by Santiago Siri and Esteban Brenman in April 2012. It received the required support of 4000 citizens (to officially exist as a party) in August 2013, and ran for a seat in the local parliament of Buenos Aires during the October 2013 elections achieving 21,000 votes (1% of the votes.) It is currently working to improve the software system they call DemocracyOS and also to elect its first congressional representative in the 2017 elections.

The Net Party created an open-source software (DemocracyOS) to be used as a new democratic participation instance, for citizens to vote on existing legislative projects being discussed in the local parliament, and so determine how the party's congressman will vote. They also maintain the people's rights to propose and vote on new law proposals, and to be officially represented by the party's congressman if they meet a threshold of citizen support.

In the DemocracyOS software model, each citizen can either cast their vote or can delegate it to a trusted peer. Delegation is transitive and can be determined by topic. That is to say a user can delegate economics-related votes to a certain user, environment-related and health-related votes to another user, and keep the remaining topics for themselves. Since this app's innovation is that it is linked to the formal political system through a "Trojan legislator", identity validation is a crucial component and is achieved through a separate app called NetIdentity.

Another is IserveU, a non-profit, direct democracy organization and web-based voting platform founded in Yellowknife, Northwest Territories, Canada. It is currently the only system in the world with an elected representative in office. The organization strives to increase citizen engagement, transparency and accountability in government through crowdsourcing decision-making to the voting public of Yellowknife.

Initially conceived of in 2012 with the intention of introducing a form of e-democracy to Yellowknife, IserveU has since become a fully-fledged web-based voting platform and volunteer driven organization, orchestrating public events and canvassing. In a letter from one of the organization's founding members, it is stated that prior to the election, IserveU operated through volunteers and a small staff.

The IserveU voting platform functions as a way to incorporate elements of direct democracy into a representative system, by obligating city council incumbents to vote in accordance with the outcome of online votes – effectively creating a way for the public to directly decide the fate of their city.

Councillors seeking greater citizen input into decision making, post all current motions before the council, on the IserveU site. These motions could be detailed, debated and voted on by the registered userbase before the final outcome is taken to council. Councillors themselves can vote on issues with the weight of the currently 'uncast' votes. That is, the outcome of a motion that has very little public participation will largely be decided by the votes of the councillors, as the votes in the uncast vote pool are equally divided between them. Whereas, a motion that has garnered a large amount of public participation will have a reduced number of uncast votes for the councillors to use, reducing the councillors' impact.

The system is still being modified to meet new concerns, and has been released under an open source license on GitHub, to allow even greater public scrutiny and control.

On the 19th of October, 2015, Rommel Silverio was elected into council, making Yellowknife the official debut of the IserveU e-democracy platform.

Then, there is PlaceAVote.com, a grassroots American organization that provides a peer-to-peer framework to review, discuss, and vote on every issue before United States Congress. The guiding principle in PlaceAVote's development is to provide a boundary-free, non-partisan forum in which the collective will of the people can be gathered and communicated to their United States Congressional Representatives in order for representation to actually take place. Since the 2014 primaries, over 50 candidates across the United States expressed an interest in running on the PlaceAVote platform. Founded in 2014, PlaceAVote's mission is to facilitate democracy and to combat government corruption in the United States and abroad.

PlaceAVote.com provides secure voting via public-key cryptography. For every vote cast, the resulting "Yes" or "No" value is encrypted via a public-key. When the vote is final, all public keys along with their corresponding signature-values and vote-values are published for a public audit. This approach prevents tampering with the system while allowing voters to remain anonymous.

PlaceAVote.com advocates criticize the current political system's tendency to only represent the organized voice of special interests, arguing that the current system is an example of the minority ruling the majority via well-funded special interests. The current delegation system assumes that representatives are experts or are given access to experts on pending legislation. However, the truth is that most of the representatives in congress are actually not experts in all the issues but come from a law background.

PlaceAVote instead creates a system where experts of differing opinions can come together and publicly debate the merits and weaknesses of upcoming legislation. Though mechanisms within the software that allow for the development of peer to peer coalitions around issues, legislation will be created based on need and public benefit rather than political payback.

In 2011 Something remarkable happened in Frome. What could that be? Well, the traditional councillors lost a resounding battle and the whole lot were replaced by candidates who ran on a refreshing unified new platform based on 'whatever may be my personal interests in the town, first and foremost - I'm for Frome.' Logically, that was what they called their party and they are now two election whitewashes in, with 100% control of the council, and this is what they have to say about their approach. Taken from the IFF website:

'The Independents for Frome - Ways of Working'
"The noble art of losing face will one day save the human race".
Piet Hein

These Values and Guidelines have been drafted by the group of 17 independent individuals elected to Frome Town Council in May 2015. They are based on the original Ways of Working adopted in 2011.

Five Core Values
Independence. We will each make up our own mind about each decision without reference to a shared dogma or ideology.

Integrity. Decisions will be made in an open and understandable manner. Information will be made available even when we make mistakes and everyone will have the opportunity to influence decisions.

Positivity. We will look for solutions, involving others in the discussions, not just describe problems.

Creativity. Use new, or borrowed, ideas from within the group and the wider community to refresh what we do and how we do it.

Respect. Understand that everyone has an equal voice and is worth listening to.

We will adhere to these values by challenging ourselves and each other to:

Avoid identifying ourselves so personally with a particular position that this in itself excludes constructive debate.

Being prepared to be swayed by the arguments of others and admitting mistakes.

Be willing and able to participate in rational debate leading to a conclusion.

Understand the value of constructive debate.

Accept that you win some, you lose some; it's usually nothing personal and there's really no point in taking defeats to heart.

Maintain confidentially where requested and agree when it will be expected.

Share leadership and responsibility and take time to communicate the intention of, and the approach to, the work we undertake.

Have confidence in, and adhere to, the mechanisms and processes of decision-making that we establish, accepting that the decisions of the majority are paramount.

Sustain an intention to involve each other and others rather than working in isolation.

Trust and have confidence and optimism in other people's expertise, knowledge and intentions. Talk to each other not about each other.' Well that all sounds pretty good to me, if only our government had these guidelines, then maybe we wouldn't be in such a mess.

Recently created in Holland, the Forum for Democracy (Dutch: Forum voor Democratie, FvD), was ironically founded as a 'think tank' by Thierry Baudet who has been the party's leader since 22 September 2016.

In March 2017 the FvD had approximately 5,000 members. The bulk of the Forum's parliamentary candidates did not have prior active experience in other political parties. The list of candidates included medical specialists, financial experts and a member of the armed forces.

Refreshingly, one of the major issues the party campaigns against is the existence of a "party cartel", in which the main ruling parties of the country divide power amongst themselves and conspire towards the same goals, despite claiming to be competitors. Is this sounding familiar?

The party promises direct democracy through binding referenda, as well as directly elected mayors and a directly elected Prime Minister. The party is also in favour of the government consisting of apolitical experts, and top civil servants having to reapply for their positions when a new cabinet is formed. Well, that would be a breath of fresh air!

The party first participated in elections during the Dutch general election of 2017. During these elections they obtained 1.8% of the vote and won 2 seats in the House of Representatives.

On the 13th February 2019 (and only days before this book was sent to print) Paolo Gerbaudo of The Guardian lead an article with, *'One person, one click: is this the way to save democracy? Digital parties may help solve a crisis of legitimacy in politics, but are they truly democratic?*

It was the biggest decision in the party's young life, a turning point that will define its reputation for years to come.

But when Italy's Five Star Movement (M5S) had to resolve whether or not to join the far-right Lega, or League, in a coalition government last May, it didn't retreat into a conclave of party leaders. It asked members to vote online. An overwhelming 94% supported the move.

Paolo goes on to tell us that the process was perhaps the most striking example of an emerging trend at the heart of 21st-century politics – the use of digital technology to bring people into the hearts of movements from Italy and Spain to France, Scandinavia to the UK.

He asks the question, that while the digital world has taken a great deal of criticism for subverting open societies, could it also be a motor for a democratic revival? Could these digital innovations – mostly confined to new, populist parties – help revitalise our liberal democracies?

The pioneers of digital democracies were the pirate parties of northern Europe who first broke through in Sweden, Germany and Iceland about a decade ago, using an online decision-making platform called LiquidFeedback. One of its founders, Andreas Nitsche, said the idea was that "empowering the ordinary members would make these parties more responsive to the demands of society".

More recently, the fiercely anti-establishment M5S and the Spanish leftwing populist party Podemos have led the way. "Ordinary citizens will become protagonists, abandoning the current system of delegate democracy in the hands of politicians," said the late Gianroberto Casaleggio, who masterminded the M5S digital strategy. Given the discredited status of Italy's political class, this narrative appealed to many citizens.

He goes on to tell us that M5S made digital democracy its core creed, with its anthem proclaiming: "We are not a party, we are not a caste, one man, one vote, one man, one vote." A variety of new parties have followed suit, to the point where digital democracy has now become a must for all new political movements that want to be seen as in sync with the times.

Paolo tells us that the central innovation is the "participatory platform". This is an online portal, often part of the official party website, that hosts a number of interactive features. These might include donations, training sessions, discussions on policy and online ballots for primaries, elections of party officers, or strategic decisions, for instance whether to enter an alliance or the position to take on a specific policy, adding that the M5S platform is named Rousseau, after the Genevan political philosopher Jean-Jacques Rousseau. Casaleggio liked to describe it as the "collective intelligence of the movement".

He also tells us that Podemos has a participation portal named Participa ("participate"). It comprises a voting area and a discussion system named Plaza Podemos (Podemos Square) that is similar to Reddit, with threaded discussions and upvote/downvote functionalities, which earned it the moniker of "Reddit party".

These sites closely mimic the logic of social media platforms, with discussions, votes, likes and other metrics to assess users' views. For Miguel Ardanuy, a former participation coordinator of Podemos, the ultimate aim of this "platformisation of the party" is to "construct a different model of party, a party more open and responsive to society, where you do not need a membership card in order to participate".

"We live in an era of disintermediation, where we are bypassing the old middlemen, such as travel agencies," said Roberto Fico, a M5S politician and the current president of the Italian parliament's lower chamber, the Chamber of Deputies. "Digital democracy embodies the same tendency applied to politics, allowing people to have a say directly on important decisions without depending on their representatives."

It is heart-warming to know that I am not alone in this mission and that there are many organisations and parties out there fighting on a platform of simply giving the power to the people so they can decide what they consider to be best for themselves. So, the million dollar question here is, are *you* beginning to see the massive possibility and potential here to wrest our planet back from the hands of the greed crazed minority? I truly hope so because, you see, without you playing your part, this is not going to happen, and the result of your apathy will be just too awful to contemplate.

CHAPTER 60

The dream

'You may say I'm a dreamer, but I'm not the only one' - John Lennon

'Hey Cindy, don't forget to do your poll, there's no point in being all for the three-day working week and not bothering to vote for it, is there?'

Cindy looks forlornly at her mobile communications computer. 'Why do I have to do all this stuff grand-dad?' she asks petulantly, her blonde fringe hanging over her blue eyes.

'Because, my dear girl, you have turned sixteen and you now have the right to enter into the process of true democracy.'

'But I don't want to vote, it's boring' she replies, knowing her obstinacy shall get a response.

'Well if you don't want to, then don't bother, that is your right too. But if you lose your chance to cut your weekly work time for the Corporation to three days for the rest of your life, don't come crying to me.'

She sits up, suddenly interested, 'what, for ever? Wouldn't I get the chance to vote on it ever again?'

'Yes, but not for at least three years, and that's why you should say what you think today. You see years ago, when I was young, we didn't have the chance to vote for anything like this. All we could do was vote for a stranger. It was ridiculous. If we didn't like something that the government were doing, and there were a lot of things, I can tell you, we would have to protest and write letters and lobby and sit down in the streets and some people even lost their lives, but the government just used to keep doing what they were being told by the Corporation, saying that it was best for everyone. It was awful'

'Yes, that does seem an unfair way to do things. How could that person have made decisions on your behalf if they didn't know you?'

'Well Cindy, the bottom-line is they couldn't. They didn't know you and they couldn't say what was right for anyone, let alone everyone. Unbelievably they couldn't even say what they thought was right, as they were controlled and told how to vote on things by the Corporation. So even if they did care, they weren't allowed to say that. It was madness.'

'So who was telling them what to say grand-dad?'

'At the heart of the problem lay the banks and corporate elite. They were ruthless and so obsessed with greed they just got the government to do all sorts of things to make them richer, while the rest of us suffered.'

'Well that doesn't sound fair!' exclaims Cindy, 'but then what happened grand-dad?'

'Well, it went on like that for a long time, and people didn't even think there could be a better way to do things, because when they were young and gullible they were told that government control was the only right way, and so of course they didn't question the situation at all. Things got worse and worse, with the government doing all sorts of crazy things in the name of the people.

They invaded other countries saying they were doing it for peace, and to ensure that country had democracy, when we didn't even live in one ourselves. Then they stole that countries wealth by taking its natural resources. They were dismantling the planets ecosystems and came very close to killing us all. All the time they just kept telling everyone it was for the best, and writing that in the daily information sheets and broadcasting on the vision box. Then they started the 'virus lie.'

'What was that grand-dad? I don't like the sound of it, whatever it was,' replies Cindy, placing a hand over her mouth.

'No my dear, would have been right to be fearful of that. Many were, but many were so brainwashed they went along with it for a while. It all happened at a time when the world had started to fall apart. We now call it 'the point of vanishing stability' when Mother Nature started shutting down. The weather got really bad, there were hundred mile an hour winds and droughts that went on for years in places that used to be green and fertile. Floods happened that drowned whole cities and the seas rose until they swamped coastal towns and river valleys. The number of poor people sleeping on the streets were outnumbering those with homes.

The 'virus lie' was their last big push. They saw a chance to end the freedom of mankind forever, by making people very afraid of dying from a virus that wasn't more dangerous than many other diseases, and promising they could protect them with an injection. They locked people in their homes and wouldn't let anyone move freely. No-one could work so they didn't have any money and the government wouldn't let them become freer until they had had the injection, but it was all a plot.

The injection contained a tiny secret microchip that could intimately report on the person all the time, and even allowed the government to use it to change their mood, using a communications method they had just invented called 5G. The infrastructure started to break down due to lack of investment, as the tax money was being stolen by the greedy elite, and so it became normal to see bodies rotting where they had died.

You see, the elite took most of the money and were buying all of the food and water to make even more money by selling it again at a huge profit to the starving people who had no choice but to give the last things they had to stay alive. They were digging up all the oil and gas and even started a thing called fracking which poisoned the water so we had to buy that from the Corporation to have anything clean to drink. They were chopping down all the trees to make even more money, and the seas were all but dead from the fleets of super fishing boats that scoured the oceans and the heaps of Corporation plastic that choked them. All the time we were being told it was the only way and that we should be happy that the government were looking after us, and not to worry because it was all under control, but some people started thinking that there had to be a better way.

'That sounds horrible grand-dad. So, what happened next? Did someone find a better way' asks Cindy, shocked.

'Well the change all started when some brave people objected to being microchipped. It started by us having to carry the compulsory identification software on our mobile communications computers. People didn't like it but we were forced to have all our biometric data taken and put on the MCC and to carry it at all times, even to the beach, not that there were actually any beaches left by then, only places where the dying sea could be looked at. Worse each MCC carried our personal information, where we had been, what we did. It even logged any times we had been talked to by an enforcer, and held a list of any trouble that person had been in when they were a child.

The MCC could be scanned by the enforcers from a distance and if people talked to each other the MCC would know who it was and log it. The enforcers could easily build up a picture of who knew who and how long they had spent together. The MCC could be tracked from space so the enforcers knew where anyone was at any time and could even tell if we were speeding in our cars, and a fine would come through automatically taking away peoples hard earnt Corporate credits.'

Cindy gulps but says nothing.

'Next they made it so people had to scan their MCC at a shop before buying alcohol or tobacco, saying it was to protect the young, but then they expanded that rule to cover unhealthy foods like pizza, and going to the meeting taverns saying it was so they could keep a health check on everyone for their own good.'

'You mean I couldn't have gone to the pizza shop without my MCC and had one whenever I liked?' Cindy gawps at her grand-dad, her eyes wide in shock.

'No. You could only have bought one if the enforcers thought you were healthy enough and if you had gone to work for the Corporation every day that week without fail.'

'But grand-dad, that's awful.'

'Yes, my lovely, awful indeed, but it got much worse. Next, they said that you needed to show your MCC every time you bought *anything*. They said it was so they could do a stock take of everything we needed so they could make sure we would never run out of anything, even though we seemed to run out of a lot of things at that time. Once they had this in place, they passed another law that said they could turn your MCC off. In this way they had complete control over anyone they wanted, because if you couldn't use your MCC you couldn't buy food or a train ticket or anything. If they thought you were going to go to a protest they would turn you off so you couldn't buy a ticket to go, and so even the peoples' right to protests started to fail. You would then starve until you went to the enforcers and took a 'rehabilitation course' in a camp where they re-programmed you and tortured you if you resisted. If you were lucky you would eventually be set free and your MCC would be turned back on again. But then you were put under 'double watch.'

The government took control of all the stories in the daily information sheets and the vision box, and if anyone tried to say anything that undermined their story, even if it were the truth it was taken down and labelled as 'fake news.'

'How terrible! Who did the government think they were?' Cindy exclaims, sitting up and angry now. 'But then you said it all changed? How did that happen if they had this card thing going?'

'When they then said that they were going to replace the MCCs with the microchip in the injection that everyone would have to take this was the final straw. So many people were upset about this that they started smashing up their MCCs even though they cost a lot of money, and shopkeepers were threatened so they had no choice but to serve people anyway. The enforcers tried to stop that of course, but the number of people doing it was too great. There were huge battles in the streets. The enforcers had guns and tasers, but they were swamped by people who sacrificed their lives to try to force a change.'

Cindy shifts in her seat, anxious to hear the next bit of the story. 'How many people died grand-dad?' she asks anxiously.

'No one knows for sure, Cinders, but it was a lot, probably over ten thousand. Eventually even the enforcers started to see the truth and started siding with the people, after all, they are just people too, and that made it so the government didn't know what to do next, so they decided to hold an election.

The elections at that time were only contested by two parties, the 'Party of Truth' and the 'Party of Light' but they were secretly working together, so if one was in trouble they would lose an election and hoped the people would be fooled into thinking they were getting something new by voting in the other party, and so be pacified. The people never were getting any change of course, and were finally starting to realise that there never was any choice and that voting for those parties was all an illusion of choice designed to keep the people under control. But this time something new happened.'

'What was that grand-dad?' Cindy asks, her mouth opening wide in anticipation.

'Well Cinders, there was a man called John Connor, and he was very clever at using the internet for social media and sharing information. He had come across a book called 'The one pill fix' that had been written by someone twenty years earlier. It had been banned by the government as they didn't like what was written inside, but the ideas of freedom and fairness had inspired him. He decided that it provided the basis to many of the answers to our problems. He worked very hard and soon had a party formed called the 'Crowd Sourced Democracy Party' which stood only on the platform of a free and fair democracy run by the people, and it attracted candidates to stand in every constituency. The groundswell was huge and at the election the CSD swept to power.'

'Oh, that must have been amazing grand-dad!' Cindy exclaims.

'Yes it was my sweet, indeed it was. People were dancing in the streets. I never saw anything like it in my life. The CSD took over government and that very day everything started to change. They updated our ancient and outdated constitution that was called Magna Carta and introduced a form of direct democracy so that the people could have control over their own destiny with more power than anyone or anything else. They turned the 'Houses of Parliament' into the 'Peoples Assistance Centre' and they started a squash ladder of ideas that people could vote on, promoting the best ideas to the top and it had all the things people wanted to change on it. Of course, the first thing at the top was a vote on the hated microchip. The people voted with a resounding ninety-four per cent to abolish them.'

'Next came the clean water vote. Fracking was banned, and then the tree vote came through and everyone planted two trees each. Next was a maximum wage vote, so the super wealthy couldn't make more than a million pounds in a year so there was no point in them plundering the countryside any more. Without the possibility of earning so much money the wealthy stopped the super fishing boats and didn't bother to dig up so much oil and gas. A vote was passed for banking to be non-profit making so the money of the country was more fairly shared out to the people and everyone could start living decent lives. Then we voted to introduce the fair home policy so that people could only own one house, which meant everyone had somewhere to live, and then the energy vote went through for home micro generation, so everyone had free power.'

'Oh wow! That's brilliant! I bet everyone was really happy!' Cindy smiles, her hand pushing her hair from her face.

'Well, not quite everyone Cinders. The Corporation didn't like what was going on at all and tried to stop it. They killed John Connor by poisoning him with polonium 210 but by this time it was too late for them. Already the world had seen what had happened and most countries had already started to copy the idea. Even the Chinese had started doing it. The people had had a taste of freedom and they weren't going to stop for anything. America was the last to introduce this fair system, but even they had to concede to the will of the people in the end. Next, we voted in the four-day week so everyone could have a share of the work and then we reduced the retirement age to fifty. Because there were no greedy banks taking the money there was plenty of wealth to support these schemes and the peoples' lives became easier and freer than ever before.'

'War was banned and the armies disbanded, freeing up so much money for the social system they could hardly spend it all. The hospitals became well-funded and waiting lists disappeared, retirement homes were made free and comfortable with lots of nice things for the elderly to do and children's nurseries became free and plentiful.'

'Next the people of the world voted together for the installing of thousands and thousands of deep-sea turbines with all the companies that had been making weapons putting them together. That provided more clean, predictable, out of sight, energy than we could ever need. With the reduction in the archaic burning of fossil fuels, and with all the millions of trees that had been planted locking up CO_2, the weather patterns started to return to normal, the polar ice reformed and the planet was saved.'

'Oh grand-pa! That's amazing! I'm so happy you explained that to me! Now I can't wait to vote online about the three-day week. I'm going to tell all my friends to do it too!'

'That's very good Cinders, because chatting with your friends about things is a really healthy way to engage, and because you all get the chance to vote your conversations aren't just talk, they are important exchanges that may affect the future of everyone.'

'OK! Got it! Now where's my MCC? Ah here it is. Now, I know my passport number. . . and that's put my pin in. . . and here's the three day working week vote reference. . . and I'm going to say. . . . it's ten out of ten importance to me! There! Done! That was so easy grand-dad!'

'And so it should be Cindy. Well done and thanks for listening'

Bzzzzzzzzzzzzz.

'What?'

Bzzzzzzzzzzzzz.

'Cindy? Where are you going? Please come back.'

'I'm so sorry grand-pa. I have to go now, but thank you and never give up. We are depending on you. . . . . . I love you grand-pa'

'I love you too Cinderella.'

Bzzzzzzzzzzzzz.

'Oh no! The alarm! Five already? Time to put on my boiler suit and get to the work-camp. Dammit. For a moment it all felt so real.'

CHAPTER 61

And finally

'And in the end, the love you take, is equal to the love, you make' - The Beatles.

So how did we get here? How did it come to pass that we teach our children love and yet wage war upon one another? How can we tell our children to care for the planet and yet support the dumping of billions of tons of gasses into our atmosphere and billions of tons of plastic into our seas? How can we teach our children to share and yet generate vast rich poor divides? How can we teach respect yet fail to demonstrate that? How can we talk of honesty being the best policy while we are suffocated by lies from those we have chosen as our leaders? Because those in power serve the Demon of greed. They pretend they have our interests at heart when they do not. Take greed out of the equation and most of the problems simply dissolve into the ether.

This book covers just the tip of the iceberg of deception and double dealing that our government hands out to us. We give them our support and they do the will of the greed driven banks and corporations. That problem has reached a crescendo where no person alive today can any longer be complacent of their treachery. The planet is failing, the species we share it with are failing and we ourselves are failing. Your fear should not be reserved only for your children and grand-children. You need to be fearful for yourself.

All of this can be changed in a few short days by refusing to support a system that is painfully and transparently corrupt. Refuse to give your power away to someone who will betray your trust. Just stop voting these self-serving and elite controlled parties into power. Vote instead for 'Crowd Sourced Democracy' and see what happens next. After all, if it is a failure you can always go back to the old system in five years. But it won't fail. And the reason for my optimism? Because *you* will be making the decisions and, unless you have no heart and soul, you shall want what is best for your family and yourself. Once this dream of freedom, that currently seems a distant impossibility, is realised there will be no turning back and mankind shall have taken the first huge step toward a fairer and brighter future. With a little love the situation might yet be saved. Just.

The world is still a beautiful place, but time is running short. It's now *your* job to spread the word. Canvass your friends, get on social media, stand in your constituency, shout it from the roof-tops and put all your spare energy into dismantling this evil corrupted menace we are being sold as democracy. Because if you don't, it's all over, and without any sign of a whimper let alone a struggle. How awful is that to even contemplate.

As Sir David Attenborough so eloquently stated: *'We are at a unique stage in our history. Never before have we had such awareness of what we are doing to the planet. And never before have we had the power to do something about that. Surely we have a responsibility to care for our planet. The future of humanity and indeed all life on earth depends on us.'*

Well?

EPILOGUE

*"I'm tired of this back-slappin' "isn't humanity neat" bullshit.
We're a virus with shoes."* - Bill Hicks

Since finishing 'The One Pill Fix' in 2019 a lot has happened while negotiating approval from the publishers.

The 'Extinction Rebellion' movement came and went. In a series of actions across the world, mass protests over the blasé approach of government to critical climate change evidence, occurred. In London, thousands took over the city centre, disrupting transport services and blocking streets.

Several things set these protests apart from others we have seen in the past. The numbers of people involved were enormous, and they came from all walks of life. We had become accustomed to 'way out, lefty, hippie sorts' protesting about climate change in comparatively small groups but here were thousands of middle-class and high-profile individuals willing to suffer the indignity of arrest and prosecution for an issue that they, rightly to my mind, felt compelled to support.

What was staggering about this was not the protests, but the reporting of them. Instead of reporting the (quite literally) burning issue (vast areas of Asia and Australia were an inferno for months), the press focused instead on the nuisance factor to people trying to get to work, and on the police saying that they were undermanned to deal with the situation.

The debates that followed in parliament were not about climate change, but whether more police should be employed, and whether the penalties for protesting should be increased to act as a deterrent, thereby completely disregarding, bolstering up opposition to even, the core issue that pointed out that if nothing were urgently done, we, and all species we share this amazing planet with, were doomed, and soon.

When Extinction Rebellion, with great ceremony, handed over a petition signed by thousands to then Prime Minister, Theresa May, my heart sank as, clearly, they were under the impression that she had control over the way the banks were, and are, tearing the world apart. They might just as well have handed a petition to a soldier outside Buckingham Palace, fully expecting his input to force an abdication of the Queen.

And there lies the issue at the heart of this book. The illusion that governments make decisions that control the money people. This, sadly, while widely believed, is no more than a cleverly maintained lie.

Bigger and more startling yet, is the Covid-19 pandemic. When it first reared its ugly head there was confusion and panic. People knew nothing of this 'deadly' virus and were terrified of it, fully expecting mountains of corpses to be seen rotting in the streets. I was sceptical from the outset and when the unprecedented move was taken to lock down society, at a stroke removing peoples' freedoms and rights, my concerns were not about any virus, but about the totalitarian control that the government was able to exercise over the people.

More frightening, perhaps, was how acquiescent the people were to the outrageous curtailments to their lives. There was almost no resistance at all and within moments citizens became self-appointed watch-dogs, informing on their neighbours and taking those who resisted 'lockdown' to task. The further step of introducing measures such as distancing and mask wearing which, without a huge public backlash, shall never be rescinded, only served to remove peoples' identities and divide us, like splitting sheep in a pen.

What was interesting was to see the claims made by me in this book play out in front of my eyes. The government made statements on a daily basis and cleverly made the campaign not about saving ourselves, but about saving others and the NHS. At a stroke they had removed every person's right to reject the measures on the basis that they were willing to take the risk upon themselves. If you thought you had sovereign rights over your own life, you were now wrong.

To support the mask and lock down theories, several lies had to be perpetrated upon the people. The first was that the virus took up to twelve days to incubate to a level where you were aware you had it. Covid-19 is a flu like virus, and flu has been around us all our lives. It does better in colder climates and is less virulent in hot weather. Flu takes between two and three days for the symptoms to appear, so why would such a supposedly deadly strain take twelve? That made no sense. If anything, the time for it to get a grip should have been shorter. The next, and way bigger, lie was that you could spread the virus without even knowing that you had it. Any doctor shall tell you that if you are not suffering dyer symptoms the amount of virus you can exhale is minimal and no threat to any healthy person because they have an immune system perfectly capable of fighting off such a tiny threat.

But great! How perfect those two lies were, fooling people into thinking they couldn't tell if they were infectious, meaning totally healthy people thought they might kill each other as they passed on the street. Unbelievably, the majority of people swallowed this information without a murmur. Why? Because they were carpet bombed with propaganda to make them fearful, in the press. It's exactly how Adolf did it, so you might have thought we would have the wisdom to spot the same manipulations.

Remember how you only have to control a couple of companies to control the whole reporting network? Hitler used the same tactics to get hysteria going about the Communists and Jews. While the World Health Organisation (WHO) and Centre for Disease Control (CDC) were both saying that it was unlikely that the virus could be spread by people with no symptoms, or through touching something (like money) the press were banging out very different stories of, amongst other things, taxi drivers dropping down dead after accepting change, and people accidentally slaughtering their parents because they went to the pub.

The government chopped and changed their position on tackling the virus, and countries opened and closed their borders with boring regularity to ensure the virus was never off the front page. They spent gazillions of your money on advertising the deadly effects and strict measures. Every gap between records on every local radio station, every ad break on national TV, whole front-page ads on every Sunday newspaper. The tsunami of covid propaganda was continual and of Himalayan proportions.

Even more sinister was the control of any dissenting voice. It was impossible for highly qualified doctors (or even coalitions of more than a thousand doctors) to have their opinion heard if it were contrary to government rhetoric. Sound advice that the wearing of face masks was actually detrimental because mammals are designed to exhale impurities went unreported and unheeded.

The government then went further and instructed GCHQ, their intelligence agency who won fame for breaking the WWII Nazi Enigma Code, to trawl the internet and take down any post that dared to suggest that mass vaccination might infringe human rights or that the proposed vaccine might not be safe (and at time of writing it certainly has not been fully tested) or have another hidden purpose.

Brigade 88, a division of civilian techies, were enlisted into the fray with the remit of generating fake news to undermine genuine, but not mainstream, media comment by trying to bundle the whole together and so discredit any voice that tried to warn people of the risks and potential agendas behind the government push for mass vaccination.

But then something happened that started to undermine it all. After a single spike, the massive predicted death toll never happened. To make up for this they started reporting numbers of cases. When have you ever heard reports of numbers of cases for any disease or illness? Did you ever in your life get a daily count of cancer patients? Flu cases? Tetanus cases? Malaria cases? Of course not. If someone gets something but then recovers that is not newsworthy, nor should it be. PCR testing (Polymerase Chain reaction) was encouraged and found to be hugely faulty, as it specifies amplification of DNA samples of thirty-five times when the whole industry knows that anything above a nine times amplification can produce a large proportion of false positive results. So, the more tests they did the greater problem the virus appeared to be. So, what did they do next? Made sure the number of tests went through the roof with mandatory testing of cities and school children thereby ensuring that the numbers of false positives also rocketed giving them the bogus 'proof' to do whatever they wanted.

As summer came the numbers dropped through the floor, but still the press kept going, reporting numbers of covid related deaths. How can four people dying of something in a country that naturally loses one thousand seven hundred people every day, be newsworthy? The CDC released the actual risk data that showed the under twenties had virtually no chance of dying from the virus unless already desperately ill from something else. And the figure was not much higher until you reached your seventies, even then the risk was low. The average age of covid deaths came out at 82, a year higher than normal life expectancy in the UK of 81.

In all this time children were unable to visit ailing parents, families were not allowed to console each other at funerals and fathers were not permitted to walk their daughters down the aisle. Who thinks up these sorts of spiteful measures? And the anomalies were ridiculous. The virus would apparently be harmless at some times of the day but deadly at others, so a curfew was required. The virus was safe when you were seated but deadly if you walked about. It was harmless if you had five friends but deadly if you had six. It was safe to walk your dog for an hour but deadly if you went ten minutes over that. Safe in supermarkets but deadly in other shops. Safe at work but not at the pub. The utter nonsense was transparent to anyone who cared to question, and some people decided to do just that, by doing the job that the press should have been doing.

Their findings were yes, there was a virus, although it's similarity to flu put a question mark over its originality, and yes, some people died, but no, it was not significantly worse than any bad flu year, and no, it never warranted the dictatorial measures that were imposed upon us. Then there was a second lockdown in November – when flu cases naturally increase. Their reason for imposing it was the doubling and redoubling of (wildly inaccurate) positive tests, from miniscule numbers to tiny numbers.

Some of those positive tests were shown to appear from unsullied, untouched swabs being returned, with impossible positives resulting with instructions to self-isolate. A false positive can appear as any previous infection, including the flu vaccine, can provide the DNA they are looking for. Further, anyone testing positive became a covid victim no matter how long later, or how they died. Someone in a car accident four months after a positive test was put down on the covid death database that formed the heart of the argument for the unprecedented removal of liberties. This approach was questioned and the timescale reduced to, a still over-inflated, 28 days but the numbers were never adjusted downwards.

Most people die in hospital, and what do you have to do before entering hospital? Have a covid test. And as the test is flawed and producing false positives that 94 year old lady who sadly passed away after battling cancer for three years is now a covid victim. Many older people were now testing weekly, with any that died for another reason forming part of the nonsensical daily data base 'the number of people who have died within 28 days of testing positive' that was portrayed as factual covid deaths. This figure is what drove a fearful population into submission to the governments totalitarian policies

Further, the inflated death toll was never presented against the backdrop of normal deaths in the UK – which is 1,700 per day. At time of writing supposed covid deaths account for about 70,000 people, but there is no mention of how many of those people were likely to pass on in that time anyway, estimated at around 80%. Since the beginning of the first lockdown 500,000 would have naturally died and it is estimated that 200,000 of those shall have died prematurely due to withheld treatment at hospitals for cancer, stroke, heart attack and all manner of other medical issues, which were unavailable due to this amplified covid 'pandemic.'

And then came the dash for a vaccine. Dr Micheal Yeadon, who spent 30 years leading new allergy and respiratory medicines research at Pfizer said *there is absolutely no need for vaccines to extinguish the pandemic.'* His reasoning is that 30% of people have now been infected and so have immunity, and 30% of people shall in any case hardly feel any effect more than a harmless cold, which is enough to establish herd immunity, and a very slow transmission rate.

The Great Barrington Declaration was made by over 51,000 medical and health science professionals affirming that due to the relatively mild danger of the virus to the vast majority of the population, *'those who are at minimal risk should be allowed to simply build up natural immunity to the virus.'*

Over 3,000 doctors in Belgium have labelled the episode 'a fake pandemic' with the purpose of creating a world dictatorship. World renowned microbiologist Dr. Sucharit Bhakdi went as far as to call the mass vaccination *'downright dangerous.'*

It transpires that early treatment with hydroxychloroquine is a safe and inexpensive method of treating the virus however this drug was mysteriously removed as being safe to be administered by doctors after thirty years of use. Ivermectin was another drug that was said to have 'miraculous' results in dealing with covid transmission but was irrationally impeded by the National Institute of Heath (NIH) and the Food and Drug Administration (FDA). Don't tell me they weren't trying to stop anything that would make the vaccine redundant.

Clearly, we were not being told the truth, the whole truth and nothing but the truth (so help us God.) The question now was why? Why would they want to put the people in fear? And why would they want to purposefully collapse the economy? Well, this is where we start trying to find out how deep the rabbit hole really goes.

The golden rule when considering government policy is to remember that if it makes no sense, they are lying to you. If they are lying to you, they have an agenda that you don't know about. The cover, as always, is incompetence, and the greater the apparent incompetence the greater is the cover up and the more worrying the agenda.

So let's look at the effects that the covid virus has had, to ascertain who is likely to benefit from the situation, which is normally a pretty good clue as to what is really going on.

Effect one, the economy is suffering. Badly. Closing businesses for long periods is going to undermine their ability to stay afloat and threatens employment. This collapse shall devalue the whole country within months, making it easy for an outsider with extreme wealth to pick up assets like shops, pubs and service companies (like airlines), or possibly control of the whole country, at a fraction of the pre-covid cost. The Rothschilds did exactly this in 1929 America. They purposefully created the great depression (by selling seemingly lucrative stocks that offered ten times the normal returns but which could be ordered to be cashed with only a 24 hour notice. They subsequently demanded liquidation of *all of them on the same day* making every investment worthless, (after having quietly removed their own investments of course.) This collapsed banks, losing savings and driving the people into abject poverty. In short, they made their billions on the back of thousands of suicides.

Effect two, the 'money is dangerous' lie means that many people have been driven to use cards only, so banks take more of their 2% or 3% cuts thereby significantly increasing their earnings. This is leading to a cashless society where your every expenditure is known and logged, your movements tracked, and taxes are collected on everything. Without a cash option, banks can turn off your card and flush you out as you would no longer be able to purchase anything, including food. Travel could be curbed against your will. Without competition there would be nothing to prevent the banks from increasing the rates for their 'services' to 30, 40 or 50%. (I already experienced a bank wanting a 30% cut for me using an ATM in Greece recently.)

Effect three, the wearing of masks dehumanises us all and stops people interacting. The social distancing also has that effect. The result is a frightened population who feel isolated and cut off from each other. This is very good for a government who wishes to control people through fear, and the masks reinforce the message of terror every day.

Effect four, the pubs are closing down. This is a very good thing for a government who want people to obtain their news from official sources and do not want people chatting and spreading their views of dissent, and shall make their value for any future sale plummet.

Effect five, some people believe there is a massive health issue and some believe there is nothing out of the ordinary. This is very good for a government who wants to 'divide and conquer' the people. While we are asking questions of each other we miss who the real problem is by not looking upwards. The timely introduction of the 'black lives matter' movement was a furthering of this separation policy, causing turmoil and trouble over issues several hundred years old, while deflecting attention away from the serious and universal freedom issues that are being inflicted upon all of us today.

Effect six, the possibility of introduction of something else in the vaccination that is the real agenda, as the death toll does not justify this measure. What the elite are trying to achieve is open to conjecture, however a thousand doctors consider the vaccine is highly likely to incorporate nanobots or a microchip tuned into 5G.

This is mass medication, and very good for Pfizer, Moderna and AstraZeneca the pharmaceutical companies that enjoy the lucrative contracts that they want to be rolled out to every person on the planet, with a rescinding of rights for those that try to refuse. Microchipping the population would provide intimate surveillance via the 5G satellite ring (so there would be no escape) and once in place would pave the way for absolute and draconian new laws curbing freedoms to levels experienced by criminals today.

There would be nothing to stop a new law, for example, (to save the NHS of course,) saying you could only go to the pub once a week, or not at all – and they would know if you tried to go. Your speed would be monitored at all times so automatic fines would arrive at 31 mph. Laughable as it sounds there could be taxes put in place for having sex, as they would know exactly when, where and for how long relations took place. Scarily the chip could be bi-directional providing a third party with the power to affect your mood. If you get 'uppity' and start to protest they can simply turn you down to a lethargic state. Experiments on charging bulls stopped by the push of a button demonstrate that this is not a science fiction.

Effect seven, the lockdowns prevent the normal movement of people and so dramatically cuts the carbon footprint for each of us. I am a believer in climate change and know that we have all experienced it first-hand, if we can be bothered to consider the seasons shifts, extreme weather and raising sea levels. Certainly, while the first lockdown was in place the roads became quiet, smog disappeared and the skies became blue again. I believe this would be beneficial to the people, and of course those with the power to implement these covid-justified measures are themselves people, albeit insanely wealthy, who are doomed to live on planet earth with us.

Effect eight, in no time at all, the people surrendered themselves to the rule of government and capitulated their right to choose their destiny for themselves.

Effect nine, well this all depends on what else is in the vaccine. There is no hard evidence but the terrifying desire of the establishment to vaccinate everyone they can, as fast as they can, combined with the contrary testaments of tens of thousands of highly qualified individuals in the medical profession, who are placing their jobs and credibility on the line, and who's posts have been rapidly removed, we know for sure that the government, and those that control them, are up to something big. Bill Gates is a driving force in the mass vaccination program, with huge profits to be made from his stock in Moderna and Pfizer. He has been recorded numerous times at presentations (that can be viewed online) talking about mind control and sterilisation via vaccines, which is deeply concerning.

According to Dr Miklos Lukaks de Pereny, a research professor of science in Peru, the plan may be to globally advance 'transhumanism', literally the fusion of human beings with technology, by using a new 'messenger RNA' (mRNA) which could potentially alter our DNA, our genome, the blueprint for how we develop, reproduce, function and repair ourselves. The process is called 'transfection.'

Dr Lukaks said that *'We are told that the mRNA shall go into our cells and make an alteration that shall fight the virus, but who can say that it wouldn't do a different process like limiting our ability to capture oxygen or disrupt the ability to manufacture sperm. The possibilities are endless.'*

Dr Michael Yeadon, ex-Pfizers' most senior researcher in allergy and respiratory medicine, together with a Dr Wolfgang Wodarg, filed a petition with the European Medicines Agency (EMA), which is responsible for approving drugs in Europe. They claim that the vaccinations produce anti-bodies to attack spike proteins (like covid), however spike proteins also includes syncytin-homologous proteins, which are essential for the formation of the placenta. If the vaccine triggers an immune reaction to that protein it would *'trigger infertility for an indefinite period.'*

Dr Carrie Madej warns that the vaccination may carry 'Luciferase' with the potential to insert a digital code, barcode or brand under the skin that can be read with a smartphone, making the recipient like a bar-coded product or identifiable like an animal to its owners.

I think it's fair to say that whatever else it is that they are wanting to pump into us, it's not going to be good, and the fact they have been underhanded about it can only double and re-double the likelihood of an agenda, as, remember, the numbers of deaths for this vast operation do not justify it.

And there we have it. Nine effects providing four benefits to the banks directly, seven to the government (and so the banks that control them), and one for us. Oh, but they are trying to save us! Sorry – I nearly (and not unreasonably) forgot that one.

But, something then happened that the players at the helm of this episode did not expect. The President of Belarus, Aleksandr Lukashenko, appeared in the press stating that he had been offered a bribe of $940,000,0000 from the IMF and World Bank to impose a strict lockdown on his countrymen including the wearing of facemasks. He refused and went public with the information about the bribe saying that he was *'not going to dance to anyone else's fiddle.'*

In a moment the veil had been lifted, and we could see what lurked behind. Belarus cannot be the only country to be offered such a bribe and, as theirs is nearly a billion dollars, one can only imagine the size of the bribe for a country like Britain with eight times the Belarus population. It then came to light that in 2020 the UK had in fact borrowed another £400 billion from the World Bank.

Now why would the IMF and World Bank want to throw such fantastic sums of money around? Because attached to the bribe/loan, is a slew of conditions to do with lockdowns and curtailments of liberties. Locking down a country smashes its ability to make ends meet, and when the economy goes into free fall guess who will be there to snap up the pieces at a bargain price. And who is in control of the World Bank? Yep – you guessed it – it's those naughty Rothschilds again with their hundred trillion dollars, that isn't, seemingly, enough wealth for them.

So, what has our government been doing with all this money they have been given/lent? Bribing! Bribing who? Us! As a business owner I was given a £10,000 bribe for my capitulation to the covid claims and to close, others were given as much as £30K. All companies had their staffing costs paid and (temporarily) interest free loans were handed out to anyone who wanted them. The first mandatory testing of people in Liverpool was softened by a £500 bribe for anyone who tested positive. When was the last time you ever heard of the government just handing out money like that? Never? This on its own should have had your warning sensors on red alert, as it smacks of corruption and an agenda.

The director of the C.D.C. came clean by saying that hospitals in the U.S. were being paid a bonus for putting a death down as covid related, and so each leaned toward doing just that. Every covid entry to a hospital earnt it $13,000, and if the patient went onto a ventilator, $39,000. This is very good for bolstering up the figures needed to go to a mass vaccination plan. In the UK the hospitals can claim for a slew of expenses to cover the additional virus costs, but at the same time have been told to cancel all non-urgent operations and care, and to empty patients from the wards, meaning many hospitals are almost standing idle while pocketing millions in extra cash.

As mentioned earlier, the World Bank - IMF is owned and controlled by NM Rothschild and 30 to 40 of the wealthiest people in the world (including Goldman Sachs, Rockefellers, Lehmans, Schiff, Kuhn Loebs, Warburgs, Harriman, Lazards, Brown Brothers) For over 150 years their collective ambitions have been to evoke a planned takeover of the world through money. Former chief economist of the World Bank, Joe Stiglitz, was fired in 1999 when he pointed out to the top executives that every country the IMF/World Bank had got involved with ended up with a crashed economy and a destroyed governmenta, sometimes leading to flames and riots

Before Stiglitz left, he took a large stack of secret documents out of the World Bank and International Monetary Fund, that revealed that they both required nations to sign secret agreements with up to 111 items in which they had to agree to sell off their country's key assets (water, electric, gas, transport and so on), to take devastating economic steps, and to pay off the politicians, with billions of dollars going into Swiss bank accounts to ensure their agenda was carried though.

If the government did not agree to these steps the country was cut-off from all international borrowing. If you cannot occasionally borrow money in the international marketplace you cannot survive, whether you are a people a corporation or a country.

If the strangle hold doesn't work, they have been known to overthrow the government, plant lies about them and even rewrite history.

So where is this leading? A common phrase now is 'The Great Reset', where everything we understand about how the world works, changes. For years it has been referred to the 'one world order' or as I revealed earlier in the book, from the Latin on the dollar bill, 'Annihilate to bring about a new order of the ages.' The covid situation is no accident, but is a long considered and carefully drawn up plan providing the big players with the opportunity to bring this collapse of the world economy, and subsequent take-over, about.

The ambitions are many, with complete control, not only of people's movements, money, spending and habits, but with intimate biological surveillance, thought assessment and control. It looks increasingly likely that very enterprise in our community shall become the domain of some huge corporation and the economy shall collapse. This may rise unemployment to around 50%, thereby driving people into abject poverty and starvation, unless you are part of the 1% club, where your wealth shall spiral to fantastic and un-spendable heights. A one world order means a world bank, a world army and dictatorial constraints on liberties that just a year ago would have been thought impossible.

This is a quiet, bomb-less world war three, the people versus the uber-wealthy, where faith, spirituality, prayer, meditation, sacrifice and downright doggedness are going to be key factors in deciding the outcome. A ray of hope lies in the winter equinox of 21 –12-2020 which astrologists say begins the age of Aquarius. Before you dismiss this as mumbo-jumbo you should be aware that all of the decisions for lockdowns were made on solstices, which cannot be a coincidence.

As I speak today the government are carrying out the agenda of the uber-wealthy, making them the mouthpiece and tool of the enslaving enemy, and forsaking the people they are sworn to defend,. An independent group have emerged to create Magna Carta 2020, a strong use of common law and historical stipulations in laws written to protect the common man from abuse from government and the Crown. This is a tool that may prove to be extremely useful, as the government still has to satisfy the law and can be brought to account through the courts. The longer-term problem, of course, is that the government also makes the laws up, and so it is simplicity itself for them to continue re-writing the rights and wrongs (as they have been doing the all the way through this covid episode), moving goalposts, changing rules, bribing the referee and making up the scores to suit the overlords whom they serve.

But there is another way.

A simple solution. A solution that is within our grasp, and which is more urgently needed than ever before in the history of our planet.

Remember that 'One Pill Fix' I was telling you about?